DATE DUE

THE LANDMARK HISTORY OF THE
AMERICAN PEOPLE

THE LANDMARK HISTORY

illustrated with prints and photographs

OF THE

AMERICAN
PEOPLE

FROM APPOMATTOX
TO THE MOON

DANIEL J. BOORSTIN

RANDOM HOUSE · NEW YORK

Author's Acknowledgments

My wife, Ruth F. Boorstin, has given this volume the full benefit of her expertise and her editorial skill and judgment. The book would not have been written without her assistance and has been much improved by her close collaboration. Dr. Peter C. Marzio has helped immensely—with scholarly advice, editorial suggestions, and in the selection of illustrations. Others who have helped include: Perry R. Duis, Professor John Hope Franklin of the University of Chicago, James W. Seymore, Jr., and Dr. Louise C. Wade. While all these persons have offered critical suggestions, in many particulars my judgments have differed from theirs, and none of the interpretations in this book should be ascribed to them. Mrs. Vincent Haynes and Miss Genevieve Gremillion have given important help in preparing the manuscript. Miss Karen Tobias, assisted by Miss Agnes Maier, has been principally responsible for collecting the excellent illustrations. Miss Janet Finnie of Random House, having proposed this two-volume *Landmark History* to me in the first place, has helped shape it from beginning to end. Once again, I thank her for her scrupulous and unstinting editorial assistance. My friendly colleagues and the research resources of the University of Chicago, together with those of the Smithsonian Institution, and especially of The National Museum of History and Technology, have helped make this book possible.

PICTURE CREDITS: Bethlehem Steel Company, 32; The Bettmann Archive, 3, 4, 7; Black Star (Eugene Anthony) v, (Fred Ward) 135, (John Bennewitz) 167; Brown Brothers 11, 41, 54, 56, 59, 60, 69, 83, 91, 120, 124, 132 left, 162, 180; Camera 5 (Ken Regan) 185; Culver Pictures, 6-7 margins, 12, 14, 16, 18, 21, 23, 27, 29, 33, 35, 39, 45, 49, 51, 62, 64, 66, 70, 71, 74, 76, 81, 82, 113, 117, 121, 129, 131 both, 132 right, 144, 149 top, 149 bottom, 151; Defense Department Photo, Marine Corps, 169; DeWys Inc., ii; Drake Well Museum, 9; Richard Erdoes, 128; Library of Congress, front endpaper, 36, 37, 42, 79, 98, 103, 104, 111, 123, 126, 173, 174; Magnum, Inc., back endpaper; Montgomery Ward Catalog (1895) 18, 30; Museum of the City of New York, 73, 100 both; National Aeronautics and Space Administration, 141, 182; New York Historical Society, 1, 24–25 top, 57, 65, 67, 84, 114; New York Public Library, Picture Collection, 28, 53; Pictorial Parade, 139; Pix (James Pickerelle) 170, (Charles Simonpietri-Gamma) 171; courtesy Joseph Pulitzer, Jr., 145; Radio Corporation of America, 176; Remington Art Memorial Museum, 146; courtesy Epes Winthrop Sargent (from *Queen of Populists*, by Richard Stiller), 107; Sears Roebuck Catalog (1897) 20; Smithsonian Institution, 31, 88, 92, 94, 95, 96, 101, 108, 109, 154, 159; Union Pacific Railroad Company, 77; United Press International, reverse of front endpaper, 119, 138, 165, 178; official United States Air Force Photo, 164; Wide World Photos, 136, 155, 160, 186.

COVER CREDITS: Amon Carter Museum of Western Art (lower-middle left); DeWys, Inc. (lower-middle right); National Aeronautics and Space Administration (upper-middle center); New York Historical Society (upper-middle right); Pictorial Parade (bottom); Steve Schapiro, Black Star (top left); United Press International (upper-middle left).

For Frances Olsan
with love and admiration
from
her nephew

CONTENTS

A Word to the Reader

Part One: The Go-Getters

1. *Cattlemen and Cowboys*   *3*
2. *Rock Oil to Light up the World*   *8*
3. *City Goods for Country Customers*   *15*
4. *One Price for Everybody!*   *22*
5. *A Democracy of Clothing*   *25*
6. *Things by the Millions*   *30*

Part Two: People on the Move

7. *To Punish—or to Forgive?*   *41*
8. *A Two-Nation South*   *47*
9. *Filling the Land*   *52*
10. *Crowding the Cities*   *58*
11. *Whose Country? Oldcomers and Newcomers*   *63*
12. *Reformers and Self-Helpers*   *68*

Part Three: Bringing People Together

13. Everybody Shares the News   *75*

14. Letters in Every Mailbox   *80*

15. The Sun Is No Longer Boss   *83*

16. Company Towns and Garden Cities   *89*

17. Bridge-Building Heroes   *93*

18. Going Up!   *97*

Part Four: Champions for the People

19. The Farmers Find a Voice   *105*

20. From Umpire to Guardian   *110*

21. Who Killed Prosperity?   *116*

22. Nothing to Fear but Fear Itself   *121*

23. Who Was Left Out?   *127*

24. "A Triumph for Freedom"   *133*

Part Five: To This Whole World—and Beyond

25. Ocean Paths to World Power   *143*

26. How Submarines Killed the Freedom of the Seas   *148*

27. Winning a War, Losing a Peace   *153*

28. The Battlefield Is Everywhere   *158*

29. The Exploding World of the Atom   *163*

30. "Little" Wars and Big Risks   *168*

31. Windows to the World   *172*

32. Footprints on the Moon   *179*

Postscript: The Mysterious Future   *184*

Index   *188*

A Word to the Reader

For the American people, everyday life changed in the century following the Civil War more than the life of earthlings had changed in the thousand years before.

As millions from everywhere became Americans, they invented a new Way of Life. And they gave a new meaning to almost everything.

Americans, for example, changed the meaning of day-and-night. Indoors, after sundown, could now be brighter than during the day.

Americans changed the meaning of the seasons. Wherever they lived, with central heating and air conditioning, they could be warm in winter and cool in summer. Foods of all seasons could be eaten any time. The United States became the land of strawberries in winter.

Americans changed the meaning of country-and-city. Every day the farmer, like the city man, could read his city newspaper. He wore city-made clothes and he bought city-made furniture in the latest styles—delivered right to his door.

Americans changed the meaning of distance. Faraway events were heard and seen in everybody's living room. Now millions could afford to go out by jet plane to Paris or Rome or Tokyo and see the world for themselves.

Americans even changed the meaning of the earth. Ever since the beginning of history this had been a lonely planet. The heavens were where living men could never go. Now, once again, Americans accomplished the "impossible." They walked on the moon and planned trips to Mars and beyond.

The United States is plainly the most modern of nations. But with 1976—the nation's two-hundredth birthday—not so far away, we are already the oldest of the new nations. Now we live by the world's oldest written constitution.

Since the Civil War our grown-up nation has been seeking ways to stay young. And the nation has been kept young by Americans always asking again what it means to be an American. Like the Pilgrims who risked the ocean-crossing, or the men who fought the American Revolution, or those who struggled to write a Constitution, or those who died in the Civil War, later Americans continued the search.

In this book I tell the adventures of Go-Getters and inventors and cowboys and businessmen and factory workers and farmers and soldiers and others (including a few politicians!) who have been seeking to keep our New World new.

Their search is what made modern America, and what keeps America modern. It is the story of the making of your life and mine. This is a book about us.

D. J. B.

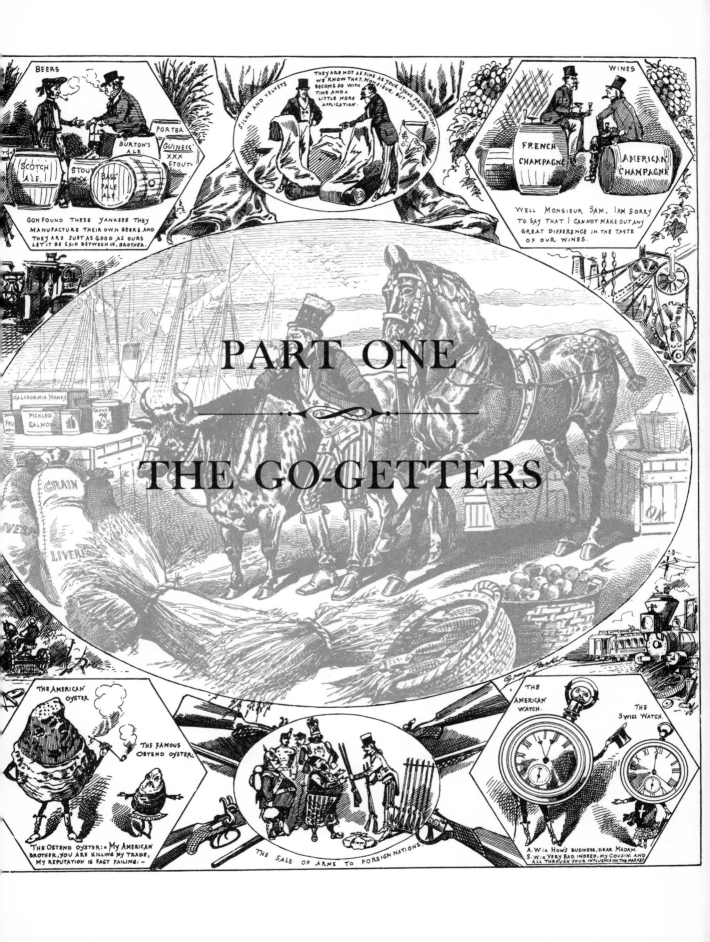

PART ONE

THE GO-GETTERS

THE GO-GETTERS

By the time of the Civil War, Americans had only begun to discover America. The land was still half-explored. The highest mountains were still unclimbed and the swiftest rivers still unmapped. Nobody had yet reached the top of Long's Peak or Mount Whitney. The Colorado River, which began somewhere high in the Rockies, had not been traced in its dangerous meanders. The shores of the Great Lakes were still a mystery. The bayous of Louisiana and the everglades of Florida seemed dark and threatening.

The Gold Rush to California in 1849 was only a first finding of the treasures in mountain streams and deep under the earth. America was full of secret resources.

A new kind of American, the Go-Getter, helped discover these treasures. Just as the nation was founded by people with assorted dreams and hopes, so a new American Way of Life was invented by a wide assortment of Go-Getters.

Some were outdoor men riding the range, leading thousands of cattle on new trails. Some were adventuring miners, risking fortunes to drill deep in search of mysterious new minerals. Some were businessmen—new-style storekeepers finding ways to make the whole nation their customers. Some were engineers and inventors, anxious to build bigger engines than the world had

ever seen, and machines which could turn out things by the millions.

E Pluribus Unum was the Latin motto of the young nation. It meant "one made from many." The Go-Getters were experts at bringing people together. Just as earlier Americans had organized thirteen new colonies and a new nation, so now the Go-Getters brought later Americans together in their cattle-trains and oil companies and department stores, and in thousands of other new enterprises. The new American Way of Life was designed for everybody.

America would be not merely a democracy of people but also a democracy of things. It would be a long time —maybe forever—before no one was poor. But after the Civil War it became easier for more and more Americans to share the good things of life. The Go-Getters, without even intending it, were bringing the whole nation together.

Some of the Go-Getters were more honest than others. Some made their fortunes by new ideas, by hard work, by being clever. Some were simply lucky. All prospered from the continent's hidden wealth.

The Go-Getters were not satisfied with the slow pace of the Old World. They wanted to see things happen fast. And by the early years of the twentieth century they had helped transform American life.

CHAPTER 1

Cattlemen and Cowboys

About the time of the Civil War, the Western cattle trade became big business. The men who made money from it were as different as possible from the European peasant who kept his few cattle at night in the room where he slept. The peasant could keep only a few because his house was small, and he had to feed his animals by hand in winter.

The Western cattleman numbered his stock by the thousands. He did not have to give them a roof, for Western cattle were tough enough to look after themselves on the range. And on the great Western plains there grew "buffalo grass" which survived drought and provided free food right on the ground throughout the winter.

Western cattlemen were bold and adventurous, willing to take big risks in a wild country. In the Old World, the expression "Man on Horseback" meant a military man, a commander of troops which he might use to take over the government. But in the American West the "Man on Horseback" was a cowboy. And the Western cattleman was a Go-Getter on horseback.

One of the first and most energetic of these was John Wesley Iliff. His father, an Ohio farmer, had offered him $7,500 if he would settle nearby on a respectable Ohio farm. But in 1856 he heard of the fortunes farther west. Young Iliff, who wanted adventure, told his father he would be satisfied with $500 if he could use it to make his start out there.

A cowboy and his horse, working together, could rescue a Longhorn from the mud. In the days before the camera could take action pictures, the artist Frederic Remington became famous for his drawings and sculptures of men and horses in action.

A cowboy in his "uniform," fully equipped with lariat and six-shooter. A drawing by C. M. Russell, who was born in St. Louis and went to Montana as a cowboy at the age of sixteen.

Iliff did not find gold in the Colorado mountain streams. But he did find it in the cattle that came there with Americans pushing westward.

During the Colorado Gold Rush the thousands of covered wagons that arrived near Denver—just before the climb into the mountains—wanted to lighten their load. They shed most of their belongings, so they could go ahead on foot or with a few pack mules. They were glad to sell to Iliff the footsore oxen that had pulled their wagons across the plains.

He fed these cattle free on the open range that belonged to everybody. He began breeding a herd. When the animals were fattened, Iliff sold them either to butchers in the mining camps or to travelers returning east who needed oxen to pull their wagons.

Of course there were risks, especially from winter weather and from Indian attack. Iliff became friendly with a man named Gerry, a pioneer fur trader who had married the twin daughters of Chief Swift Bird of the Oglalas. Using the information from his wives, Gerry warned Iliff whenever the Indians were about to attack, so that Iliff's cattle could be moved to a safe place.

For a Go-Getter like Iliff, even the Indians became a source of profit. He made a small fortune supplying meat to the remote western outposts where troops had been sent to fight the Indians. At the same time he sold beef to government officials so they could feed the Indians on reservations.

When railroads—promoted by Eastern Go-Getters—pushed West, they opened another new market. Now Western beef could be shipped to the growing Eastern cities. At the same time, hard-working crews building the railroads had to be well fed, and what they most wanted was meat. Iliff agreed to deliver cattle by the thousands to the Union Pacific Railroad construction gangs and to the troops guarding them against the Indians.

This was easier said than done. He had to find more beef than anyone had ever yet seen in one place. And he had to bring it to the middle of nowhere, where railroads were still to be built.

Iliff was helped by still another brand of Go-Getter, the Western Trailblazer.

One of the oldest of them was a remarkable man with the unlikely name of Charles Goodnight. His family had taken him to Texas when he was a boy of nine. In 1868 Goodnight agreed to deliver to Iliff's camp near Cheyenne, Wyoming, forty thousand dollars worth of cattle from Texas.

When Americans had come to Texas in the 1830's thousands of Longhorn cattle were running wild. These were the great-great-grandchildren of a few animals brought over by Spanish explorers in the sixteenth century. To get your herd all you had to do was to hunt and capture. Hunting wild cattle became a prosperous business. But it was not child's play. For the wild cattle of Texas, one hunter reported, were "fifty times more dangerous than the fiercest buffalo." Armed with sharp horns that they were not afraid to use, these bold beasts could not be managed by men on foot. They made the Texas cowboy get onto his horse, and they kept him there.

It was a thousand miles from the cattle country of central Texas to Goodnight's promised delivery point in southeastern Wyoming. You had to cross some of the driest, most unfriendly land in the whole continent—what maps before the Civil War called the "Great American Desert." In all that country there was no town worthy of the name. There was not even any trail. To deliver his cattle, Goodnight had to find his own way.

It would be a risky business. But it seemed worth trying, when a steer bought for four dollars in Texas sold for forty dollars in Wyoming. Multiply that by three thousand (the number of cattle Goodnight hoped to take on each

trip) and it added up to a handsome profit.

The Texas Longhorns were well equipped for long trips. Their sense of smell, the cowboys said, was as much superior to that of an ordinary Eastern cow as the bloodhound's was to that of a parlor poodle. Where water was hard to find, the Longhorn's nose for water could make the difference between life and death. Cowboys who let the leading steer act as guide sometimes found remote lakes they had never seen before.

The real problem was how to keep all those three thousand cattle together and moving at just the right speed. If they were allowed to stop or dawdle, they might never reach their goal. But if they were allowed to trot they might get out of control or exercise off the weight that was worth money in Wyoming.

Stationed at the front, or "point," of the herd were two of the most experienced men, called "pointers." They navigated for the whole herd, following the course set ahead by the foreman. Bringing up the rear were three steady cowboys whose job it was to look out for the weaker cattle—the "drags." To prevent the herd from straggling out for miles, the whole party moved no faster than the weakest "drags" at the rear. The rest of the cowboy crew were stationed along the sides to keep the herd compact and all the same width.

Every herd of cattle on the trail needed its own herd of horses to give the cowboys fresh mounts for their tricky jobs. To feed the men you needed a chuck wagon which the cook would drive fast ahead of everybody else. His job was to have food ready as soon as the weary cowboys arrived.

Communication between the front and rear of the herd was difficult. The rumbling of hoofs smothered words. The cowboys, then, borrowed a clever system of hand signals from the Plains Indians.

Apart from Indians, the greatest peril was a stampede. Suddenly at night the three thousand cattle, which a moment before had been quietly dozing, might rouse into a thundering mass. To stop a stampede, experienced cowboys made a circle to keep the animals churning and circling, always round to the right. Then by tightening their circle they squeezed the stampeding cattle tighter and tighter together till they had no place to run. The milling herd was forced to halt.

If the encircling tactic failed, all was lost. The stampede would get out of control. Then the cattle would fly out like sparks into the night, and they might never be seen again.

The cowboys had their own trail-tested ways of preventing stampedes by soothing the jumpy Longhorns. At night the men guarding the herd would sing and whistle while they made their rounds. The purpose of this "serenading," the veteran cowboy Andy Adams explained, was "so that the sleeping herd may know that a friend and not an enemy is keeping vigil over their dreams."

The cowboys called these songs "hymns" because they were sung to tunes which the cowboys remembered from their mothers' songs in childhood or from church services. But the words the cowboys sang usually were not church-words. What they sang might have shocked or startled the cattle if they could have understood. For these cowboy songs told the exploits of famous horse races and notorious criminals, or they repeated advertising texts from coffee cans or whiskey bottles, or they recited profanity sprinkled between nonsense syllables.

At the end of the Long Drive came the "Cow Town," which was as American as the cowboy. It was simply another smaller kind of "instant city" like those already dotted over the West. The Cow Town was where cowboys delivered their herd to the cattle dealers and the railroads. There, after long lonely weeks on the trail, cowboys enjoyed the company of strangers, bought liquor, and gambled away their money.

Go-Getting cattlemen made these instant towns prosper. One cattleman, Joseph G. McCoy, picked a place along the Kansas Pacific Railroad. In 1867, when he first made his plans for Abilene, it was (as he later recalled) "a very small, dead place, consisting of about one dozen log huts, low, small rude affairs, four-fifths of which were covered with turf roofing; indeed, but one shingle roof could be seen in the whole city. The business of the burg was conducted in two small rooms, mere log huts, and of course the inevitable saloon, also in a log hut, was to be found."

Within sixty days the place was transformed. As if by magic, Abilene had a shipping yard for three thousand head of cattle, besides a large pair of Fairbanks Scales to weigh the cattle on, a big barn and office, and of course "a good three-story hotel." The idea was to ship out thousands of cattle from Abilene to Chicago and other big cities.

Texas cowboys trying to end a stampede of Longhorns frightened by thunder (1881). In the margin of this and the facing page are cattle brands.

On September 5, 1867, when the first shipment (twenty carloads of cattle) left Abilene, the Chicago stockmen had come there to celebrate. In tents specially erected for the occasion, they feasted, drank wine, sang, and listened to bombastic speeches. Before the end of that year Abilene shipped out 35,000 head of cattle.

The Go-Getting McCoy had paid only $2,400 for the whole Abilene townsite. Before long he was offered more than that for a single city lot. He received from the Kansas Pacific Railroad a commission of one-eighth of the freight charges on every carload of cattle. Before the end of the second year,

the railroad company owed McCoy a quarter of a million dollars.

Soon there were other prospering Cow Towns sprinkled all over the West: Schuyler and Fort Kearney and North Platte and Ogallala and Sydney in Nebraska, Pine Bluffs and Rock River and Rock Creek and Laramie and Hillsdale and Cheyenne in Wyoming, Miles City and Glendive and Helena in Montana.

The Cow Towns did not suffer from modesty. More than one boasted that she was the "Queen of Cow Towns." But Dodge City, in Kansas, and others competed for the title of the "Wickedest Little City in America."

While town-building was profitable

and exciting, prosperous cattlemen still fondly remembered their days on the trail. "All in all, my years on the Trail," Charles Goodnight remembered on his ninety-third birthday, "were the happiest I ever lived. There were many hardships and dangers, of course, that called on all a man had of endurance and bravery; but when all went well there was no other life so pleasant. Most of the time we were solitary adventurers in a great land as fresh and new as a spring morning, and were free and full of the zest of darers."

Western cattlemen and cowboys were among the first and bravest of the Go-Getters. They tried the impossible and succeeded in making something from nothing. They captured wild cattle that belonged to nobody. Then they fed the cattle on buffalo grass that nobody even imagined could be food, and grazed them on range that belonged to everybody and nobody. And they finally transported the cattle on their very own feet for thousands of miles to places where they could become beef.

Who could have imagined that the "Great American Desert" would become the greatest beef factory in the world?

CHAPTER 2

Rock Oil to Light up the World ꙮꙮꙮ

The Indians had taught the early settlers how to raise new crops like corn and tobacco, and how to find new medicines in the forests and underground. One of these medicines was a curious black oily substance that the Seneca Indians of upstate New York saw floating on ponds. They laid their blankets on top of ponds where the oil was floating, until the blankets had soaked up the oil. Then they wrung the oil out of the blankets into a bowl. They treasured the oil as an ointment, which they thought would cure all sorts of ills.

Before the end of the eighteenth century, the American colonists had learned to use this oily medicine, and it became an item of trade with the Indians. It was called "Seneca Oil" after the Indians who sold it.

Down in Kentucky in the 1830's, when a salt well was ruined by the oil which bubbled into it, the owners discovered that the black stuff was really Seneca Oil. They stopped selling salt, and instead went into the medicine business. They put the stuff in bottles, called it "Rock Oil" or "American Oil," and sold it as a remedy for rheumatism and nearly everything else. They sold these bottles by the hundreds of thousands.

Other salt manufacturers, who found this black stuff ruining their salt wells, also went into the medicine business. One of them, Samuel Kier, put out leaflets boasting of his Rock Oil's "wonderful curative powers" for rheumatism, chronic cough, ague, toothache, corns, neuralgia, piles, indigestion, and liver ailments. He printed advertisements in

A bottle and wrapper for Kier's "Genuine Petroleum" which he sold as medicine. The scene from the Biblical story of the Good Samaritan (who helped his suffering fellowmen) was supposed to show what Kier's Genuine Petroleum could do for you.

the shape and size of paper money. These featured the number 400—the number of feet below the earth's surface from which the oil was drawn—as if every drop of the oil was worth its weight in gold.

To attract customers, Kier sent salesmen out over the countryside in circus wagons. They played music, sang songs, displayed animal freaks, and used every possible means to attract attention and sell their magic fluid. Within a few years, Kier had disposed of a quarter-million half-pints of his wonderful Rock Oil at a dollar a bottle.

But Kier's wells gushed out even more than his clever salesmen could sell. What could be done with the rest?

About the same time that Kier and other salt manufacturers found themselves flooded with Rock Oil, there was a growing need for some inexpensive kind of lighting. In those days before electric lights, home lighting came from tallow candles and oil lamps, not much different from the ones used in ancient Rome. A wick made from a twisted rag burned in a dish of fish oil or animal oil or vegetable oil. That weak flickering light of burning oil was all that people

had to read and play and work by after sundown.

But oil was expensive. So most homes were usually not lit at night. And people went to bed when the sun set.

In the years before the Civil War, American cities were growing. Homes built close together lacked sunlight. At the same time city people wanted to get together more in the evenings. New factories and railroads also required more and better artificial light. As early as 1830, gas (manufactured from coal) was used to light a few streets and public buildings in Baltimore, Boston, and New York. But gas was not yet used in houses.

Some help came when Isaiah Jennings invented a new lamp oil, which he called "camphene." He used American turpentine—the yellowish sticky fluid that seeped out of holes made in certain pine trees. When this sticky stuff was heated and the product was mixed with alcohol, it made an excellent lighting fluid. It was much cheaper than the other lighting oils, and when it burned it gave a brighter, whiter light. But it had an unpleasant smell and it gave off explosive gases.

Nearly everybody agreed that American homes would not be bright at night until there was a safer inexpensive lamp oil. Where could it be found?

A hint of the great new source came when a clever Canadian doctor, Abraham Gesner, in 1850 found a way to make lighting oil from coal. He called his new product "kerosene" (from *keros,* the Greek word for wax). It had an unpleasant odor, but it could be used without danger of explosion. Doctors who had warned against the "horrors of burning fluid" now urged people to fill their lamps with the safe new "coal oil." Before the end of 1859 nearly two million coal-oil lamps had been sold. But since there were about thirty million people in the United States, the country was still a long way from the goal of "a lamp in every room."

Dr. Gesner had showed that lamp oil could be made not only from plants and animals but also from coal, which was a *mineral.* Was it possible that the new mineral product, Rock Oil, could also be used for lighting?

About this time a New Haven businessman, George H. Bissell, formed the Pennsylvania Rock Oil Company to buy lands in western Pennsylvania, where Rock Oil was found floating on ponds. He hired a famous Yale professor of chemistry, Benjamin Silliman, Jr., and agreed to pay him $500 to find out what the Rock Oil was good for.

Professor Silliman's report opened a new age for Rock Oil. He discovered that Rock Oil—by now also called "petroleum" from *petrus,* Latin for rock, and *oleum* for oil—would make an excellent oil for lamps. His process was cheap. He simply distilled the Rock Oil

—that is, heated it and collected the gas that came off. When the gas cooled down into a liquid, it was lamp oil. This, he discovered, was a new way to make kerosene that was just as good as kerosene made from coal. Kerosene made from Rock Oil also gave a bright, white light, with almost no smoke, and would not explode.

The Rock Oil itself also had wonderful lubricating powers. It would keep the wheels and gears of machines from wearing out and would make them run quiet and smooth.

Rock Oil, with these valuable uses, could surely be sold in large quantities. But until then the only known way to collect it was to find it on the surface or accidentally in a salt well. Sometimes people would dig a shallow ditch to increase the flow where it was already bubbling up.

Then one day, the story goes, Bissell saw one of Kier's advertisements. It was the sheet printed to look like paper money that featured the numeral 400. "A.D. 1848," it read. "Discovered in *boring* for salt water . . . about FOUR HUNDRED FEET below the Earth's surface." Boring! If oil could be obtained when you bored for salt water, why not simply bore for the oil?

"Oil coming out of the ground!" exclaimed a friend. "Pumping oil out of the earth the way you pump water? Nonsense! You're crazy."

But Bissell and the other Go-Getting businessmen in the Pennsylvania Rock Oil Company decided to try. From New Haven they sent Edwin L. Drake out to the oil fields. One reason they picked him was that since he had been a railroad conductor, he still had a free pass on the railroads. He could go out to western Pennsylvania without it costing anybody anything.

When Drake reached Titusville, the town closest to the biggest finds of surface oil, he decided to drill for oil. But at first he could not find a driller willing to do the job. The drillers all thought that boring for oil was silly.

Then, luckily, he found an old salt driller, "Uncle Billy" Smith, who was also a skilled blacksmith and knew how to make drilling tools. Uncle Billy began drilling in June 1859. But after he reached bedrock thirty-two feet down,

Uncle Billy could drill no more than three feet each day. Drake thought that to find oil they might have to drill a thousand feet.

On Saturday, August 29, 1859, the hole still reached down less than seventy feet. When Drake and Smith came back on Monday morning the hole was full of oily black stuff.

"What's that?" Drake asked.

Uncle Billy replied, "That's your fortune!"

Soon there was an oil mania. Everybody wanted to get rich from oil. The map of northwestern Pennsylvania was

---

The first oil well, Titusville, Pennsylvania. The pointed wooden structure held a derrick for pulling up the drilling tools.

Barrels of oil being loaded on flat-bottomed barges for shipment by water. Shallow boats like these had to navigate the torrents of the Pond Freshet.

dotted with such new names as Oil City, Oleopolis, and Petroleum Center.

Like the instant Cow Towns, these instant Oil Towns boomed. They were good places for salesmen and for swindlers. Some well drillers began "doctoring" their wells. They would pour buckets of oil into their holes at night to trick buyers who came to look the next morning.

When Drake's first well began to gush oil, the oil was put into old whisky barrels, washtubs, and any other container in sight. But since the oil was inflammable, it was dangerous to store in the open. The oil was usually sealed in barrels before being loaded on wagons to

be hauled to the railroad or to docks on the nearest rivers. As roads were poor, the best way to move the oil barrels was on flatboats. But in the streams nearest the oil wells the water was too low to float the loaded flatboats.

The clever oilmen then invented their own way of filling the creeks with water to float their oil barrels to market. The name for their system was the "Pond Freshet" ("freshet" meant a sudden flood of water). For example, on Oil Creek, each oilman made his own artificial pond held back by a dam. Then, at a signal, each quickly opened the dam of his own artificial pond. This suddenly flooded the creek.

Only a few minutes before, the creek was much too shallow for the big flatboats. Now this man-made wave floated down the stream. All the flatboats along the way were alert and ready. At just the right moment, each oilman pushed his loaded boats into the flood, which carried them quickly down to the railroad center.

Just after a successful Pond Freshet, as an oilman recalled, the Oil Town was very much like a Cow Town after the arrival of a large Texas herd.

Shippers are busy paying off the boatmen, the citizens of the creek are laying in a stock of the necessaries of life, and all is bustle and business. You see men dripping with the oleaginous product. Our hotels are filled to repletion with these greasy men who are supplying light for the world. Oil is the only topic of conversation, and the air is redolent with its sweet perfumery.

The great success in oil—one of the most spectacular of all American Go-Getters—was John D. Rockefeller. He was not an inventor or an explorer. He was an organizer. His talent was like that of Charles Goodnight, who had collected thousands of cattle for the Long Drive.

Young Rockefeller went to school in Cleveland, but he never went to college. His father, who traveled through the West selling patent medicines, left young John in charge of the family long before he was grown. John D. Rockefeller was ambitious. "I did not guess what it would be," he recalled. "But I was after something big."

Even as a boy he was systematic and well organized. While still struggling to make his way, he gave one-tenth of his income to the Baptist Church and to charities. But when it came to organizing his oil business, he did not always use Sunday School methods.

Cleveland was a good place to organize "something big" in the oil business. At the receiving end of two railroads which came from the western Pennsylvania oil fields, Cleveland was also on a lake big enough for large ships. Rockefeller determined to make Cleveland the center of the oil business, and from there to command the biggest oil company in the world. Beginning with a small sum he had made in a grain-trading business, in 1865 he bought his first Cleveland refinery. There crude oil from the fields was made into kerosene for lighting and oil for lubricating. Then he bought up the smaller refineries in Cleveland and many oil wells in western Pennsylvania.

As other oilmen went out of business, the railroads needed Rockefeller's freight more than ever. He was clever at making the two Cleveland railroads compete for his business. He bargained with one railroad by threatening to give all his business to the other. And he finally forced them to charge him lower prices than they charged anybody else. He did this by secret arrangements so other customers of the railroad could not know for sure what was happening. He pretended to pay the same prices the railroad charged everybody else. Then the railroads secretly gave him back a "rebate"—a refund on each barrel of his oil that they had hauled.

After he perfected these tactics he went to the small refiners in other parts of the country and asked them to sell to him. "If you don't sell your property," he would say, "it will be valueless, because we have advantages with the railroads."

"But we don't want to sell," they would say.

"You can never make money," Rockefeller would reply. "You can't compete with the Standard Oil Company. We have all the large refineries now. If you refuse to sell, it will end in your being crushed."

He would then offer a price far below what the owners thought their refineries were worth. But they usually sold because they realized that Rockefeller could drive them out of business.

When it became cheaper to pump oil through pipelines instead of carrying it in barrels, Rockefeller organized his own pipeline. Then, when a different kind of oil was found in Ohio, Rockefeller hired chemical engineers to invent new kinds of refineries.

Rockefeller's Go-Getting business reached around the world. To the Chinese, his Standard Oil Company sold inexpensive lamps by the millions—and then sold the oil to fill them. Before long, people on all continents were

A magazine cartoon published two years after Drake's first oil strike. Whales (whose blubber had been an important source of lamp oil) had good reason to celebrate the discovery of "mineral oil." As the new oil industry prospered, the whaling industry declined.

using lamp oil from American wells. Between the Civil War and 1900 over half the American output went abroad. In those years the giant Go-Getter, John D. Rockefeller, helped light up the world. Now Americans could afford a lamp in every room.

In the twentieth century, Rockefeller's business would grow in ways even he had never imagined. After the automobile was invented, petroleum was refined into gasoline—and Rock Oil made it possible for a whole nation to move on wheels.

CHAPTER 3

City Goods for Country Customers ⌘

During the colonial years, an American farmer made for himself almost everything he needed. He built his own house (with the help of a few neighbors) and he made his own furniture. His wife and daughters spun the thread, wove the cloth, and then made the family's clothes. The pots and pans and metal tools which he could not make for himself he would buy from a peddler. But he bought very few things. There were not many ready-made things for him to buy.

Then, in the years before the Civil War, American know-how built on ideas from Europe's Industrial Revolution to develop a new kind of manufacturing. Lots of new things were produced in vast new quantities. The new American System of Manufacture, which Eli Whitney and Samuel Colt had organized to make guns and revolvers, also turned out clocks and locks, and countless other items—both better and cheaper. Now farmers could afford to buy them.

But when a farmer wanted any of these things he had to go to the nearest village and visit the general store.

Children loved the place because it was where you could buy candy and toys. Since the storekeeper kept a good fire in his stove, the store was where you could stay warm in winter. Year round it was where you could meet friends and exchange ideas.

But it was no place for bargains. The country storekeeper, who bought only a little bit of everything, could not command the best wholesale prices from the big-city manufacturers. Each item had to be hauled by wagon over bumpy backwoods roads. Things would get dusty and out-of-date before they could be sold.

Soon after the Civil War an energetic young salesman, who had covered the West selling goods to the owners of general stores, began to think of a new plan. His name was A. Montgomery Ward. He had done all sorts of things, from working in a barrel factory and in a brickyard to selling drygoods. Often in his travels he had heard farmers complain about the small choice of goods and the high prices.

Young Ward's idea was to sell goods

An old general store with the village post office. The storekeeper often doubled as postmaster.

in an entirely new way. Instead of the old general store which stocked only a few of each item, Ward imagined a mail-order store. The storekeeper would stay in the big city where it was easier to collect a large stock of all sorts of goods. He would send out to farmers lists of his goods with descriptions and pictures. The farmer would not need to come to the store because the store—in the form of a catalog—would go to the farmer. And the farmer would order by mail, picking out whatever he wanted from the catalog. Then the storekeeper would mail the farmer his goods.

If this new scheme worked, the store-keeper would be selling not only to the few customers in one particular village. He could sell to farmers all over America—to anyone within reach of a mailbox.

The possible customers of this new kind of store would not be just a few hundred, they might be millions! And then Ward could buy his goods from the manufacturer by the hundreds and thousands. The manufacturer could afford to give him a lower price.

For the customer, too, there were advantages. He had a much wider selection of goods. And he paid a lower price since the mail-order storekeeper, with so many more customers, could take a smaller profit on each item and yet would make more money in the long run.

Young Montgomery Ward had lost nearly all his savings in the Chicago fire of 1871, but in the very next year he managed to scrape together enough to make a start with his new idea. He put in $1,600 and a partner added $800. They rented a small room over a stable, and started modestly. Their single price-sheet listed the items for sale and told how to order. Within two years Ward was issuing a 72-page catalog with illustrations. By 1884 the catalog numbered 240 pages and listed nearly ten thousand items. Within another thirty years it was over a thousand pages and included every conceivable object for animals or men.

One way Ward rounded up customers was to get himself appointed the official supplier for the "Grange." This was one name for a large farmers' club, the Patrons of Husbandry, founded just after the Civil War. By 1875 its members numbered 750,000 and all these were likely customers. Ward offered Grange members a special discount. He stocked the official Granger hat and in his catalog printed recommendations from Grange officers. This encouraged other farmers to trust Ward's.

Trust was the most important thing for a mail-order store. If you bought in a general store you were buying from a storekeeper you knew. You could see the goods and handle them to satisfy yourself. But when you bought from a mail-order store you had to trust somebody you had never seen. You had to believe that the storekeeper would really send you the exact thing described in the catalog.

Ward was a spectacular success. The first secret of his success was not a secret at all, but simply to be honest, give good value, and always let the customer be the judge. On everything Ward's gave an ironclad guarantee. "Satisfaction or your money back!" If a customer did not like the goods when they arrived, he could always return them. If something arrived damaged, he could send it back to Ward's to be replaced. The company paid the postage both ways.

Of course there had to be trust on the company's side, too. The company had to be willing to cash the customer's checks, to believe his complaints, and to replace damaged goods without a lot of investigating. Ward was willing to do this, and to take the risks.

The catalog showed pictures of Ward himself, of the other executives, and of the men in charge of the different departments. This was to convince the customer that he was dealing with real people. Some customers wrote in to say how pleased they were to deal with such "fine looking men." Some even named babies after Ward, and said he would be an inspiration to their children.

Ward saw that their letters were promptly answered—even if they were not ordering goods but only asking advice. One customer asked how to find a baby to adopt. Others tried to sell Ward their secondhand furniture or their livestock. Parents asked help in finding boys who had run away from home. They wanted to know how to handle disobedient children. Some wrote him simply because they were lonely and had nobody else to write to.

SHOPPING by CATALOG

From the Montgomery Ward catalog, 1895. At that time both wages and prices were much lower than today. A typical workingman earned about $500 a year.

Children's Suits.

32434 Boys' Shirt Waists, striped cotton cheviot, light ground, double ruffle down front, sailor collar with 1 inch ruffle.
Each.............. ..$0.30
Per dozen......... 3.24

32436 Boys' Shirt Waists, light ground striped chambray, double ruffle down front, sailor collar, turned over cuffs with ruffle. Each.......$0.45
Per dozen..........$4.86

32438 Boys' Shirt Waists, indigo blue, fancy figured penang; double ruffle down front, sailor collar, turned over cuffs with ruffle, pleated front and back. Each. $0.55
Per dozen.................... 5.94

32440 Boys' Shirt Waists, medium heavy stripe, cotton cheviot, double ruffle down front, sailor collar with ruffle, pleated front and back.
Each...............$0.60

32434 to 32440

Spinning Wheels.

39583

39583 Quill or Spooling Wheel, like cut. Each.$3.60

39585 German or Flax Spinning Wheel, with foot power. Price, each............$4.00

39585

Bathing Suits.

ONE-PIECE SUITS.

Knit goods, very elastic, not cloth goods. Button well down to the front, making them easy to get on or off. Extra, by mail, 5 to 10 cents. Give chest measure.

	Each.
49150 Cotton, striped........	$0.75
49151 Cotton, navy blue.......	1.50
49152 Cotton, fast black......	1.50
49153 Cotton, navy with stripes	1.25
49154 Worsted, navy blue....	2.90

TWO-PIECE SUITS.

Consisting of quarter sleeve shirts and knee pants.

	Per Suit.
49155 Cotton, striped........	$1.00
49156 Cotton, navy, with stripes.................	1.50
49157 Worsted, navy blue....	2.40
49158 Worsted, black.........	2.40
49160 Best Worsted, striped.	5.25

Extra, by mail, 15 to 20 cents.

Style N2. Case only. 14k filled $8.80

36570 Child's La... Hat, extra shir... brim. Colors: C... dinal, white, pi... or light blue. Each.. ......$0...
Per dozen..... 5...

36571 Child's Shir... Hat, made... Swiss embroid... shirred brim, tri... med all round w... embroidered edgi...
Each..........$0...
Per dozen..... 5...

5704 Ladies' Newport Suit, same style as 5700, made of heavy all-wool storm serge, trimmed with two rows of folded satin rhadame on collar, cuffs and bottom of skirt. Colors: Black or navy blue only. A stylish and splendid wearing suit. Per suit....................$5.

5705 Ladies' Newpo... Suit, same style... 5700, made... heavy English wh... cord, trimmed... narrow folds of s... in. Navy blue... black only. Ve... serviceable and e... gant. Per suit.$7...

5708 Ladies' Newpo... Suit, same style... 5700, made of fi... all wool broadclot... high finished; co... lar, cuffs and botto... of skirt trimm... with narrow fold... moire silk, very e... gant. Colors: Blac... brown, light or da... navy blue. Per suit... ..$8...

5709 Ladies' Newpo... Suit, made of a... wool cheviot ser... in navy blue; ne... organ pipe ski... double breaste... jacket, doub... stitching aroun... skirt and jacke... immense sleeve... made in first-cla... style. Per suit $8...

5711 Ladies' Newpo... Suit, made of styli... tweed suiting... light brown a... white mixtur... Very neat and se...

The Razor Toe.

Weight 15 ounces.

52034 This style shoe is becoming very popular on account of the long narrow toe, and patent tip, which has a tendency of giving the foot a very graceful appearance. The stock is a very soft dongola, with light flexible soles and medium but slightly concave; for a neat stylish dress boot, it has no equal and for the quality, compares favorably with many of the three dollar and a half grades now on the market. Sizes, 2½ to 7 widths, C, D, E and EE.
Per pair....................$2.50

5709
viceable, will not show dust or wear. Same style 5709. Per suit.. ....$9.

Just as the colonial tobacco planter might ask his London agent to send him whatever he needed, now the lonely farmer asked Ward's. One customer wrote:

Please send me a good wife. She must be a good housekeeper and able to do all household duty. She must be 5 feet 6 inches in height. Weight 150 lbs. Black hair and brown eyes, either fair or dark. I am 45 years old, six feet, am considered a good looking man. I have black hair and blue eyes. I own quite a lot of stock and land. I am tired of living a bachelor life and wish to lead a better life and more favorable.

Please write and let me know what you can do for me.

Ward's answered that it was not a good idea to select a wife by mail. "After you get the wife and you find that she needs some wearing apparel or household goods," Ward's added, "we feel sure we could serve both you and her to good advantage."

Some felt that Ward's would be disappointed at not hearing from them.

I suppose you wonder why we haven't ordered anything from you since the Fall. Well, the cow kicked my arm and broke it, and besides my wife was sick, and there was the doctor bill. But now, thank God, that is paid, and we are all well again, and we have a fine new baby boy, and please send plush bonnet number 29d-8077.

This friendly customer received a friendly reply. Ward's said they were sorry about his arm, glad that his wife was better, and sent congratulations on the son with hopes he would grow up to be a fine man. The order for the bonnet was acknowledged. Then, finally, Ward's asked whether the customer had noticed that there was an anti-cow-kicker for sale in the catalog.

It is not surprising that the mail-order store was a roaring success. Of course, in an age of Go-Getters, Ward was not the only man who tried his hand at building a mail-order store. One of the cleverest of these others was a young railroad station agent, Richard Sears. When a stray package of watches arrived at his station in North Redwood, Minnesota, the Chicago watch company offered to sell them to Sears at $12 apiece. Sears bought the watches and then sold them by mail to other agents along the line for $14 apiece.

Sears was in business. By selling watches to other station agents, Sears made five thousand dollars in six months, gave up his railroad job, moved to Chicago, and began selling other jewelry by mail. He found a partner in Alvah Curtis Roebuck, a watchmaker who ran a print shop where they could turn out their catalogs.

Sears was a clever man, and a near-genius at selling by mail. One of his schemes was a club plan for selling watches. He persuaded men to form a "Watch Club" of thirty-eight members. Every week each member would pay the Club one dollar. And every week when the members drew lots, one of them would win a watch. At the end of thirty-eight weeks, every club member had a watch. And they had bought all thirty-eight watches from Sears!

Of course, Sears could not have succeeded for long in the mail-order business unless he, like Ward, had been honest. He too gave good value for the money, and let customers return any goods they did not like.

But Sears was not afraid of a good joke. He knew that lonely farm families were glad to be entertained. In a rural weekly newspaper in 1889 he made an "Astonishing Offer." It was illustrated by a drawing of a sofa and two chairs, all of "fine, lustrous metal frames beautifully finished and decorated, and upholstered in the finest manner with beautiful plush." Sears offered to ship all this furniture "as an advertisement only" and "for a limited time only" for the ridiculously low price of ninety-five cents.

The customers who sent in their money really were astonished. They received a set of doll's furniture, made exactly according to the description. They had not noticed in the first line of the advertisement, in tiny print, the word "miniature."

There were lots of stories about how clever Sears was. One of his advertisements offered a "sewing machine" for a dollar. When the customer sent in his dollar, he promptly received by return mail a needle and thread. But Sears used such stunts only to attract attention.

Like Ward, Sears actually built his business on trust and on the personal touch. After the typewriter first came into general use, about 1900, some farmers still preferred to get a letter written by hand. Sears still went to the trouble of hiring people to write out handwritten letters for the company. Then farmers would not have their feelings hurt by receiving a letter that was "machine-made."

Sears knew that his catalog was both his shopwindow and his salesman. And he invented schemes for getting his catalogs around. He would send them in batches of twenty-four to people who had agreed to distribute them. But how could he be sure that the distributors would give their catalogs to the people most likely to be good customers? Sears kept a record of purchases by the new customers to whom each distributor had given his catalogs. The distributor then received a prize in proportion to the amount of money spent by his new customers. When, for example, total orders from his new customers amounted to $100, the distributor was awarded a bicycle, a sewing machine, or a stove.

Sears was constantly improving his catalog. He developed a new quick-drying ink, new systems of color printing, and thinner paper that would take color but was cheaper to mail. He found, for example, that four pages of

A four-passenger surrey advertised in 1897 by Sears Roebuck for $44. The buyer also needed a horse.

advertisements in color would sell as much of the same goods as twelve pages in black and white. His improvements were widely copied by other advertisers and by publishers of newspapers and magazines.

As Sears's catalog grew bigger and bigger it also reached more and more customers. He sent out two big catalogs a year, one in the spring and one in the fall. By 1904 each of these had a circulation of over one million. By the 1920's the figure was seven million. And it kept on rising.

As the mail-order catalog reached more and more people on remote farms, it became more and more important in their daily lives. While the farmer kept his Bible in the living room, he kept his Sears or Ward catalog in the kitchen. That was where he really lived.

There were all sorts of stories about how much faith people put in this big book. When one little boy was asked by his Sunday School teacher where the Ten Commandments came from, he said he supposed they came from Sears.

Just as Puritan boys and girls in colonial times had studied the New England Primer with its stories about God and the Devil, now Americans on farms studied the Sears catalog. In country schoolhouses, where there were few textbooks, teachers made good use of the catalog. They used it to teach reading and spelling. For arithmetic, pupils filled out orders and added up items. And they learned geography from the catalog's postal-zone maps.

In a school that had no other encyclopedia, pupils used a Ward or Sears catalog. It had a good index, it was

COMBINATION OF LACE, JET, IMPORTED ROSES AND FINE RIBBON.

Price, $3.95

Ladies' hats, like this one advertised in the Sears catalog of 1910, offered the latest fashions for the farmer's wife—and for his daughter's paper dolls.

illustrated, it told you what things were good for, what they were made of, how long they would last, and even what they would cost. Mothers gave the catalogs to children to keep them occupied. When a new catalog arrived, the old one would be given to the girls, who cut it up for paper dolls.

Nothing did more than the new mail-order stores to change life on the farm —and to make life in America something new. Before the twentieth century most Americans still lived on the farm. Now that the American farmer could order from Ward's or Sears, his life became increasingly different from that of a European peasant. His view of the good things in the world was no longer confined to the shelves of the little village store. The up-to-date catalogs brought news of all kinds of new machines, new gadgets, and new fashions. Now American farmers could buy big-city goods at prices they could afford and from someone they could trust.

CHAPTER 4

One Price for Everybody!

Meanwhile other Go-Getters were inventing ways to attract the new millions of city customers. The big stores which now grew up in American cities were as different from the little shops in London's West End as the grand new American hotels were different from the modest Old World inns.

The new American hotels were People's Palaces. Anybody could meet his friends in the elegant lobby or, if he had the money, could entertain in a dining room with a crystal chandelier. The new department stores were Buyers' Palaces. And they, too, were democratic.

In London, nobody was admitted to the elegant shops unless he looked like a "gentleman" or a "lady." Unless the shopkeeper knew who you were, he would not let you in. You had to be a "person of quality" (as the upper classes were called) to see "goods of quality."

Department stores changed all this. Suddenly there were vast Buyers' Palaces, some large enough to fill a whole city block—specially designed to display goods of every shape, price, and description. Anybody could walk in. Now everybody could have a close look at elegant jewelry, clothing, and furniture of the kind once reserved for rich men's eyes.

Like many other American achievements, this happened quickly. English ways of selling had not changed much in five hundred years. But this department-store revolution, which began shortly before the Civil War, changed the lives of American customers within a few decades.

Stewart's Cast Iron Palace, completed in 1862 in New York City, was one of the first big department stores. It was the product of two different kinds of Go-Getters—a businessman and an inventor.

A. T. Stewart, the merchant who built up the business, came to the United States from Ireland at the age of seventeen. He started by selling the Irish laces he had brought with him. But he soon branched out into all kinds of goods. He was a bold, ambitious businessman. And he decided to spend a fortune on an enormous building in an entirely new style. When Stewart decided to build his grand new store he picked an inventing genius who was sure to try something new.

James Bogardus, the man Stewart chose, had started as a watchmaker's apprentice in upstate New York. He first became famous by his new design for an eight-day clock. Then he invented all kinds of new machines—for making cotton thread, for mixing lead paint, for grinding sugar, for metering gas, and for engraving postage stamps. He patented a metal-cased pencil with a lead that was "forever pointed."

His most important new idea was to construct buildings of cast iron. Bogardus' own five-story factory, built in 1850, was probably the first cast-iron building in America. The building Bogardus built for Stewart overwhelmed everybody at the time by its height—eight stories. It quickly became famous as the biggest store in the world.

Bogardus used cast iron to make an impressive Buyers' Palace. The outside looked palatial and dignified. Graceful columns which held up thin beams made a neat repeating pattern like that found in Old World palaces. The molded iron panels between columns were painted to resemble stone. Fancy cast-iron shapes decorated the window frames.

On the ground floor the outside walls no longer needed to be thick—as they had to be when a tall building was made of stone. Now there could be larger windows on every floor. Slender iron columns held up the high ceiling of display rooms a city-block wide. The ground floor was made even more palatial by a grand central staircase and a great rotunda reaching up the full height of the building, topped by a glass roof down which the sunlight streamed. You could enjoy long indoor vistas of appealing merchandise—gloves, umbrellas, suitcases, coats, furniture, all kinds of things in all shapes and sizes and colors. All the people busy looking, buying, and admiring helped make a splendid spectacle.

Naturally the Go-Getting department-storekeepers wanted to display their

A London furrier giving personal attention to upper-class customers. Only select "gentlemen" and "ladies" would be shown the elegant stock.

goods to everybody who walked down the street. The thin cast-iron building frames made this easier, but it would not have been possible without a new kind of window. Before the age of the department store, glass was expensive. Windows had to be small. They were made to admit a little daylight or to look *out of*.

Then, not long before the Civil War, an Englishman invented an inexpensive way of rolling out glass in large sheets. These large sheets of glass now at last made possible the "show window." Americans invented this new expression for the new kind of window that was made to look *into*. Now the goods could advertise themselves.

In a store where thousands of customers were buying and hundreds of people were selling, other things had to

"Buyers' Palaces"—open to all—were soon found in the larger American cities. A cutaway view of Abraham & Straus department store in Brooklyn about 1892.

change. The old way of selling goods was for the storekeeper to bargain with each customer separately. He did not mark a price on the goods. Instead he asked from each customer the highest price he thought he could get. This price depended upon how rich he thought the customer was, on how much he thought the customer wanted the goods, and on how anxious he was to make a sale at that time. You could never be sure in advance how much you would have to pay. If you were a good bargainer, you could always get it for less. But bargaining took time. It did not suit Americans in a hurry.

The big department store brought the age of the "fixed price." A. T. Stewart's Cast Iron Palace employed two thousand people. Stewart himself could not know all his salesmen. How could he let them bargain for him? At Stewart's, then, everything carried a price tag. Everybody could see the price, and it was the same price for all.

When you went shopping now, you could no longer get your fun from bargaining. But you got better value, and there were new experiences to enjoy— like looking at all the elegant things you could not afford. The department store was a new, very American, and very democratic kind of entertainment where the admission was always free.

CHAPTER 5

A Democracy of Clothing ⟳⟲⟳⟲⟳⟲⟳⟲

At the outbreak of the Civil War in 1861 the government had to provide hundreds of thousands of uniforms for men in the army. This was the first time in American history that so much clothing had been required all at once. During the American Revolution the colonial army had been relatively small, and most soldiers brought along their own clothing. In the later wars too—the War of 1812 and the Mexican War—

the armies were only a few thousand strong.

So in 1861 there was no large ready-made clothing industry. The simple explanation was that it had always been the custom for each family to make its own clothes. Just as the meals that American families eat today are usually made at home, so it used to be with coats, suits, socks, and nearly everything else a person wore. Only the rich few, who could afford to look elegant, would hire a skilled tailor.

In New England in the early nineteenth century there were a few shops that sold ready-made clothing. But these offered only the cheapest grades. In New Bedford, Massachusetts, for example, sailors who had just returned from a three-year whaling voyage needed new clothing quickly. Other sailors who had just signed on for a new voyage hastily had to collect supplies for their months at sea. The stores that sold them their clothing were called "slop-shops" because the clothing they sold was sailors' "slops." ("Slop" was an Old Norse word for the sailors' wide-bottomed trousers.) What sailors bought there they put on board ship in their "slopchests." Slopshop clothing was of poor quality, and the customer did not expect a good fit.

In the South, too, some plantation owners bought cheap ready-made clothing for their slaves. In Western mining towns the men who had quickly joined the Gold Rush had usually left their families behind. There were too few women to provide homemade clothing, and not enough rich people to support a tailor. Miners had to go to a store. "Store-boughten" clothing was better than nothing.

People took it for granted that if you bought ready-made clothing from a store, it could not possibly fit you well. They believed that everybody was a quite different size. Therefore, they said, the only way to make clothing fit was to have it made specially (either at home or by a tailor) to your very own measurements. How could a manufacturer possibly turn out thousands of suits, each a different size, for thousands of different people? A suit you bought in a store would surely be too loose in some places and too tight in others. Manufacturers—without even trying—had given up the effort to provide sizes that would really fit.

Take shoes, for example. Before the mid-nineteenth century, even after shoe-making machinery had been invented, the shoes you could buy ready-made in a store were usually "straights." That meant there was actually no difference between the shoe sold for the right foot and for the left foot. If you really wanted your shoes to fit, you had to hire a shoemaker to make a pair especially for you.

The uniform-makers in the Civil War learned a lesson. They found that if they made quite a few different sizes they could provide almost everybody with a reasonably good fit. They noticed that certain combinations of measurements were more common than others. For example, lots of men with a 36-inch waist also had a 30-inch trouser length. They kept track of the sizes of the uniforms they made.

When the War was over in 1865 and hundreds of thousands of veterans suddenly needed civilian clothes, the United States actually had a clothing industry. Manufacturers had learned so much about the commonest measurements of the human body that they could produce ready-made suits which fitted better than most homemade suits and almost as well as the best tailor-made. Merchants now began to open clothing stores for everybody because their assortments of sizes would fit any customer. Americans of all classes and occupations were glad to buy their suits ready-made.

The age of statistics—a new age of careful measurement—had arrived in the world of clothing. A statistically-minded tailor named Daniel Edward Ryan, after years of collecting facts, in 1880 published *Human Proportions in Growth: Being the Complete Measurement of the Human Body for Every Age and Size during the Years of Juvenile Growth*. The new Science of Sizes gave clothing manufacturers a scientific guide for customers of all ages.

To put this new science to use, and to stock clothing stores with all the different sizes, there had to be a whole factory full of new machinery. The old tedious way of making garments—cutting cloth for one suit at a time and then sewing each seam by hand—was not good enough.

Most of the labor went into sewing. So the most important new machine would be a sewing machine. In 1831 a Paris tailor had made a workable sewing machine, and had begun to use it making uniforms for the French army. But Paris tailors, afraid that they would lose their jobs, smashed the machines and drove the inventor out of the city. Soon afterward, several Americans made sewing machines.

Walter Hunt was one of the most ingenious inventors of the age. Once when he needed money to pay a debt, within the space of only three hours he invented the safety pin, made a model of it, and sold the idea for $400. But he was more interested in making inventions than in making money. Among his new devices were a knife sharpener, a stove to burn hard coal, an ice plow, a repeating rifle, a street-sweeping ma-

chine, and paper collars. The vast new department stores and the catalogs of the new mail-order firms offered ways to show and sell such gadgets to Americans wherever they lived.

Most inventors who tried to make a sewing machine had not got very far, because they tried to make their machines imitate hand sewing. So they put the point of the needle at one end, and the eye, or hole, of the needle at the other. Hunt was more original. He put the hole at the pointed end. The thread was attached there. Then the other end of the needle was attached to a machine that simply pushed it up and down while another thread was thrust through the loop underneath the cloth. Using this original idea, by 1832 he had perfected a machine that sewed a lock stitch which would not unravel. But Hunt was not at all a businessman, and he did not even bother to patent his invention.

A few years later Elias Howe, who had been raised on a Massachusetts farm and then worked as apprentice to a scientific instrument maker in Cambridge, made the same invention on his own. He patented his machine in 1846.

The sewing machine that Howe patented in 1846. The spool at the left held the thread.

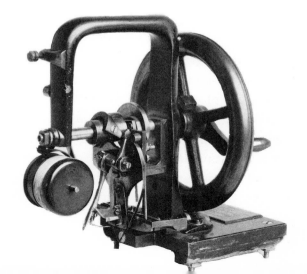

Before Thomas Edison brought electricity into homes, some people used small steam engines (fired by the kitchen stove) to run their sewing machines.

To prove that his machine really worked, Howe staged a public sewing race at the Quincy Hall Clothing Manufactory in Boston. He challenged five of the speediest seamstresses. Ten seams of equal length were prepared. One was given to each seamstress, and five were given to Howe at his machine. To everybody's amazement, before any of the seamstresses had finished her one seam, Howe had finished his *five*. His sewing machine was declared the winner.

But people feared that the sewing machine would put needy seamstresses out of work. As late as 1849 the sewing machine was still so rare that a man carried one around western New York State charging an admission fee of 12½ cents to see "A Great Curiosity!! The Yankee Sewing-Machine." Ladies took home specimens of machine sewing to show their friends.

Not for long would machine sewing remain a curiosity. For a remarkable Go-Getting salesman and organizer had become interested. When Isaac Merrit

Singer saw his first sewing machine in 1850 his main aim—like that of Henry Ford after him—was to make machines so cheap that he could sell them by the hundreds of thousands. When he used Howe's patented designs without permission, the courts eventually made him pay for the right to use Howe's design. But in 1856 Singer persuaded Howe to join a great Sewing Machine Combination to make machines with all the latest improvements.

Singer's dream came true, for by 1871 more than a half-million sewing machines were being manufactured each year. The combination of Howe design and Singer salesmanship sent American sewing machines all over the world. "Every nook and corner of Europe," the advertisements boasted, "knows the song of this tireless Singer."

The women who still had the job of making all the family's clothing were, of course, happy to have a machine to ease their work. And the sewing machine was only one of the first of many new machines—washing machines for clothes and dishes, vacuum cleaners, mixing machines for the kitchen, and many others—which would make the life of the twentieth-century American housewife both easier and more complicated.

Next to sewing the seams, what took most time in a man's coat or suit was cutting the cloth to the pattern. To cut heavy cloth for one suit at a time was tedious. But it was hard to make a knife that would cut through thick piles of cloth. The knife tended to twist the cloth so that the bottom pieces came out a different shape. This problem was solved in the 1870's when new high-speed, steam-powered cutting machines sliced neatly through twenty or more thicknesses. In the 1880's a Boston inventor perfected a machine that saved more hours by automatically cutting and finishing buttonholes.

Each factory-produced suit had to be neatly pressed. But the old heavy pressing iron (called a "goose" because it was so large and had a long awkward handle) was slow. A clever apprentice, Adon J. Hoffman, who was using a "goose" in a tailor shop in Syracuse, New York, dislocated his shoulder so that he could not handle the cumbersome iron. So he invented a presser he could operate with his feet. A foot pedal controlled the steam pressure which pushed down the top pad. All the operator had to do with his hands was to lay the garment between the pads. Within a few years Hoffman had become rich by selling thousands of his new steam pressers.

As the population grew and the American worker prospered, the demand for good ready-made clothing went up. At the same time, too, near the end of the nineteenth century, the flood of immigrants from Germany, Russia, and Poland included many who had been tailors over there. They naturally went to work in clothing factories here. But the new sewing machine was mak-

In their slum apartment a whole immigrant family (crowded together with their sewing machine) worked at making garments.

ing the tailor's skill less needed than ever. In the new clothing factories, the wives and children of these immigrants found quick employment.

Some of these factories became "sweatshops," where women and children worked long hours in stuffy rooms for low wages. But soon new laws required the children to stay in school. Meanwhile labor unions, led by enterprising immigrants, organized the clothing workers to demand better wages and shorter hours. Eventually the unions themselves would become rich enough to provide hospitals, clubhouses, and scholarships for their members.

By the end of the nineteenth century the United States saw a revolution in clothing. Here for the first time in history there was beginning to be a democracy of clothing. Here you did not have to be rich to dress well. A new industry was finding ways to make a stylish suit that any man could afford. Before 1900 nine-tenths of the men and boys in the

This fashionable man's suit was offered by Montgomery Ward (in 1895) for $7.50. For $2.25 his son could have a suit with extra pants and a cap.

United States were wearing ready-made clothing that they had bought in a store. Even the rich who once hired a tailor found a ready-made suit to fit. Americans dressed more like one another than people in any Old World nation. The new immigrant could go into a clothing store and buy a ready-made outfit that made him an instant American.

CHAPTER 6

Things by the Millions ✑ ✑ ✑ ✑ ✑ ✑ ✑ ✑

On July 4, 1876, the nation celebrated its hundredth birthday with a Centennial Exposition held at Philadelphia. On the fairgrounds there were no rifle ranges or roller coasters or freak shows. There was no need for any. American products of all shapes and sizes—from shiny new bicycles to a new machine that sent your voice over a wire—were

themselves quite enough to entertain and amaze.

Visitors from Europe were astonished at how fast the United States had moved ahead. One hundred years before, the country had been thirteen weak and separate colonies—of a few towns and many scattered farms. Even twenty-five years before (when the Great Exhibition

The festivities at the Centennial Exposition in Philadelphia in 1876 included concerts like this one, held in the Music Pavilion.

had been held in London) England was plainly the leading manufacturing nation in the world. But now the United States was already threatening to take her place.

At this Philadelphia Fair, Machinery Hall, which drew the biggest crowds, was dominated by the gigantic Corliss Steam Engine. The largest ever, it was forty feet high, weighed seven hundred tons, and produced over two thousand horsepower.

George H. Corliss, the man who made the great engine, showed how to combine the Go-Getter spirit with American know-how. When timid businessmen would not buy his improved steam engine, he offered it to them free—in return for the money his engine would save them by using less coal. From one engine alone he received in five years nearly twenty thousand dollars, which was several times what the engine cost him to make.

But it was not only size and quality that impressed visitors from the Old World. They were astonished by how cheaply Americans could make so many different things. Early in the nineteenth century one ingenious Connecticut manufacturer, Eli Terry, had already managed to turn out new clocks that sold for so little it was not worth having an old

one repaired. Even before the Civil War, American clocks sold for less than fifty cents apiece, and New England factories were producing a half-million clocks each year.

Now in 1876, Europeans who saw the Philadelphia exhibits were convinced that Americans would change the world. The American machines, one Swiss engineer predicted, would "overwhelm all mankind with a quantity of products which, we hope, will bring them blessing."

To make things by the millions, Americans first had to create whole new industries and whole new ways of thinking. Newest and most essential was the industry for making machine tools. Machine tools were the parent machines—the machines for making the sewing machines, the gun-making machines, the clock-making machines, and all the rest. Since all these machines themselves were made of metal, machine tools were mostly metal-cutting tools.

In the early nineteenth century, a number of clever British machinists perfected the art of metal cutting. They invented a new measuring tool called a "micrometer" (from the Greek *meter* for measure and *micro* for small) which could measure thousandths of an inch.

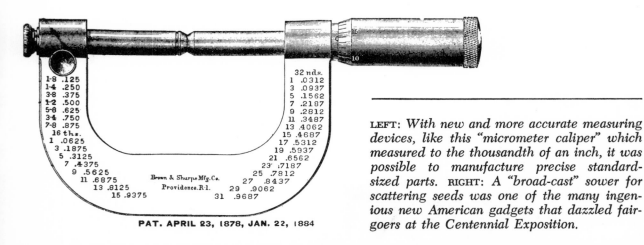

LEFT: *With new and more accurate measuring devices, like this "micrometer caliper" which measured to the thousandth of an inch, it was possible to manufacture precise standard-sized parts.* RIGHT: *A "broad-cast" sower for scattering seeds was one of the many ingenious new American gadgets that dazzled fairgoers at the Centennial Exposition.*

The Englishmen had a head start. But England was an old country, with many craftsmen skilled at making things the old way. In America there were fewer skilled craftsmen, and few craft traditions. Workers here were more willing to try new ways. Soon after the Civil War ingenious Americans were making and improving their own machine tools.

One of the most remarkable of the American machine-tool makers was William Sellers of Philadelphia. By the time of the Centennial Exposition his work was already famous. He had invented machines that could measure and cut metal at the same time. These were essential for making standard-size screws.

And now screws were more important than anyone could imagine before. The millions of metal parts of the new machines were held together by metal screws. In the old days nobody could make one screw exactly like another. Each screw had been specially made to go into one particular hole in one particular machine. Then if you took a piece of machinery apart you had to label each screw so you could put it back in the same place.

Now that would not do. What good was it to make guns or clocks with standard-size parts unless you could hold them together with standard-size screws?

In his *System of Screw Threads and Nuts* (1864), William Sellers offered his own standard designs for the tiny grooves. After that, if you said your machine used a "Sellers Number 6" screw, then everybody knew exactly what you meant. The United States Government officially adopted Sellers' system in 1868. Before the end of the century an international congress in Switzerland made it the standard for Europe too.

Sellers was also interested in the appearance of the large new machines. Earlier machines had been decorated like fancy furniture. They were painted red and green and purple and were prettied up with iron beads and carvings. To Sellers, this made no sense. A machine, Sellers said, ought to look like a machine. He began painting his machines "machine gray"—not for decoration but to prevent rusting and to make cleaning easier. He took off the gimcracks and set the modern machine style which lasted into the twentieth century.

While Sellers was pioneering in new shapes and colors, other Americans were inventing a whole new way of thinking about factories. In the old days, the individual craftsman in his shop would simply do things the way they had always been done before. This was called the "rule-of-thumb." You did the job in a rough, practical way, using your thumb instead of a precise measure.

But the new American factory could not be run that way. If the old gunsmith was crude or inefficient, it meant simply that he made less money, or that people stopped buying guns from him. But in a factory where thousands of men worked elbow-to-elbow, everybody suffered if one man blundered. If your work was not precise, your mistakes were carried all over the country in the thousands of misshapen parts that came off your machine.

Now there was need for a new science —a science of avoiding waste. "Efficiency" was another name for it. The Go-Getting engineer who invented it called it the "Science" of Management.

The efficiency pioneer, Frederick W. Taylor, was born in 1856 in Philadelphia. His mother, a passionate abolitionist, was determined to liberate men from slavery. Taylor hoped to liberate men from waste. He was astonished that people who worried about conserving forests and water power and soil and minerals paid so little attention to conserving human effort.

He believed that there was one best way to do anything. But the one way that was most economical and least wasteful was not necessarily the way it had always been done.

Early in life he experimented to find the most efficient way to walk. He counted his steps and measured his stride. Then he figured out the best way to walk at different times and to different places. He did not drink alcoholic beverages or tea or coffee, and he did not smoke. He said these wasted human energy.

Taylor loved sports and thought they were important in education, not so much because they were fun as because they helped to give a man endurance for his productive work. He designed his own tennis racket, with a curved handle that made it look like a spoon. People laughed at him—until 1881 when Taylor and his partner (with Taylor using his spoon-handle racket) won the United States doubles championship.

The Bethlehem Iron Company hired Taylor to help make their enormous plant more efficient. Every year millions of tons of coal and iron ore were shoveled into furnaces. Paying the men to shovel was one of the largest expenses of making iron. Each man brought his own shovel and shoveled any way he wanted. But wasn't it possible, Taylor asked, that there was actually only one best way to shovel?

Taylor and his crew went into the factory and wrote down exactly what the men were already doing. Each worker was using his one favorite shovel no matter what kind of coal he was shoveling. A shovelful of the extremely light "rice coal" weighed only 3½ pounds, but a shovelful of the heavy iron ore weighed 38 pounds.

"Now," Taylor asked, "is 3½ pounds the proper shovel-load or is 38 pounds the proper shovel load? They cannot both be right. Under scientific management, the answer to the question is not a matter of anyone's opinion; it is a question for accurate, careful, scientific investigation."

Taylor counted the number of shovelfuls of the heavy ore that one man handled in a day. He found that with 38 pounds of ore in each shovel-load, a man in one day handled about 25 tons. Then Taylor cut off part of the metal scoop on the man's shovel so it would hold only 34 pounds. He discovered that this same man now managed to shovel *more* ore in the same length of time. Now the worker handled 30 tons. Yet the worker was less tired. Day after day Taylor kept cutting off a little bit of the shovel.

He found that when the shovel carried 22 pounds in each load, the man moved the most ore in one day.

Taylor had discovered a Science of Shoveling! He designed several different shapes and sizes of shovels and then tested each one to see that it was best suited to the stuff it had to carry. His small flat shovel was for the heavy ore and his immense scoop was for light rice coal. Soon there were 15 kinds of shovels in the Bethlehem tool room. Instead of the 600 men needed to do the shoveling before, with Taylor's Science of Shoveling the same work was done by only 140. Taylor had abolished the waste.

This system, according to Taylor, made it possible to pay each shoveler 60 percent more in wages. The wages of workers actually were increased. But,

naturally enough, many workers were afraid they would lose their jobs. Others were afraid that, even if they kept their jobs, they would have to work harder. Many were afraid they would be regimented. They liked their own shovels. They did not like anybody telling them how to do their simple job.

Still, all over the country, "Scientific Management" became more and more popular with employers. They discovered that by making a science of the simplest jobs, they usually could find a better way.

In an astonishingly short time, the American factory took on a new look. Scientific management engineers invented a whole new way of organizing a factory. Instead of having the worker walk around to pick up parts and bring them to his workbench, the manage-

One of the last steps in the Ford assembly line. The body (assembled on the second floor) was dropped down onto the chassis and motor (assembled on the ground floor), to be attached and fitted by alert mechanics.

ment engineers designed a workbench that moved. Then each worker could stay in one place and keep his mind on his proper job. The bench (now a moving belt) would carry along the heavy parts from one worker to another.

This new kind of moving workbench was called an "assembly line," because on it the whole machine was put to-gether or "assembled."

In early April 1913 a bold mechanic named Henry Ford decided to try an assembly line for making automobiles. He wanted to make automobiles so cheaply that he could sell them by the millions. He made some improvements of his own in the assembly line. For example, he arranged the moving belt so that it

---

When Edison's new phonograph was still rare, this man made money by giving programs of recorded music and talk. Here he holds one of his cylinder-shaped records, chosen from a case decorated with Edison's photograph.

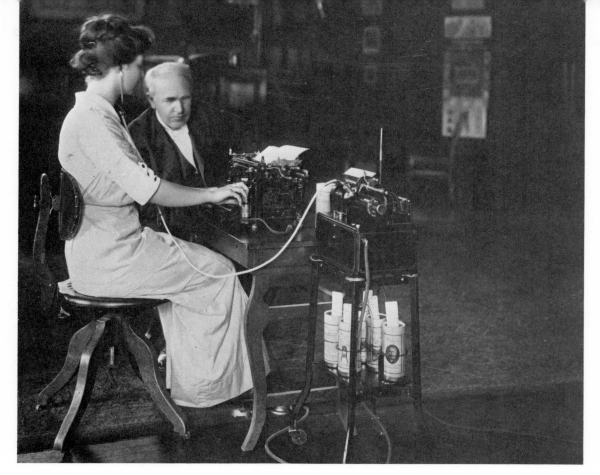

Edison's main interest in the phonograph was not for music but for office use. In this picture Edison watches while a secretary listens to the recorded voice of her employer and copies the words on a typewriter. Like the typewriter and the telephone switchboard, the new device helped to open a whole new world of office work to American women.

would always be "man-high." He changed the height according to the job so that nobody had to waste energy bending down or reaching up.

Ford also varied the speed of the belt. He explained:

The idea is that a man must not be hurried in his work—he must have every second necessary but not a single unnecessary second. . . . The man who puts in a bolt does not put on the nut; the man who puts on the nut does not tighten it. On operation number 34 the budding motor gets its gasoline. . . . On operation number 44 the radiator is filled with water, and on operation number 45 the car drives out.

In the early years when Henry Ford had been trying to perfect a gasoline-driven motor, many people laughed at him. They put him in the same class with crackpots who tried to make perpetual-motion machines. It was hard to imagine a self-propelled machine that would run not on steam but on a liquid fuel.

Luckily, in 1897, Ford met the already famous Thomas A. Edison. Some of Edison's own friends had been working on an electric automobile which worked on storage batteries that had to be recharged frequently. When Ford explained his "gas car," Edison cheered him on. "Young man, that's the thing!

You have it! The self-contained unit carrying its own fuel with it. Keep at it." Edison said the fuel could be a "hydrocarbon"—a chemical name for fluids like gasoline. Although Ford then did not even know the meaning of "hydrocarbon," he was encouraged and later said that the talk with Edison was a turning point in his life.

Ford and Edison became best friends. Even before they had met, Edison (who was sixteen years older) had been an inspiration to Ford, as he was to many other inventors.

Edison had invented a new kind of factory—an "invention factory." It's purpose actually was to invent new kinds of things to make. In the 1870's Edison set up his first "invention factory" with $40,000 he received from his own early inventions.

To his "invention factory" he brought the most ingenious men he could find. He inspired them with loyalty and hope, and built them into a team. Following the example of earlier Go-Getters like Benjamin Silliman and others who had found ways to make "Rock Oil" into fuel to light American homes, these men tried to find new uses for old materials, and also to invent new machines for all sorts of purposes.

Edison and his associates were tireless testers and imaginative mechanics. One of their first feats was to help make electric lighting possible. The most difficult problem had been to find a thread, to put inside the bulb, that would give light when electricity was sent through it and yet would not quickly burn out.

They tried all sorts of materials—carbon, bamboo, hair, platinum, copper, and scores of other substances. They finally discovered that a filament of charred paper served well if it was in a vacuum. This made possible the commercial production of light bulbs, which soon replaced Rockefeller's oil lamps.

Edison and his fellow inventors, looking for a way to record the human voice, invented the phonograph. They worked on a way to use the new art of photography to show "moving" pictures. In 1891 Edison patented a "kinetoscope"—a kind of peep show which showed moving pictures inside a box.

Edison's own ingenuity seemed endless. But he was also a great organizer, and when he could not make an invention of his own to solve a problem, he bought up the patent rights of others. Then he found ways to manufacture the new products cheaply and efficiently. He was most interested in the improvements in daily life that could reach everybody.

Edison fired the imagination, not only of Henry Ford, but of the whole American people. He was nicknamed the "Wizard." When Congress awarded him a special gold medal in 1928 it was announced that his inventions had been worth $15,599,000,000 to humanity! But this was only to say that there really was no way of measuring his enormous contribution to American life. By the time of his death at the ripe age of 85, in 1931, he had become an American hero —a truly democratic hero, because his work benefited every living American.

PART TWO

PEOPLE ON THE MOVE

PEOPLE ON THE MOVE

Americans were people on the move. There would have been nobody here except the Indians unless Old World millions had been willing to cross the ocean. The United States might have been only a string of seaboard farms and cities if brave new Americans had not then been willing to risk the move farther west. Going into the half-mapped continent was, of course, traveling into the unknown. But Americans were willing—even eager—to risk new places.

The Civil War, too, meant the moving of peoples. Great battles were fought by thousands of men in armies on the move. The fortunes of war brought Virginians to Gettysburg in Pennsylvania and sent Massachusetts volunteers deep into Georgia. Even while the armies of General William T. Sherman cut their bloody swath through the South, the Union men could not help seeing the beauties of the Southern land. They discovered that Southerners were not so different from themselves. Thousands of Americans pried into far corners of their country.

After the war, many soldiers returned to their old homes. A few stayed where they had fought, and found wives and homes in the new places. Some Northerners went south to teach school or help in the Freedmen's Bureau. From the burnt-over south, hopeful Southerners went north or west in search of opportunity. Negroes, at last free to leave the old plantation, for the first time were able to move about like any other Americans.

"Go-Ahead" became an American motto. Of course, Go-Getting Americans were eager to move up in the world. But they were just as eager to move around. The same spirit that before the Civil War had led Americans to move westward in wagon-towns, that had led them to build railroads even before there were cities to go to, now led Americans to move and keep moving.

After the Civil War, brave and needy men and women were still risking the ocean to come fill the land and crowd the cities. From impoverished European farms, many were drawn by extravagant promises. And thousands already here, who were disappointed by the American land, moved hopefully to the cities.

The Americans already here kept telling themselves: "Go ahead. Move on. Try to find a better place."

As Americans churned about the vast continent, they came to know their land —and to know one another. Most nations of the Old World were rooted to the same spot. Their people were held together because their ancestors had so long lived inside the same boundaries. It was unusual for them to move. They learned to be satisfied with their place.

But Americans would not long let themselves be confined anywhere. Americans were held together by their ways of moving and by their shared desire to move. And the freedom to move to a better place helped build the nation.

CHAPTER 7

To Punish–or to Forgive? ∾∾∾∾∾∾∾

Lee's surrender to Grant at Appomattox brought peace to the nation. But peace brought new problems. How to find jobs for the million men who left the Union and Confederate armies? How to change factories from making cannon and rifles and ammunition to making harvesters and sewing machines?

When the South agreed to unconditional surrender, they put themselves at the mercy of the North. This gave Northerners their most difficult problem —what to do with the South.

Was it more important to punish the former rebels, to teach them a lesson they would never forget, so they never again would try to break up the Union? Or was it better to forgive the rebels, to welcome them back into the Union, so they would feel at home and never again want to leave?

Of course the South had already been punished. A quarter-million Southerners had died in the war. The Confederacy was a land of cinders and desolation —of charred plantation houses, broken bridges, twisted railways, and desecrated churches. An Englishman who traveled halfway across the South said he did not see a single smiling face. But

---

Ruins of Charleston, South Carolina, by the pioneer Civil War photographer, Mathew Brady. For many people in the South, "Reconstruction" after the Civil War meant clearing away rubble and rebuilding cities.

Thaddeus Stevens, Congressman from Pennsylvania (from an old and damaged photograph).

the North had also suffered, with its own quarter-million dead. And for Northerners who had lost fathers, sons, or husbands, no punishment of the South would be enough.

Yet this was not just a question of feelings. Unless the North wanted to feed and house millions of Southerners, it was important to get the South back into working order. This meant getting crops planted, factories built, railroads running, and pupils and teachers into schools. It also meant getting the Southern States organized to govern themselves, to collect their own taxes, to keep the peace, and to protect life and property.

But it was not easy to get people to agree on how to revive the Southern States. There was wide disagreement on what the war had really meant. What the North called "The War of the Rebellion" in the South was still called "The War between the States." The

Southerners argued that their State governments had never been destroyed. Once a State always a State!

Lincoln himself had almost agreed with the Southerners on this point. He also believed, Once a State always a State! But for Lincoln this meant that the Southern States had no power to secede. And if the Southern States had never really seceded, then even after the Civil War the Southern States were still within the Union.

Naturally, once the war was over, Southerners wanted to agree with Lincoln. They said they still had their States and therefore could still run their own affairs. The most, then, that the victorious North could properly ask was that some Confederate leaders be barred from office.

But on the other side were the Northern Avengers. The most powerful of them were in a group of Northern Senators and Congressmen called Radical Republicans. They were bitter against the Southern rebels. They remained suspicious of all white Southerners. They did not want to forgive and forget, but instead wanted to rub salt in Southern wounds. The Southern States, said the Radical Republicans, had actually "committed suicide." By trying to rebel, they had not only violated the Constitution but actually destroyed their own States. They were no longer States at all.

People who thought like this believed that after the war the Southern "States" could claim *no* rights under the Constitution. They had no right to govern themselves or to be represented in the Senate or the House of Representatives. They were nothing but so much territory

—like parts of the sparsely settled West. And, like those Western territories, they could be governed in any way Congress decided.

Congress could treat them as "conquered provinces." They could be ruled by military governors—generals of the Union army. When, if ever, they would be allowed to govern themselves and take part in the national government— this would depend on how they behaved themselves and what the victorious Congress wanted. This offered anything but a cheerful prospect for the Southerners.

The leader of the Radical Republicans was one of the strangest men in American history. Thaddeus Stevens was sometimes called "a humanitarian without humanity." For he seemed to use up all his good feelings on large noble causes and then he had very little left for individuals. Stevens was a sour man. Just as Lincoln inspired love and respect, Stevens inspired fear.

Very early in life he took up the great cause of abolishing slavery. He never gave it up, nor did he ever forgive men who had ever held slaves or who had been entangled in the web of slavery. After Appomattox, Stevens made it his purpose in life to punish all "traitors." Old age never mellowed him. At the age of seventy-five he boasted that he would spend his remaining years inventing new ways to make the Southern rebels suffer.

During the Civil War, Lincoln had shown his greatness—and his forgiving spirit—by his plan for bringing Southerners back to the Union. He was less interested in the past than in the future. Back in December 8, 1863, in his Proc-

lamation of Amnesty and Reconstruction, he had explained his plan. He would pardon almost all Southerners, even if they had fought against the Union.

All Lincoln asked was that Southerners take a solemn oath to support the Constitution of the United States in the future. As soon as enough citizens of a Southern State took the oath, Lincoln would recognize the government of that State and let the people govern themselves. Of course they must agree to abolish slavery. It would be enough, Lincoln said, if a number equal to only one-tenth of the voters in the last election took the oath.

This plan did not satisfy the Radical Republicans. They were busy in Congress making a plan of their own. During the war they concocted their Wade-Davis Bill in quite another spirit. They could not take their eyes off the past. Under their plan each Southern State was to make a list of all its white men. The State could not be recognized or given the power to govern itself until a *majority* of the people on that list took a new oath to support the Constitution. Then (since these Radicals believed that the old Southern States had committed suicide) there would have to be an election to call a convention to make an entirely new constitution for each Southern State.

No one could even vote in that election, much less be a delegate to help make the new constitution, unless he took the "ironclad oath." This oath was not merely a promise of future loyalty but was also an oath of past purity. You had to swear that you had never held office under the Confederacy or fought in the Confederate army. By the end of the war, most white men in the South could not honestly take such an oath.

Under the Radicals' scheme it would be years before any Southern State could set up a majority government for itself. It would have to wait until the whole Civil War generation was dead. But that did not bother the Radical Republicans. They were quite willing to keep the Southern States under military rule by Northern generals. They said they were in favor of liberty, but they were not willing to give it to white Southerners.

This was the Wade-Davis Bill, which passed Congress on July 2, 1864. It could not be law unless Lincoln signed it. What would Lincoln do?

Lincoln refused to sign the bill. But he was shrewd. Instead of attacking it, as he might have, for being evil and vengeful—or instead of saying simply that the plan for the South was the business of the President and not of Congress—he issued a new proclamation. He would not sign the Wade-Davis Bill into law, he said, because he did not think it should be the *only* way a Southern State could get back into working order. Any "seceded" Southern State that wanted to follow the Wade-Davis plan should feel free to do so.

But there were now, Lincoln said, two possible paths. Any Southern State could choose between Lincoln's one-tenth plan and the Radicals' majority-ironclad-oath plan. In the long run, of course, no Southern State would prefer the vengeful Radical plan. But still Lincoln had done his best to avoid a head-on clash with Congress.

On April 14, 1865, Lincoln called his Cabinet together to explain his policy to them. He urged them to use charity. He begged them to help bring the wartime spirit to an end.

That very night when President Lincoln and his wife went to Ford's Theater in Washington to attend a play, there occurred one of the great disasters of the Civil War era—and of all American history. It was less than a week after Lee had surrendered to Grant at Appomattox. The demented actor John Wilkes Booth rushed past the Secret Service men guarding the President's box and shot President Lincoln. The President died the next morning.

We cannot be sure what would have happened if Lincoln had lived. But we do know that Lincoln's combination of qualities was extremely rare. He was, of course, a strong man who would fight for what he believed. Yet he was also a simple, gentle man who understood other people. And, most important for a President, he was a clever politician. He knew how to give up less important things in order to persuade people to support him on what was more important.

Andrew Johnson, the new President, was in many ways like Lincoln. With no schooling, he began as a poor tailor. He, too, was a self-made man. Like Lincoln, he had been born in the South. And though he came from Tennessee, he had been against secession. When he was the Democratic Senator from Tennessee he was the only Southern Senator to support the Union after the Confederates fired on Fort Sumter.

Still, in some important ways, Johnson was no Lincoln. He was not good at persuading. He did not know how to use a joke to make a serious point. Just as Lincoln was gentle, generous, and compromising, so Johnson was crude and obstinate. His weaknesses would not have been serious in an ordinary citizen. But they were disastrous in a President.

When Lincoln was assassinated in April 1865, Congress was not in session. Many Republicans distrusted Johnson because he had been a Democrat. They had added him to the Republican ticket as their candidate for Vice-President in 1864 in the hope that he might draw the seceded States back into the Union.

Now, when the death of Lincoln had brought Johnson to the White House, the Radical Republicans wanted President Johnson to call Congress into special session to make new rules for the South. But he refused. President Johnson would follow the rules already declared by Lincoln. And *he* alone would decide when the Southern States had satisfied Lincoln's requirements so they could govern themselves.

Lincoln's requirements were not too hard for the Southern States to satisfy. By December 1865, when President Andrew Johnson made his first report to Congress, every one of the old Confederate States (except Texas, which soon came along) had done what Lincoln asked for. Each of these now had its own State government in working order. President Johnson reported happily that the Union was restored.

When the Congressmen from these "restored" Southern States came to take their seats in Congress, they were shut out. The Radical Republicans who controlled the House of Representatives told them that they were not really Congressmen at all—because the Southern States were not really States at all. Even if the Confederate States had followed

President Andrew Johnson, who had no Vice-President. If he had been removed from office, a Member of Congress (the Speaker of the House) would have become President.

the President's rules, the Radicals said, the President had no power to make the rules. Only Congress (by which they meant, of course, the Radical Republicans themselves) had that power. Their Punishing Bill—the Wade-Davis Bill—had declared what Congress wanted. The South would have to be "restored" by Congress or not at all.

Congress set up its own Committee on Reconstruction led by the Radical Avenger, Thaddeus Stevens, to make its own plan. The watchword of Stevens' Congressional plan was, Force! The South, he said, was a "conquered province" and nobody would be allowed to forget it. Northern troops would be sent to occupy the South.

The committee divided the old Confederacy into five military districts. The boundaries of the eleven seceded States were not to be respected. Each of the five districts would be ruled by a Northern general. The Northern Radical Republicans in Congress laid down new rules for building new Southern States. They wished to see the new States designed so as to keep political control in Republican hands.

Some of the Radical demands, such as abolishing slavery and giving civil rights to Negroes, were of course just and necessary. But others were not.

Worst of all was the Radical refusal to forgive. They denied many leading citizens in the Old South the right to vote, or even to work at their regular jobs. Hungry for power, the Radicals wanted to rule the South through a small group of their puppets. Anxious to hold their Republican majority in Congress, they were afraid the new Southern Congressmen might be against them. Although they said they loved liberty, they really were afraid of it. They were afraid to give political liberty to their old enemies.

What was President Johnson to do? Under the Constitution he was supposed to enforce the laws of Congress. Though he believed these laws unwise, he tried to enforce them. But the Radicals were out to "get" Johnson. They could not bear the idea of a President who was not in their pocket. They passed laws taking away powers which the Constitution had given to the President. For example, even though the Constitution made the President the Commander in Chief of the Army, the Radicals passed a Command of the Army Act taking away his power to command.

They were spoiling for a fight, hoping to tease the President into violating one law so that they could have him removed from office. They hoped that then they could seize the powers of the President.

But Johnson was careful to obey every law, to follow all the instructions of Congress.

Still there was a limit to his patience. When the Radicals passed the Tenure of Office Act which took away the President's control over his own Cabinet, that was too much. Secretary of War Stanton, whom Johnson had inherited in the Cabinet from Lincoln, had become Johnson's enemy and was actually plotting against him. So the President fired Stanton to test the Tenure of Office Act, which he believed to be against the Constitution. This was a small thing, but enough to give the Radicals their chance. They took it.

The framers of the Constitution, being wise men, had provided a way to remove a criminal President. But they saw that if they made it too easy to remove a President, opponents would be tempted to use it to get rid of any President they could not beat at the polls. Then every President would live in terror—afraid to do his duty, for fear some political enemy would make a crime out of it.

The Constitution said (Article II, Section 4) that the President could not be removed except "on Impeachment for, and Conviction of, Treason, Bribery, or other high Crimes and Misdemeanors." First the House of Representatives would have to "impeach" the President. This meant a majority vote to support a list of accusations. Then the President would actually be tried by the Senate. The Chief Justice of the United States would preside. But to remove a President a mere majority of the Senate was not enough. The framers showed their special wisdom when they required a vote of *two-thirds* of the members present.

When the Senate met on March 30, 1868, to try President Andrew Johnson on the impeachment brought by the House of Representatives, the nation was in breathless suspense. Few really believed that Andrew Johnson had been guilty of "Treason, Bribery, or other high Crimes and Misdemeanors."

Johnson, like Lincoln, was a man of rock-ribbed honesty. No one could prove otherwise. Earnestly he had followed his inaugural oath "to preserve, protect, and defend the Constitution of the United States, against all enemies foreign and domestic." Perhaps he had sometimes lost his temper, had shown bad judgment, or had used language that a President should not use. But these were not crimes. His only "crime" had been that he believed it *his* duty to obey the Constitution. And he was determined to follow a policy of forgiveness. He could not have satisfied the Radicals without surrendering all the powers of the Presidency into their hands.

On May 16, 1868, when the vote of the Senate was finally taken, 35 Senators voted "guilty" and 19 voted "not guilty." This was a big majority. But, luckily, it was *one* vote less than the two-thirds which the Founding Fathers required. Andrew Johnson remained President.

This was the first and the last time American politicians came near ousting a President during his term of office. We can all be thankful that they failed. If they had succeeded they would have opened the way for a new kind of dictatorship—a dictatorship of Congress.

CHAPTER 8

A Two-Nation South

Peace and reunion brought an end to slavery. But the roots of slavery ran deep. They reached into every nook and cranny of Southern life.

One of its roots was racism—the belief that one race was naturally better than another. This belief had helped keep slavery alive. At the same time slavery had kept racism alive. Under slavery, nearly all the Negroes in the South did lowly tasks. Therefore, it was easy for white people—and sometimes even for Negroes themselves—to believe that God had meant it that way.

Slavery could be abolished simply by changing laws. But it was much harder to abolish the belief that one race was better than another. Many generations of Southerners had taught that to their children. After the war it was still rooted in their minds and hearts.

And after the war it became clearer and clearer that the South was still split into two "nations." There was a White South and a Negro South. Much of the time these two "nations" lived at peace.

Some of the time they lived in a nervous truce. Occasionally they were actually at war. Obviously the United States could not be truly united until the South ceased to be divided.

Lincoln and Johnson had their eyes mainly on the abolition of slavery. The future they looked to—a South without slavery—seemed not too hard to accomplish. Stevens and the Radicals also wanted to abolish slavery. But for them, abolishing slavery was not enough. They believed that slavery would not really be abolished until the Negro was treated as the equal of the white man. Their hopes were wider and deeper—and much harder to accomplish—than the hopes of Lincoln or of Johnson.

The Radical Republicans saw the wickedness of slavery. But they did not really see its full tragedy. Part of the tragedy was that the roots of slavery could not be removed in a year or two— nor perhaps even in a generation. The Radical Republicans were right when they said that the problem was not *only* slavery. But they were violent and impatient men.

For the deep problem they had no deep solution. They knew what they wanted, but they did not know how to get it. To transform the life of the South, to bring equality to the Negro, to cure both the white man and the Negro of the disease of racism, would take a patience and a charity and a wisdom which the Radicals lacked. They were wrong when they believed that the old cancer of slavery could be ripped out quickly and by force.

The Thirteenth Amendment to the Constitution, which abolished slavery, was proclaimed on December 18, 1865.

But when the legislatures of the Southern States (under the Lincoln-Johnson one-tenth plan) had their first meetings, they promptly adopted "Black Codes." These were supposed to provide for the new situation of the Negro now that he was no longer a slave. They provided, for example, that now the Negro could own property, and they gave him certain other rights.

But, under the Black Codes, the freedom of the Negro was still strictly limited. He could not vote. He was not allowed to marry a white person. He could generally be a witness only in trials against other Negroes. He could not leave the land where he had been a slave. He could not look for a new job. In Mississippi, for example, if a Negro was convicted of being a "vagrant"—a wandering person without a job—he could be fined $50. If he could not pay the fine, he could be hired out against his will to anybody who would pay the fine in return for his labor.

Had Northerners died in a Civil War merely to preserve slavery under a new name?

The Radical Republicans in the North, who anyway expected the worst from the Old Confederates, were not taken by surprise. Even before the war was over they had set up the Freedmen's Bureau. Its purpose was to help war refugees, to get Southern farms back in working order, and to help Negro freedmen make their new start in life.

The Freedmen's Bureau did a great deal of good work that nobody else could do. It handed out millions of free meals to Negroes and to white refugees. It built hospitals. And it brought thousands of Southerners back onto farms

A school for freedmen, Vicksburg, Mississippi, in the year after Appomattox. For the first time, many Negroes had a chance to learn to read.

where they could make a living again. The Bureau also helped Negro freedmen find jobs, and helped protect them against a new slavery.

The Bureau's most important work was in building schools and in providing teachers—to give Negroes the education they had been denied under slavery. Howard University, Hampton Institute, Atlanta University, and Fisk University were set up for Negro students of college age. A quarter of a million Negro children were sent to school for the first time.

Few white Southerners were grateful for this help. They were worried that Negroes were no longer being kept in their "place." And they were especially annoyed at this interference by "outsiders."

It took courage to go south to teach for the Freedmen's Bureau. One young lady teacher who went to North Carolina reported that while the men who passed her on the street only rarely lifted their hats, "the ladies almost invariably lift their noses."

Northern teachers in the South found it hard to survive. In South Carolina, for example, grocers charged them especially high prices hoping to starve them out. One Southern farm woman said she "would not sell milk to Yankees to save her life, she hated the very ground they trod." Some Yankee teachers were afraid to buy the food anyway, because they thought it might be poisoned. Some found that no one would rent them a room to live in. Even in church they were shunned and insulted.

The South was now at war with itself. Many Southerners said they were only fighting against meddling "outsiders." But they were really fighting their fellow Southerners—Negroes who wanted to be free and equal.

Before long, the Old Confederates in the South had organized a secret army. Its purpose was really to carry on the Civil War under another name. Although slavery was abolished by law, the Old Confederates still desperately hoped to preserve as much as possible of their old Southern Way of Life.

Late in 1865 a half-dozen ex-Confederate soldiers in Pulaski, Tennessee, founded an odd new club. It was the first unit in this secretly revived Confederate army. It called itself the Ku Klux Klan—nobody knows exactly why. Soon many branches appeared all over the South.

Almost everything about the Ku Klux Klan was peculiar, and many of its features were ridiculous. Its members met in secret and tried to keep everything about it a mystery to outsiders. Each member swore never to reveal the names of other members—nor even to admit that he was a member himself. At the initiation of a candidate the Grand Cyclops ordered, "Let his head be adorned with the regal crown, after which place him before the royal altar and remove his hoodwink." The "royal altar" was a big mirror, and the "regal crown" was a high hat sprouting donkey's ears.

According to the Klan's constitution:

The officers of this [secret lodge] shall consist of a Grand Wizard of the Empire and his ten Genii; a Grand Dragon of the Realm and his eight Hydras; a Grand Titan of the Dominion and his six Furies; a Grand Giant of the Province and his four Goblins; a Grand Cyclops of the Den and his two Night Hawks; a Grand Magi, a Grand Monk, a Grand Exchequer, a Grand Turk, a Grand Scribe, a Grand Sentinel, and a Grand Ensign.

No wonder some people thought this was only a "hilarious social club."

But there was nothing funny about the Klan's activities. The Klan actually pretended to be (as it said in its constitution) "an institution of Chivalry, Humanity, Mercy and Patriotism." It pretended to protect the weak and the innocent, and to support the Constitution of the United States. It soon became a weapon of violence and terror.

Klan members traveled the countryside flogging, maiming, and sometimes killing Negroes who tried to vote or who in other ways presumed to be the white man's equal. The Klan uniform was a pointed hat with a white hood to conceal the face, and a long robe, either white or black.

In the beginning, Klan members included some respectable citizens. A famous Confederate cavalry general, Nathan Bedford Forrest, was the Grand Wizard. But the Klan's "Invisible Empire" also included many hoodlums. They wanted to frighten Negroes into *not* claiming their rights under the Constitution. The object of these Klan members was to keep the South separated into two *un*equal nations. They could not do their work except by blackmail and bloodshed. In 1869 when the crimes of the Klan became too scandalous, General Forrest resigned as Grand Wizard and pretended to "dissolve" the organization. The Klan then simply went underground.

Nobody knows exactly how many people joined the Klan. In 1868, General Forrest said the Klan had forty thousand members in Tennessee alone and a half-million in all the South. Scores of other organizations joined in the bloody work—the Tennessee Pale Faces, the Louisiana Knights of the White Camelia, the North Carolina White Brotherhood, the Mississippi Society of the White Rose, the Texas Knights of the Rising Sun, the Red Jackets, and the Knights of the Black Cross. In 1871 alone, in a single county in Florida, 163 Negroes were murdered, and around New Orleans the murders came to over 300. Thousands of Negroes were driven from their homes, maimed, or tortured.

Under pressure from Northern Radical Republicans, some Southern State governments passed laws against these crimes. On December 5, 1870, President U. S. Grant—who as general had commanded the Union forces to victory—delivered a special message to Congress. "The free exercise of franchise," he warned, "has by violence and intimidation been denied to citizens of several of the States lately in rebellion." Congress then passed the Ku Klux Klan Acts to outlaw these organizations and to protect the rights of all citizens. But these laws had little effect.

For the State governments set up in the South by the Radical Republican Congress were being replaced by old-fashioned Southern State governments. Confederate heroes were back in charge. The land and the factories were still owned by white Southerners. The last few Northern troops were not withdrawn from the South until 1877. But by 1875—within ten years after Appomattox—eight of the eleven old Confederate States had already come back under rule of Old Confederates.

The work which only a few years before had been done by disreputable terrorists was now being done "legally" by the State governments. Although the Southern States had approved the Civil War Amendments (Thirteenth, Fourteenth, and Fifteenth) to the Constitution, although they had abolished slavery and their laws "guaranteed" the Negro his rights, all these proved to be

Members of the Ku Klux Klan, hooded and armed, 1868.

mere technicalities. Before long it was pretty plain that slavery itself was just about the only thing the Civil War had abolished.

Thaddeus Stevens died in 1868, and soon enough his avenging spirit—along with his special concern for the Negro's rights—was dead. Now more and more Northerners were anxious to "leave the South alone." In practice this meant putting the South back in the hands of white Southerners. And the South then remained divided into the same two nations—a "superior" race and an "inferior" race.

The South would not really become united with the rest of the United States until the South itself had become one. And this would take time.

The Two-Nation South was a One-Party South. When the Old Confederates came back into charge of the Southern States, they had no love for the Republican Party. That was the party of the Yankees, the party that had made war on the South and had then held the South under military rule. By keeping their control of the State governments, the Confederate heroes also kept those governments under the control of the new Democratic party. And the Negro was to have no voice in Southern politics for many years.

A divided South remained afraid of equality, afraid of change. This was at the very time when the American people —and newcomers from the whole world —were filling up the land and churning about the rest of the country faster than ever before.

CHAPTER 9

Filling the Land

From the earliest colonial days, America's leading import had been people. Before the Civil War nearly all immigrants arriving in New York or other American ports had come by sail. The passage from the Old World to the New had been a risky adventure lasting as long as two or three months. Sailing vessels depended on the wind, and the old sailing routes went only to certain places. Built mainly for cargo, these vessels stowed their poorer passengers like cattle.

Within a decade after Appomattox nearly all immigrants from across the ocean were arriving by steam. They were coming more speedily and in larger numbers than ever before. During the Civil War the need quickly to import supplies had encouraged the development of steamships. After the war the nation was eager to renew a free-flowing commerce with the world.

Steamships, unlike sailing vessels, could run on a reliable timetable. The uncertainty of the winds was replaced by a ten-day transatlantic schedule. The new steamships were actually planned for passengers. They were a good deal less uncomfortable—even for those who

Waiting room of the Union Pacific Railroad in Omaha, Nebraska, in 1877. Here immigrants from many countries, lured by promises of choice land advertised by the States and the railroad companies, could stock up for the journey farther west.

came most cheaply in steerage. Steamships could now pick up new thousands of immigrants in remote ports of the eastern Mediterranean and of Asia.

German and French and Italian and other steamship lines competed for passengers, offering lower rates, better accommodations, and a new easy system of prepaid passage. Prosperous immigrants who had already settled in the United States could pay in advance for the tickets of friends or relatives who wanted to come. The steamship companies opened offices all over the United States. By 1890 the Hamburg-Amerika Line had three thousand of these. More than one-quarter of the immigrants in that year came on tickets that someone in the United States had paid for in advance.

Before the Civil War, revolutions in France and Germany and Italy and famines in Ireland prodded Europeans to leave. So too, in the later years of the nineteenth century, multiplying miseries drove out European peasants by the thousands.

Many of those peasants in western Europe who were lucky enough to own a few acres of land were losing their ancestral plots. The price of wheat in their home countries went down as the new railroads and cargo steamers brought wheat from the United States, from Russia, and even from India. A strange disease (phylloxera) was killing the grapevines in the Balkans. When Americans began raising their own oranges and lemons in the 1880's and when the French began keeping out Italian wines, Italian farmers with orchards and vineyards found themselves on the edge of starvation.

The Jews of Russia were being bar-

barously persecuted, and whole villages were murdered for their religion. Turks were slaughtering Syrian Christians.

Once again, there was plenty to get away from. And now that the United States was at peace, this country seemed more attractive than ever.

To generations of European peasants, owning a piece of land had been the sign of dignity, the beginning of freedom.

When President Lincoln signed the Homestead Act on May 20, 1862, America seemed to offer everybody the chance to be a landowner. The whole American West was begging for people. All you had to do was come. You only needed to be twenty-one years of age and to say that you intended to become a citizen. Then you picked a 160-acre plot of "homestead" land somewhere on the vast Public Domain that belonged to the United States government. If you simply lived on it and cultivated a part, then the whole 160 acres would be yours at the end of five years. You paid nothing but a small registration fee.

This was an Old World dream come true. Every man a landowner!

Before the Civil War, the Southern States had opposed this Homestead Act. They were afraid it would strengthen the anti-slavery forces by increasing the population of the Free States. As soon as the Slave States left the Union it was possible to pass the Act through Congress. Lincoln's simple aim was "settling the wild lands into small parcels so that every poor man may have a home."

But the "free" land was not really as free as it seemed. In the Western plains where most of the best homesteads were found, it cost labor and money to make wild land into a farm. Before anything could be planted, the ground had to be broken. The prairie grass had roots that grew in thick mats, unlike anything known in Europe. The familiar Old World plow would not cut through but was quickly twisted by the heavy sod.

The Oklahoma "Land Rush" which began at noon, April 22, 1889. At the firing of a starter's gun and the sound of a bugle, more than 20,000 people rushed in to stake their claims. Oklahoma was then still called "Indian Territory" because it was supposed to be reserved for Indians removed from the East.

It was slow work to plow up enough land to support a family and it was expensive to hire a man with the right tools to do the job.

Then you needed to find water. Where streams and springs were rare, the only answer was to dig a well. And to pump up the water you had to build a windmill. On the treeless plains you had to buy the lumber for your house. Posts and barbed wire for fencing had to be brought from great distances. All this added up. You needed about $1,000 to make your homestead livable. That was a big fortune for a landless peasant.

Still, if you were healthy, willing to work year round, and not afraid to shiver for a few winters in a crude house of earth or sod, you might manage. The Homestead Act allowed you to be away from your land for six months each year without losing your claim. Some energetic homesteaders used this time to earn money by working as lumberjacks in the pine forests of Minnesota, Wisconsin, and Michigan. Others helped build the short "feeder" railroads that branched off through the countryside. Or they worked as farm laborers for their more prosperous neighbors.

Even if life was hard on the "free" lands of the West in the post-Civil War years, it still was not so bad by comparison with peasant life in Europe. What had been little trickles of immigrants from faraway places now became wide fast-flowing streams. For example, the old Austro-Hungarian Empire in eastern Europe, which had sent only seventeen thousand in 1880, sent over one hundred thousand in 1900, and seven years later, over a third of a million.

Americans worked hard at finding ways to attract the dissatisfied peoples of the world—to persuade them to come here instead of going to those English, French, or German colonies in Africa, South America, or the South Pacific which also wanted new settlers. Even before the Homestead Act, Western States sent their agents abroad. They helped immigrants with information and with loans.

More people in Wisconsin, for example, would mean more business for everybody there. Everybody's land would be more valuable. The State of Wisconsin therefore appointed a commissioner of immigration in 1852. He enlisted the aid of the United States consul in Bremen, Germany, and of other consuls elsewhere. He advertised in European newspapers and in a single year distributed 30,000 pamphlets about the glories of Wisconsin.

The Americans used the empty lands of their vast Public Domain to help pay for building the first railroads here. These were the lands that belonged to the United States government—land given to the new nation by the States at the time of the Revolution, land acquired from Napoleon in the Louisiana Purchase in 1803, land taken from Mexico in 1848.

After all, the government land might be worth very little if there was no way to reach it. The railroad companies would give the land value—in two ways. While they provided the transportation to open up the West, they would also be working as real-estate salesmen.

So the federal government assigned large tracts of land to the States with the understanding that the States would grant these lands to the companies that

A sod house of the type common in the early West. This family was fortunate to have glass for a window. The teen-age daughters had perhaps been ordering the latest fashions from a mail-order catalog.

built railroads. And the federal government also granted some of its land directly to the railroad companies. These companies suddenly found themselves in the real-estate business.

Like the State governments, the railroad companies themselves became colonizers. They sent their own agents to Europe to attract immigrants to live along their tracks. These agents, too, helped with information and with loans. Sometimes they actually provided newcomers with a house while they were getting settled.

Often the railroad builders were granted the best lands in the West. And, anyway, once the railroads were built, the land near the tracks—since there were no automobiles and few roads—would be the most valuable. While railroad lands sold at higher prices, they were usually much more attractive than the more remote lands left over for dis-

tribution under the Homestead Act.

Land grants to the railroads finally amounted to about 150 million acres—an area almost as big as the whole State of Texas. Nine-tenths went to the companies that built railroads west of the Mississippi.

The first railroad company to receive a land grant from the federal government was the Illinois Central. The land along its future track was divided into a checkerboard pattern extending six miles from the track on each side. Each "section" in the checkerboard was one mile square (640 acres). The railroad was given every other square all along the way. The squares in between were kept by the federal government.

The Illinois Central Railroad extended four hundred miles from Chicago, the whole length of the State of Illinois. When it was completed in 1856 it was the longest railroad in the world.

And the company paid for the construction mainly by selling its two and a half million acres.

"Homes for the Industrious," the Illinois Central land salesmen announced, "in the Garden State of the West!"

> There is no portion of the world where all the conditions of climate and soil so admirably combine to produce those two great staples, Corn and Wheat, as the Prairies of Illinois. . . . Nowhere can the industrious farmer secure such immediate results for his labor as upon these prairie soils, the fertility of which is unsurpassed by any on the globe.

The railroad printed brochures, bought space in newspapers and magazines, and hired "runners" in New York City to mingle with arriving immigrants.

To Norway and Sweden, the railroad sent a super-salesman. Oscar Malmborg was a Swedish immigrant who had succeeded. After serving in the Mexican War, he had helped build the railroad in Illinois. From personal experience he could convince people that the railroad lands were really fertile. He sang the praises of Illinois Central land from Gothenberg at one end of Sweden through all the big cities to Bergen at the other end of Norway. He published 2,500 brochures in Swedish and a thousand in Norwegian. He planned meetings at churches and country fairs until he had covered the countryside of both nations.

Swedish farmers began to fear he would lure away all their laborers. To keep their laborers at home they invented horror stories. The Swedes who

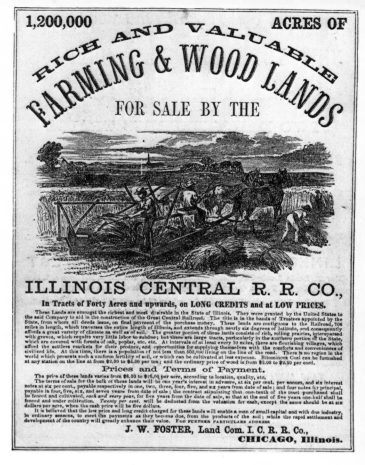

Advertisement by the Illinois Central Railroad to attract settlers to its lands.

arrived in New York, they warned, would be shipped to Siberia or sent as slaves to the Southern States. But in 1861, after Malmborg's successful campaign, nearly ten thousand Norwegians —a third more than in any earlier year —were planning to leave for America. The Swedish exodus was just as large. Even before the end of 1862 substantial new communities of Swedes and Norwegians had taken root near Chicago.

Scandinavia was only one of the immigrant sources. The Illinois Central hired the best-known German-born citizen of Illinois, Lieutenant Governor Francis Hoffmann, to cover Germany with a crew of salesmen. Within four years he settled Germans on eighty thousand acres of Illinois Central land.

To attract settlers from nearby Canada, an Illinois Central booklet claimed that while Canadian farms "are covered with huge boulders of granite, the summers are very hot, and the mosquitoes abound," the Illinois Central lands were a cool, mosquito-free earthly paradise. Colonies of hopeful Canadians were soon settled along the Illinois tracks.

CHAPTER 10

Crowding the Cities

Within the United States during these same years after the Civil War, there was another great movement of peoples —from the country to the cities. When the Civil War began, only one American in five was living in a city. By 1915, cities held half of all Americans. And this was only a beginning.

They came from everywhere. First of all they came from the countryside. While the railroad builders sent abroad their super-salesmen boasting the wonders of American farms, many American farmers were actually moving to the city. Older sections of New England offered visitors the sad spectacle of farms that had lost their farmers.

Many deserted farm villages seemed relics of a departed civilization. A traveler to one such village saw an abandoned church and a school half-taken-apart for its lumber. There were only two inhabitants, one living on each side of the broad street. Some of these farmers had gone west, but most had gone to the cities. By 1910 over a third of all people who were living in American cities had moved in from American farms.

Of the twenty-five million immigrants who came to the United States between the Civil War and World War I, most stayed in the cities. Outside of cities many of them would have felt lonely and lost. They loved the friendly bustle and wanted to be close to people like themselves. And some of them had no choice. They had spent everything to cross the ocean and had no money left for the trip west.

Within the big American cities there grew little immigrant cities. By 1890 New York City held twice as many Irish as Dublin, as many Germans as Hamburg, half as many Italians as Naples. And besides, there were large numbers of Poles, Russians, Hungarians, Austrians, Norwegians, Swedes, and Chinese. Four out of every five New Yorkers either were born abroad or were the children of foreign parents. The Germans and Irish who had come before 1880 were found nearly everywhere in the United States. There were also lots of Canadians in Boston and Detroit, Poles in Buffalo and Milwaukee, Austrians in Cleveland, and Italians in New Orleans.

Crowded Hester Street, on the lower East Side of New York City (shown here about 1900), was where many immigrants settled on their arrival. Some who later became famous department-store owners started by selling from pushcarts like these.

In a public school like this, the children of immigrants from many lands learned to speak and read English—and also learned American ways.

Cities were sometimes called the nation's "melting pots." Perhaps they should have been called "mixing bowls." The individual adult immigrant sometimes became Americanized only slowly. But very quickly his whole colony found its special place in American life. Just as the new United States had first been made from thirteen different colonies, now a great nation was being made from countless colonies of immigrants.

In New York City, for example, there were separate colonies from different parts of Italy. Italians from Naples and Calabria lived around Mulberry Bend,

those from Genoa had settled in Baxter Street, and Sicilians clustered about Elizabeth Street.

Wherever you came from, you could find a neighborhood in New York or in the other big cities where you could feel at home. Whether you were from Germany, Italy, Hungary, or Poland, you could shop in your own old-country language, buy familiar old-country foods, and attend a church offering your old-country services. By 1892 nearly a hundred newspapers in German were published in American cities. And there were dailies in French, Italian, Japanese,

Polish, Yiddish, and a dozen other languages.

In the making of Americans nothing was more important than the public schools. They were free, and the States passed laws requiring all children to attend. There the children of Irish, German, Italian, and all sorts of other families learned and played—and sometimes fought—together. They came to know one another better than their parents knew people from other countries.

At home many families spoke only Polish or Italian, but in school everybody spoke English. Even if the parents spoke English with a foreign accent soon the children sounded like all other Americans. And the children taught their parents. They not only taught them English, but all sorts of American customs. One little girl in New York City who had learned to use a toothbrush brought it home from school. She showed it to her mother, who had been born in a peasant hut in Poland and had never seen such a thing. Her mother, too, was soon brushing her teeth like an American.

Although these immigrant colonies tried to keep separate, they could not stay separate forever. People from the different colonies became more and more alike. Children who stopped speaking their parents' language sometimes stopped going to their parents' church. They were afraid to seem foreign. Then, too, a young man from the Italian colony might marry a girl whose parents spoke German. In the city, people could not help feeling closer to one another.

If the crowds were the joy of the city, crowding was the curse. Old World cities had grown mostly by children being born to the people already living there. The parents put a cradle in the room with the other children. As the family grew larger everybody was more crowded.

The American city was different. It grew by adding not just new children but whole new families.

In the crowded cities after the Civil War land was expensive. Unless you were rich you could not afford a private house. Still the thousands who came pouring in had to be put somewhere.

New York—the nation's biggest city and busiest seaport and the magnet of the world's immigrants—was where the problem was worst. And in New York, American know-how, which at the same time was building grand cast-iron palaces for department stores, produced another, but unlucky, American invention. This was the "tenement house."

New Yorkers, of course, did not invent the slum. European cities had their streets of ancient rickety buildings and evil-smelling hovels where the poor were tumbled together. But in the years after the Civil War, New York City produced a new kind of slum—the tenement-house slum.

Most newcomers to the city could not afford to pay much rent. Back in the early years of the nineteenth century the poorer people of New York had lived in shacks on the swamps at the edge of Manhattan Island. But as the island filled with people, specially designed buildings went up for the city's new poor. A tenement house was a building six or seven stories high designed to hold the largest possible number of families. They were solid blocks of deep buildings whose inside rooms had no windows or ventilation. There were also helter-skelter buildings of many other kinds.

Then in 1878, to help find something better, *The Plumber and Sanitary Engineer,* a builders' magazine, announced a contest for architects. The editors offered a $500 prize for the best plan for tenement apartments for the poor.

The winning plan was the "dumbbell" tenement. The floor plan of the whole building, looked at from above, had the shape of a dumbbell. And it had a good deal to be said for it compared with some of the flimsy firetraps that were

common before. The dumbbell tenement, built of brick, was meant to be fireproof.

It was specially designed to fit on a narrow lot twenty-five feet wide and a hundred feet deep. It was six or seven stories high, with the stairway running up the middle. On each floor were four sets of apartments—two in front and two in back. The front and back rooms got some light and air from their windows on the street.

What was new about the plan was that the inside rooms were also supposed to get some light and air. The building was slightly narrower in the middle.

Although the prizewinning tenement design was supposed to provide "light, air, and health" for working people, actually whole families (like this mother and six children) were crowded into little rooms. The new art of photography made it easier for reformers like Lewis W. Hine (who took this picture) and Jacob Riis (who took the picture on page 59 above) to awaken the conscience of other Americans.

When another tenement like it was built alongside, between them there was a narrow air shaft on which each inside room had a window. This became the standard plan for tenements.

By 1900 the island of Manhattan alone had over forty thousand buildings of this type, holding over 1,500,000 people. A prizewinning plan had produced the world's prize slum!

The air shaft between the buildings was only twenty-eight inches wide—so narrow that it did not really bring in light. Instead the foul air brought up smells from the garbage accumulating at the bottom. If there was a fire, the air shafts became flues which quickly inflamed all the rooms around. Up the air shaft resounded the noise of quarreling neighbors. There was no privacy.

The primitive plumbing in the hallway on each floor was shared by four families. It bred flies and germs. Sometimes the toilets became so disgusting that the tenants would not use them, but depended on the plumbing at work or at school. There were no bathtubs with running water. Nearly every one of these tenement houses had at least one sufferer from tuberculosis, and in some there were twenty or more.

When Theodore Roosevelt was Governor of New York, he appointed a commission in 1900 to report on the tenement-house slums. They were not at all surprised that these buildings festered with poverty, disease, and crime. But they were surprised that in spite of it all, so many of the people raised there managed to become decent and self-respecting. And they reported that the slums were even worse than they had been fifty years before.

Slum neighborhoods were given names like "Misery Lane" and "Murderers' Alley." This was hardly the America that the thousands of hopeful immigrants were looking for.

CHAPTER 11

Whose Country? Oldcomers and Newcomers

The bulging cities and bustling factories were full of men and women who had been raised in the quiet American countryside—or of European peasants who had come across the ocean with high hopes. Here, they had been told, anybody could succeed, if only he was honest enough and worked hard.

But many honest, hard-working immigrants found that they could not get ahead. These disappointed new Americans would not take their disappointment lying down. The United States was the land of help-yourself. It is not surprising, then, that the post-Civil War years became a time of conflict. Workingmen were organizing into labor unions. Their aim was a better life—shorter hours, higher wages—but peaceful means did not always seem strong enough.

Beginning in the 1870's labor battles

became more common. In 1872, nearly a hundred thousand builders and mechanics in New York City went on strike. They refused to work longer than eight hours in any one day. After several months, they won their point.

Miners in the eastern Pennsylvania coal fields organized a secret society called the "Molly Maguires." In 1875, on flimsy evidence that private detectives had gathered for the employers, ten Molly Maguires were hanged for murder. Then in 1877 a railroad strike, beginning with workers on the Baltimore and Ohio, spread across the country. It brought death to nine persons in West Virginia and to twenty-six in Pittsburgh.

In 1886 came the so-called Haymarket Massacre when a bomb killed seven policemen and wounded seventy after they tried to break up a meeting of anarchists and communists. In a fight at the steelworks at Homestead, Pennsylvania, in 1892, seven were killed. The Pullman Strike in 1894 again tied up the railroads. This became a minor civil war when Federal troops began fighting against workers.

A conservative and law-abiding organization of trade unions, the American Federation of Labor, became strong among skilled workers. The Federation's aim was simply better wages and shorter hours. Meanwhile a small number of radicals called "Wobblies," who aimed to take the factories away from their owners, started the International Workers of the World.

All over the country crime showed an alarming increase. In 1890 the prisons held 50 percent more criminals than ten years before. And the murder rate in the United States, already twice the rate in England or in Germany, was going up every year. National crime "rings" used hideouts in Chicago, Boston, Philadelphia, Detroit, and scores of other cities to help their members escape the police. The city crowds—at the Philadelphia Centennial Exposition of 1876, at the Chicago Columbian Exposition of 1893, and every day on streetcars or in department stores—were a pickpocket's paradise. Young hoodlums terrorized San Francisco with knives and six-shooters.

New expressions had to be invented to describe the assorted new criminals. There were "badger-game experts" and "knock-out drop" artists. "Green-goods" men tricked innocent farmers into exchanging their real money for large bundles of counterfeit. In 1880 one Go-Getting criminal from Springfield, Illinois, went to New York where he made a fortune selling "gold bricks." Before he was killed by a fellow thief,

Two Molly Maguires on trial, 1875.

IF 100 BULLETS WONT FINISH YOU 1000 WILL.

A WARNING

Police firing on strikers in East St. Louis during the railroad strike that began in 1877.

he actually had taken in over a quarter-million dollars from the lead bricks which he had painted gold before he sold them to gullible country boys. Stores with fancy goods on display naturally attracted shoplifters.

A ring working out of New York managed one of the biggest bank robberies in history. In 1878 from a single job they had planned for three years, they got three million dollars.

Meanwhile newspapers, anxious to sell more copies so they could attract more advertising, became more sensational than ever. They found that it paid to feature the worst crimes and to glamorize the worst criminals.

In business and in government too there were notorious scandals. Beginning soon after the Civil War, President U. S. Grant made a bad start. He was so honest himself that he did not know a crook when he saw one. Some found their way into his Cabinet, and then used their position in the government to make a fortune for their railroads or their banks.

All decent Americans had reason to be worried. Was this the best that could be expected from what Jefferson had so hopefully called an "Empire for Liberty?"

The early American frontier had been a line on the outer edge of settlements. Beyond was the no-man's land where Indians had not yet given up and where settlers had not yet conquered. Out there a man could make a fresh start. In the Centennial Year of 1876, the defeat of Chief Sitting Bull and Chief Crazy Horse and their braves marked the last great battle between the Indians and

Sensational magazines like the Illustrated Police News *attracted their readers by playing up stories of crimes, such as the Indiana train robbery shown here.*

the invading settlers. Fifteen years later, the Superintendent of the Census reported that the wilderness-frontier had come to an end.

By the end of the nineteenth century, then, the New World had lost much of its newness. One bright young historian, Frederick Jackson Turner, who had been raised in the backwoods of Wisconsin, proposed the theory that this disappearance explained many of the country's troubles.

According to Turner, what had made America the Land of Promise was not its cities but its frontier. The free land out west, he explained, had also been a safety valve. In earlier times if a man in an Eastern city wanted a second chance, he could move to the West. But now that the country was being filled up it was no longer possible to find your second chance by going out to the edge of civilization. If you were unlucky enough to be a newcomer in a slum, there seemed to be no escape. Was it surprising, then, that so many Americans were unhappy? And that so many felt that

they had to fight for a better life?

For a while it seemed that the country might be divided between Oldcomers and Newcomers. Oldcomers themselves, of course, came from immigrant families originally, but their families had been here for a long time. Among them were the rich and famous. Few of them were crowded into slums.

In the older Eastern States that still controlled Congress, the Oldcomers were in charge. They were most of those who had money and education and power. But the Oldcomers did not agree on how to cure the country's ills. Some were simply frightened. They wanted to keep the country the way it was. They blamed the troubles on the Newcomers. Their answer was to slam the door. Simply because *their* families had been here longer they thought the whole nation belonged to them.

At Harvard College, a group of New England bluebloods thought that their world was coming to an end. Three young men in the graduating class of 1889, Charles Warren, Robert De Courcy Ward, and Prescott Farnsworth Hall, had been taught by their professors that there was an "Anglo-Saxon" race superior to all others. The race was supposed to be separated from other races not by color but by what countries the people had come from. The "superior" people were supposed to come from England and Germany. And that just happened to be where Warren's and Ward's and Hall's families had come from.

These young men had been raised near Boston. Their parents were horrified by the hordes of "vulgar" immigrants and especially by those with unfamiliar ways—from Ireland and from southern and eastern Europe. The New England aristocrats said the nation's problems could be solved by keeping out all people who were not like themselves.

Five years after their graduation, Warren and Ward and Hall formed the Immigration Restriction League to persuade Congress to pass laws to keep out all "undesirable" immigrants. In their League they enlisted famous professors and writers. Their real object was to keep out the "new" immigrants—the Newcomers. These "new" immigrants, they argued, were the main cause of the increasing crime, the strikes, and most of the troubles of the country.

To keep out "undesirables" they pro-posed a "Literacy Test." According to their proposed law anyone over fourteen years of age who wanted to come into the United States would have to prove that he could read and write. He did not have to know English, provided he could read and write the language of the country he came from.

At first sight the test seemed harmless enough. Actually it was aimed against the Newcomers from certain countries, such as Italy and Greece, where poor peasants had no chance to go to school. The Boston bluebloods believed that because Newcomers from such countries were not "Anglo-Saxons" they must be "inferior."

But in their proposed law they did not dare list particular countries. There

Poor Newcomers arriving in America while rich Oldcomers (with their governess) leave for a vacation in Europe. A magazine illustration by Charles S. Reinhart (1878).

already were many people in the United States from those countries. They would be insulted—and they, too, elected members of Congress.

Year after year the Immigration Restriction League tried to persuade Congress to pass a Literacy Test. But even when they finally pushed their bill through Congress, they did not manage to make it into a law. One President after another vetoed the bill. President Grover Cleveland called the law "underhanded," because it did not say what it really meant. President William Howard Taft said the United States needed the labor of all immigrants and should teach them to read. President Woodrow Wilson agreed.

All three Presidents said the law was un-American. The United States had always been "a nation of nations." It made no sense to keep out people simply because they had been oppressed. America was a haven for the oppressed. Here the starving could find bread and the illiterate could learn to read.

In 1917, however, when the war in Europe was frightening Americans, the Literacy Test finally had enough votes in Congress. The law was passed, over the strong objections of President Wilson, who had already vetoed it twice.

Out on the West Coast, Oldcomers feared Newcomers from Asia. They worried about imaginary hordes that might come across the Pacific. And they had persuaded Congress to pass a Chinese Exclusion Act in 1882. Then, in 1907, President Theodore Roosevelt persuaded the Japanese government to stop their people from emigrating. For some odd reason, this was called a "Gentlemen's Agreement." This became the slang expression for any agreement to discriminate against people on account of their race when you were ashamed to admit what you were really doing. Since there were so few Chinese-American and Japanese-American voters among the Newcomers, the fearful few among the Oldcomers found it easier to have their way.

CHAPTER 12

Reformers and Self-Helpers

Not all the Oldcomers were frightened. Some became Reformers. If the whole country had troubles, they said, it was everybody's fault. If the country had too many strikes and too much crime, it could hardly be blamed on those who had just arrived.

It was mainly the fault, they said, of the Americans who had been here long-est and who had had the most chance to make the country better. Who had built the very cities and constructed the very slums where the poor were condemned to live? Who were the Congressmen and Senators and businessmen and policemen? It was not the immigrant's fault if the nation was not prepared to receive him.

One of the most remarkable of the Reformers and one of the most original Americans of the age was Jane Addams. She was born with a deformity of the spine which made her so sickly that after graduating from college in 1882 she had to spend two years in bed. Her wealthy family sent her to the best schools and colleges, she traveled abroad whenever she wished. One evening in Spain after watching a bullfight—"where greatly to my surprise and horror, I found that I had seen, with comparative indifference, five bulls and many more horses killed"—she suddenly decided that she could waste her life no longer.

The trouble with people like her, Jane Addams decided, was that they had been caught in "the snare of preparation." To become leaders they needed long years of education. But this meant that they were kept out of action at the very time when they were most anxious to rebuild the world. Jane Addams knew that she and her friends needed more education than they could find in books.

In June 1888, she stopped in London to visit the famous Toynbee Hall. There in the poorest section of the city lived a group of Oxford and Cambridge graduates while they tried to help the people of the neighborhood. She decided to try starting something like it in the United States.

Jane Addams' plan was simple. In the poorest, most miserable city slum she would settle a group of educated young men and women from well-to-do families. Like Toynbee Hall, the place would be called a "settlement house." And the well-bred young men and women newly "settled" in the midst of

A young woman settlement-house worker with girls of the neighborhood.

a slum reminded her of the early colonial "settlers" who had left the comforts of English life to live in an American wilderness.

The young men and women who came to live in the slum, seeing the struggles of the poor, would learn things they could never learn from books. At the same time, the people of the slum would use the settlement house as a school, a club, and a refuge.

With her purpose clearly in mind, she acted quickly. Since she knew Chicago she decided to do her work there. She looked for the neediest neighborhood. And she persuaded the owner of a large old house to let her have it free. She opened her settlement house between an undertaker's parlor and a saloon. She called it "Hull-House" after the man who had built it for his home years before.

In the neighborhood of Hull-House there were Newcomers from all over Europe—Italians, Germans, Polish and Russian Jews, Bohemians, French Cana-

Jane Addams (right) in a parade supporting votes for women. The Nineteenth Amendment to the Constitution, prohibiting the States from depriving women of the vote, was finally ratified in 1920.

dians, and others. For the young, Jane Addams set up a kindergarten and a boys' club. And she paid special attention to the very old people whom nobody else seemed to care about.

One old Italian woman was so delighted at the red roses which Jane Addams displayed for a Hull-House party that she imagined they must have been brought all the way from Italy:

> She would not believe for an instant that they had been grown in America. She said that she had lived in Chicago for six years and had never seen any roses, whereas in Italy she had seen them every summer in great profusion. During all that time, of course, the woman had lived within ten blocks of a florist's window; she had not been more than a five-cent car ride away from the public parks; but she had

never dreamed of faring forth for herself, and no one had taken her. Her conception of America had been the untidy street in which she lived and had made her long struggle to adapt herself to American ways.

Jane Addams' work became famous. All sorts of unexpected projects started at Hull-House. The Little Theater movement, of amateur actors putting on plays to entertain themselves and their friends, developed and spread all over the country. She started a book bindery and a music school.

Settlement houses on the Hull-House model appeared in big cities everywhere. Future playwrights, actors, composers, and musicians who had happened to be born into poor slum families now found their chance.

For the first time many thousands of immigrants discovered that somebody else cared about them. Jane Addams—without the aid of governments or politicians—had helped make America the promised land.

America had always been a land of help-yourself. Before long some of the most energetic Reformers came from the immigrants. But it was not easy for Newcomers to become leaders. So many respectable institutions remained in the hands of the Oldcomers—whose families had been here for a century or more. For example, Harvard College—the oldest college in the country, where young bluebloods had learned their ideas of Anglo-Saxon superiority—was run by Oldcomers. It was hard even to become a student there if you were not one of them.

New institutions offered the best chance for Newcomers. Among the most remarkable—and most American—of the new institutions were the scores of new colleges and universities.

At the outbreak of the Civil War there were only seventeen State universities. Then, in 1862 an energetic Congressman, Justin S. Morrill from rural Vermont, secured the passage of the Morrill Act. This act granted government lands from the Public Domain to States—30,-000 acres for each of the State's Senators and for each of its Representatives in Congress—to support new State colleges. There students would be taught to be better farmers. These were called "Land Grant" Colleges.

After the Civil War, hundreds of other colleges and universities were founded. In the later years of the nineteenth century, some of the wealthiest Go-Getters gave millions of dollars to found and endow still more institutions of higher learning. In 1876 Johns Hopkins University was founded by a fortune left by a Baltimore merchant. In 1885 a railroad builder, Leland Stanford, in memory of his son, founded Leland Stanford Jr. University. In 1891 John D. Rockefeller, the Go-Getting oil millionaire, founded the University of Chicago. And there were scores of others.

Many of these college-founders were men who themselves had never gone to college. But they shared the American faith in education. Even before the end of the century, the United States had more colleges and universities than there were in all western Europe. And a larger proportion of the citizens could afford to go to college here than in any other country. The children of poor immigrants, along with millions of other Americans, now had a better chance to rise in the world.

The new labor unions also became centers of new leadership and of self-

Mayor Fiorello La Guardia, during a newspaper strike, reading the comics aloud over the radio.

help. Samuel Gompers, who had been born in London, came to New York as a boy. He worked at starvation wages as a cigarmaker before becoming president of his Cigarmakers Union and then the first president of the American Federation of Labor (1886). Sidney Hillman, who came from Lithuania when he was twenty, led the Amalgamated Clothing Workers, the union that did most to help the new immigrants in big-city sweatshops.

In politics the support of your fellow immigrants counted for something. Crowded together in the cities, the immigrants of any one nationality found it easy to stick together to support one of themselves. Soon new political leaders from among the Newcomers themselves were livening up City Hall and even the halls of Congress, which began to sound like a United Nations. The representatives of Italian-Americans and German-Americans, and of the new arrivals from everywhere, gave a new spice to American politics.

One of the most colorful of these was Fiorello La Guardia. His mother and father had come from Italy, and Fiorello was born in New York City only three years after they arrived. His father, a musician, joined the army and soon became the leader of an infantry band. On an army post in Arizona in the 1880's Fiorello saw the pioneer West. He found it "a paradise for a little boy. We could ride burros. Our playground was not measured in acres, or city blocks, but in miles and miles. We could do just about anything a little boy dreams of. We talked with miners and Indians. We associated with soldiers, and we learned to shoot even when we were so small the

gun had to be held for us by an elder."

Out there La Guardia had his first glimpse of corruption. And it was something he would never forget. The men who had been paid to supply wholesome beef to feed the army were supplying diseased beef instead, and then pocketing the money themselves. La Guardia's father became so ill from eating this diseased beef that he had to be discharged from the army and a few years later he died. No wonder Fiorello spent his life fighting corruption.

For several years he worked at United States consulates in eastern Europe. He learned about the problems of the immigrants in their homelands. When La Guardia returned to New York in 1906 he joined the Immigration Service on Ellis Island. There the Newcomers were examined before being admitted to this country. La Guardia knew Croatian as well as German and Italian. While he worked as an interpreter, he learned the immigrants' troubles and the immigrants' hopes.

In 1917 La Guardia went to Congress, where he began his long fearless career of defending the poor and of fighting corruption. He carried on his fight when he became mayor of New York City in 1934. Now the city was his family and all the city's problems were his. With the broad-brimmed cowboy hat he had learned to wear out in Arizona, his familiar figure bounced all over the city. He especially liked to be on hand at trouble spots. Whenever there was a big fire La Guardia somehow arrived with the fire chief. In twelve years as mayor he did more than any New Yorker before him to remove the blot of the slum and to brighten big-city life.

PART THREE

BRINGING PEOPLE TOGETHER

BRINGING PEOPLE TOGETHER

After the Civil War the United States was as large and varied as all western Europe. From the alpine heights of the Rockies and Sierras to the tropical everglades around the Gulf of Mexico there stretched nearly every kind of landscape.

And this variety made the nation more attractive to immigrants from all over. Just as the English could feel at home on the rolling landscape of "New" England, the Swedes felt less strange on the snowy stretches of Minnesota and the Dakotas, and Italians found familiar sunny seacoasts in southern California. The imported people spread across the land.

From Chicago to New York was as far as from London to Rome. And if you traveled all the way from London to Constantinople and back to London you had still not gone quite as far as if you went from New York to San Francisco. How could these spread-out people ever become a nation?

People in the United States wanted and needed new ways to feel closer together. This challenged American know-how. And American know-how—using telegraph wires, rails, and new-style bridges—organized new ways to bind a nation.

The nation of many cities remained a nation of many centers. Chicago and St. Louis and Denver, even before the end of the nineteenth century, were rivaling Boston, Philadelphia, and New York—the capitals of the eastern seaboard. And by mid-twentieth century Los Angeles on the Pacific was one of the nation's fastest-growing big cities.

Even before the continent began to seem overcrowded, American know-how, with materials and techniques borrowed from everywhere, sent skyscrapers high in the air, collecting thousands to live and work in a single towering building. In American cities—in the once-wilderness of open spaces and fresh air—people were close-packed together as never before.

The telegraph instrument patented by S. F. B. Morse.

CHAPTER 13

Everybody Shares the News ⌘⌘⌘⌘⌘

Newspapers were not very newsy until nearly the time of the Civil War. They used up much of their space to print stories and poems and essays and the strong opinions of their owners. And they copied much of their "news" from other newspapers which arrived by slow mail. The best-known papers were owned or controlled by political parties. They praised their own side and slandered the other. If you wanted to know what was happening far outside your neighborhood you had to wait for a traveler to come by.

Businessmen and generals organized their own systems to send urgent messages over great distances. One of the oldest was the "semaphore" (from the Greek words meaning "signal-bearer"), sometimes called the "visual telegraph." People arranged in advance what their signals would mean. Then they built fires, sent up smoke, or arranged a pattern of boards on a high tower. All these could be seen at a far greater distance than the voice would carry. The Greeks and Romans and the American Indians had used rows of these semaphore stations to relay messages for many miles. By the mid-nineteenth century a French semaphore system used 556 separate stations to stretch three thousand miles.

In the 1840's a young New England Go-Getter, Daniel Craig, decided to try sending news by carrier pigeons. He ordered pigeons from Europe and trained them for his Pigeon Express. Soon newspapers subscribed to his service. In his boat he would go out into the Atlantic for many miles to meet a ship arriving from Europe. The captain would throw him a watertight canister containing the latest London newspapers. Then Craig would quickly summarize the news on thin pieces of paper. These he would attach to the legs of his pigeons, who swiftly flew to the newspapers.

His pigeons went all the way from Halifax, Nova Scotia, to a newspaper in Washington, D.C. The New York *Sun* even built a dovecote for its own carrier pigeons on the roof of its new building. But the pigeon service, too, was unreliable. And there was a limit to how much news a pigeon could carry.

It was hard to imagine a system that did not depend on seeing signals, or on sending written messages. Samuel F. B. Morse found a way to make an electric current do the job. Morse was a man of many talents. At Yale he painted portraits of his fellow students for five dollars apiece. Then he went to London where he studied at the Royal Academy,

In the days before the telegraph or radio, sending news "by air" meant using carrier pigeons.

the honor society of English artists. When Morse came back in 1815 he was a famous artist but he nearly starved because people would not buy his large paintings. Once again he made a living by painting portraits. At the age of thirty he went to Italy and France, the headquarters for painting at the time.

Among Morse's fellow passengers on the sailing ship *Sully* coming back from Europe in 1832 was a talkative young physician from Boston, Charles T. Jackson. In Paris, Dr. Jackson had learned a great deal about electricity. To while away the six-week ocean trip, Morse asked him lots of questions. Morse was an educated man, but he still knew very little about the new science. Would electricity flow through a long wire?

How fast did it travel? Why, Morse asked, couldn't electricity be used to send messages? Others before him had asked the same question—and got nowhere with their answers. But Morse did not know enough about the subject to be discouraged. He suddenly decided to make an electric "telegraph" (from the Greek words for "far writer").

As an artist Morse had a bold imagination about new shapes of things. Then and there he began to invent his telegraph. In our National Museum of History and Technology in Washington, D.C., we still have the shipboard notebook in which Morse every day wrote his new ideas. Before he reached New York he had drawn a picture of a telegraph instrument, very much like that used today. He had even begun to use dots and dashes for his new Morse code.

"Well," Morse told the captain of the ship as they arrived in New York on November 16, 1832, "should you hear of the telegraph one of these days, as the wonder of the world, remember the discovery was made on board the good ship *Sully*."

It took Morse five years to make a telegraph instrument that would work. During that time he supported himself by giving painting lessons.

To build a telegraph line would require a small fortune. Most people thought the telegraph was nothing but a toy—"a thunder and lightning 'jim crack.'" Morse decided to change their minds by a public demonstration. He took his machine with him to Washington, where the Committee on Commerce of the House of Representatives allowed him to demonstrate his telegraph in the Capitol. It was a sensation. "The world is coming to an end," one witness declared. "Time and space are now annihilated." President Martin Van Buren and members of his Cabinet came to see the new electric marvel.

The chairman of the House Committee, Congressman "Fog" Smith of New Hampshire, saw his own chance to make a fortune. When he asked Morse to make him a partner in a firm developing the telegraph, Morse could hardly refuse. For Congressman Smith had the power to persuade the House of Representatives to give Morse the money to build a telegraph line.

The Congressional debate was hilarious. Opponents jokingly proposed that the money be split among Morse's telegraph and the supporters of hypnotism and the crackpots who believed the world was about to end. Finally, in 1843, eleven years after Morse had his first inspiration, Congress appropriated $30,000. With this money Morse was supposed to stretch a telegraph line from Baltimore to Washington.

At first Morse and his partners tried burying the wire. They spent $23,000 before they discovered that, because the wire was defective, the buried line would not work. They then started all over again by stringing a wire on poles. They were in a hurry to get the job done before the whole Congress began to believe the telegraph was a hoax. Mile after mile, they placed 24-foot-high chestnut poles two hundred feet apart. In holes they bored in the poles, they stuck the necks of old bottles which served very well as insulators.

Luckily, at that very moment in May 1844 both the main political parties were holding their national conventions

As the railroads pushed westward across the continent, telegraph lines kept pace.

in Baltimore. This gave Morse his chance to impress all the people in Washington who were especially anxious to learn the names of the candidates. But when the candidates were actually selected, Morse's wire still reached only twenty-two miles—from Washington to Annapolis Junction.

To demonstrate his telegraph, Morse had the news brought by train from Baltimore to Annapolis Junction. Then —to beat those who had to carry the news all the way by train—he flashed it over the wire to his telegraph receiving machine in the Capitol. The politicians there were amazed when Morse told them (before anyone else in Washington knew) the names of the Whig Party candidates—Henry Clay for President and Theodore Frelinghuysen for Vice-President. This was the first news ever flashed by electric telegraph.

The telegraph soon impressed people

by other sensational uses. When a thief escaped from Washington by train, his description was telegraphed ahead to the station in Baltimore. There he was arrested as he stepped off the train. Newspaper editors predicted that before long there would be no more crime, since criminals would be too afraid to be "struck" by this telegraphic "lightning."

Morse joined two newspapermen to form the Magnetic Telegraph Company. They built new lines—from Philadelphia to New York, from Philadelphia to Baltimore, and around to all the larger cities. By 1848 the telegraphic network reached northward to Portland, Maine, southward to Charleston, and westward to St. Louis, Chicago, and Milwaukee. Regular newspaper columns offered the latest bulletins under the heading "BY MAGNETIC TELEGRAPH." Newspapermen boasted of the "mystic band" that now held the nation together.

The Mexican War of 1846–48, the Gold Rush beginning in 1848, and the national troubles that foreshadowed a Civil War—all these whetted the Americans' appetite for news. And the more news people had the more they wanted.

Because it was expensive to gather news by telegraph, the newspapers came together in groups. Since they all shared the latest dispatches, each of them had to pay only part of the cost of telegraphing the news. In 1848 six New York daily newspapers formed the first Associated Press. Their man in Boston took the news brought by ships from Europe and put it in one telegram to the New York office. Then the Associated Press sold its speedy and reliable dispatches to newspapers in Boston, Philadelphia, and elsewhere.

Gathering and selling news became a big business. With the news-gathering experience of the Civil War behind them, Go-Getting newsmen extended the Associated Press throughout the nation. Then every member newspaper supplied its own local news to all the hundreds of other members. Since there were so many members, they could also afford to open offices with full-time reporters all over the world. This increased the quantity and improved the quality of news. The Associated Press stories tried not to be prejudiced or one-sided, for their readers were members of all political parties. Papers would not buy the "A.P." news unless it gave the straight facts. By the early twentieth century there was also a United Press and an International News Service.

At the same time many other new inventions were helping to turn out papers fast and by the millions. In the early nineteenth century an ingenious Englishman improved the presses used by big-city newspapers. Instead of using a frame that went up and down he used a cylinder. The blank paper was attached to the cylinder and rolled evenly against the type. This was much faster because the cylinder could be kept going continuously and a new piece of paper put in every time it went around.

Then Richard Hoe, a young New Yorker, had a still better idea. Why not put the *type* itself on a cylinder and roll the type smoothly and rapidly against the paper? By 1855, his Hoe Rotary Press was printing 10,000 newspapers in an hour.

The next step was to manufacture paper in long rolls instead of sheets. In 1865, a Philadelphian, William Bullock, made the first machine that printed on a continuous roll of paper—and it printed both sides of the paper at once. The finishing touch came with a gadget that actually folded the papers as they came off the presses.

Some metropolitan papers soon put out six different editions each day. Newspapers became larger and larger. Sunday newspapers—including advertisements, comics, magazine sections, book reviews, and everything else—became big enough to fill the whole day for Americans who did not go to church.

Richard Hoe's speedy web printing machine was among the new wonders shown in Machinery Hall at the Centennial Exposition in Philadelphia. This new-style press, instead of printing on separate sheets, used a continuous roll of paper, which could be more than four miles long.

CHAPTER 14

Letters in Every Mailbox ⌇⌇⌇⌇⌇⌇⌇⌇⌇⌇

A workable national mail system was slow in coming to the nation. The framers of the Federal Constitution in 1787 had given Congress the power "to establish Post Offices and Post Roads." A Post Road was a main road with special stations to provide fresh horses for the riders who carried the mail. For some years, almost all postal service was on one Main Post Road along the Atlantic coast. People used the mail very little. When George Washington was President the letters in the mail averaged less than *one* for every *twelve* Americans each *year!*

In those early years the postage on a letter was usually paid by the person who received it. If he did not want to pay the postage he never got your letter.

Of course there was no home delivery. To get your mail you had to go to the post office. Even after Philadelphia had a population of 150,000 everybody in the city who wanted his mail had to wait in line at the post office.

Then in 1825 came the dim beginnings of modern mail delivery. The postmaster in each town was allowed to give letters to mail carriers to deliver to people's homes. The carriers still got no government salary. They lived by collecting a small fee from anybody to whom they delivered a letter. If you were not at home to pay they would not leave your letters in your mailbox.

By the 1840's the growing country desperately needed a cheap and efficient postal system. The government service was still so haphazard and expensive that there was widespread demand to abolish the Post Office. People called it an "odious monopoly" and said that private businesses could do much better.

As a result in 1845 Congress passed a law establishing cheap postage and tried to reform the whole system. At first each postmaster printed his own stamps and there was chaos. Then, in 1847, the reformed Post Office Department issued the first national postage stamps—a five-cent stamp showing the head of Benjamin Franklin and a ten-cent stamp with the head of George Washington.

Now the postage would be paid by the person who mailed the letter. Some people objected. They said that if a person really wanted to receive a letter, the least he could do was pay the postage. Before postage stamps, people would simply fold their letters and write the address on the outside. But now letters became more private because everybody began to use envelopes which could be sealed.

With the growth of the railroads just before the Civil War it was possible to carry the mail much faster than on horseback or by stage coach. But when a train arrived at a railroad station and dropped several large bags of mail they had to be sorted all at once. That caused annoying delays. Then in 1865 the Railway Mail Service began using specially designed railway cars to sort the mail while it was in transit.

There were still problems of how to pick up mail from small towns along the track where the trains did not even stop for passengers. With a clever new gadget—the mail-bag catcher—the speeding train, as it passed, could snatch a bag of mail hanging beside the track.

Postage stamps, too, became a way of bringing Americans together. The pictures on stamps reminded the nation of its heroes (like Franklin and Washington) and told of great events, past and present. The first "commemorative" series of American postage stamps appeared in 1893 at the time of the World's Columbian Exposition in Chicago. Sixteen large stamps in different denominations showed scenes of Columbus and the discovery of America. In 1938 the Post Office issued a complete series of Presidents. From the very beginning the Post Office had a rule against using the images of persons still alive.

Even after postage stamps were introduced, at first they paid for delivery only as far as the post office. They did not include delivery to anybody's home. About the time of the Civil War, when private letter-carrying businesses were actually delivering mail to the home address on the envelope, they were often speedier than Post Office mail. To compete with them the Post Office began to provide the same service.

Finally in 1863 Congress provided a regular salary for letter carriers. They took the mail from the post office and delivered it to home addresses. This serv-

Paying the postman for a letter received.

ice was offered only in the cities. By 1887 a city had to have at least 10,000 people to be eligible for free home delivery. But most Americans still lived on farms or in small towns. As late as 1890 nearly three-quarters of the people in the United States never received a letter unless they went to the post office to collect it.

The old-fashioned system had its points. People did not receive "junk" mail they didn't want. The general storekeeper was commonly the village postmaster. When the post office was in a corner of the general store—between the drygoods and the farm tools—the system brought customers to the general store. There, too, farmers would enjoy meeting friends from the whole countryside who had come for their mail.

But it was also a nuisance. The farmer never received mail unless he came to town. He was out of touch with the news. No wonder the farmer had a reputation for being out-of-date.

In 1889 a Go-Getting department-store pioneer from Philadelphia, John Wanamaker, became Postmaster General. He saw that it was time for a change. The whole nation would profit if *everybody*—not just the city dweller—had mail delivered to his mailbox. Wanamaker's plan would finally bring the mail to the farmer. It would be called "Rural Free Delivery"—RFD for short.

"RFD!" became the farmers' battlecry. And there really was a battle. On one side were the farmers who wanted mail-order catalogs and mail-order packages and newspapers delivered to their doors. They wanted to be in touch with the world every day. On the other side were the village storekeepers. They wanted to keep the farmers coming into their stores to get their mail—and incidentally to do some shopping. If it became too easy to shop by mail, the farmers

might buy all their goods from Sears and Ward's and the country stores would lose their customers.

At the same time, in the 1890's, many American farmers in the West were suffering from drought and hard times. Farmers were organizing in their Grange Clubs (which had supported Ward's) and in their Populist political party. And many city people, too, wanted to help the farmer—especially if it could be done in some way that would help make the cities prosper.

In 1896 Congress adopted RFD. Incidentally, Congressmen were glad to create lots of new jobs—and perhaps win new votes. In one of the great American organizing achievements of the nineteenth century, the Post Office laid out nine thousand new routes in one year. The Postmaster General approved the design for a standard rural mailbox, which ever since has been the trademark of country life.

RFD helped open the world to the farmer. Now when he ordered from Sears and Ward's, his goods came promptly by RFD. Soon farmers insisted on—and were getting—the latest styles and the newest improvements. The farmer was no longer a "back number" as he used to be called.

Now, at last, he shared with other Americans all the news of the world. When his only way of receiving mail had been his weekly trip to the village, no sensible farmer would subscribe to a daily newspaper. Who wanted an armful of stale newspapers once a week? But now the newspaper came to the farmer's mailbox every day. In 1911 over a billion newspapers and magazines were delivered over RFD.

A Railway Mail Service employee aboard a moving train, using the improved "catcher" to snatch a mailbag from a post beside the track.

In the days before the automobile, mail wagons like this brought letters and packages by Rural Free Delivery to the farmer's own mailbox.

CHAPTER 15

The Sun Is No Longer Boss

In the days before the railroad, people did not worry much about being on time. George Washington or Thomas Jefferson did not consider a person late simply because he arrived fifteen or twenty minutes after the time they had agreed on. When Benjamin Franklin listed in his *Autobiography* the thirteen virtues he would practice till he became perfect in them, he included "sincerity" and "cleanliness"—but he did not include punctuality.

In colonial days it was hard to be on time anyway, because watches were expensive and not many people carried them. Most people depended on the clock they saw—or heard—on the town hall or the church steeple. "Grandfather clocks" struck the hour and the half-hour to tell time to people who had no watches. If you took a trip, there was no regular timetable. Stagecoaches left whenever they had arrived from some other place or whenever the driver and

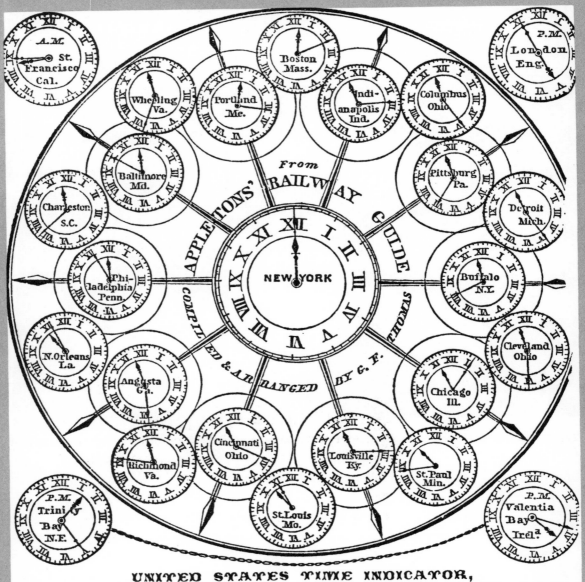

UNITED STATES TIME INDICATOR,

Showing the Difference of Time between the various Cities of the United States: including San Francisco, California; Trinity Bay, Newfoundland; Valentia Bay, Ireland; and, London, England.

It will be perceived, by glancing at the "Indicator," that when it is noon at New York, it is 12 minutes past 12 00 at Boston, 25 minutes past 1 00 at Trinity Bay, 24 minutes past 4 00 p. m. at Valentia Bay; when it wants 15 minutes of 9 00 a. m. at St. Francisco, Cal., it wants 5 minutes of 5 00 p. m. at London, England. Thus, by a little calculation, the reader will readily perceive the difference of time between the several points, and obviate the necessity of moving the hands of his watch to be in time. There is no standard railway time in the Union,

each Railway Co. adopting the time where its princ pal office may be located; we would, therefore, su gest to the traveller the necessity of consulting t "Indicator," and, if possible, to be at the depot son few minutes previous to the departure of the trains

TO TRAVELLERS.—As our object is to publish *reliable Guide*, regardless of expense, we woul thank the travelling community if they will notif us of the incorrectness of a Time Table, and we wil not only exclude it from the "Guide," but notif the public of the same.

Before Standard Time. This cover of Appletons' Railway Guide *shows the time in different cities when it was noon in New York.*

the horses were ready.

In a stagecoach on a good road you might average five miles an hour. After the railroads were built you could average forty. And you could travel on schedule. When a single track was used for trains in both directions, the engineer had to know exactly what time the train was due from the other direction so he could be on the siding to let it pass. Trains ran by the minute.

And now, with trains speeding from city to city, there were strange new problems that nobody had ever noticed before. The trouble was that every town had its own clocks set to its own particular time. The astronomers said that it was "noon" when you saw the sun reach its zenith—the highest point in the heavens. Since the earth was constantly in motion, and since the sun rose sooner when you were more to the east, then when it was noon obviously depended on *where* you were. Since you saw the sun rise earlier if you were in New York than if you were in Chicago, and still earlier in Chicago than in San Francisco, the time was different in those places.

There actually was a difference in the "astronomical" time, between any two places if one was to the west of the other —that is, if the places were on different longitudes. When it was precisely noon (that is when the sun had reached its zenith) in Boston, it was still only 11:56 in the morning in Worcester (slightly to the west). And when it was precisely noon in Chicago it was already 12:06 in Indianapolis (slightly to the east).

Cities became as patriotic about their own time as about the splendor of their city hall or the grandeur of their hotel. In every city the people said God had given them their "own" time, when He fixed the sun in the heavens.

Imagine what this meant for a railroad! The Pennsylvania Railroad tried to use Philadelphia time on its eastern lines. But that was 5 minutes earlier than New York time and 5 minutes later than Baltimore time. In Indiana there were 23 different local times, in Illinois 27, and in Wisconsin there were 38.

Even in any one town people disagreed about what the time really was. Each jeweler might have his own special time, which his customers were loyal to. To keep business running smoothly, and so that people would know when the stores would open and close, and when to meet their appointments, each city somehow had to announce its own time. Some used chimes on a town clock. Others blew a whistle or used a ball, called a "time ball" (held up on a pole in a conspicuous place) which was dropped at the precise moment of noon.

Generally the railroads used the local time for their arrival in each station. In between cities there was the greatest confusion. Yet for speeding express trains a few minutes could make the difference between a clear track and a fatal collision.

It is not surprising, then, that railroad men were among the first to try to bring order out of this confusion. But it was not easy. If you began tampering with their time, citizens were as outraged as if you tried to change the name of their city. And, of course, the astronomers really had a point. If you measured time by the sun in the heavens, then it was not man but nature that had made the confusion. And then perhaps nothing could be done about it.

But maybe, others said, this way of handling time was only a matter of habit. Suppose people simply stopped using sun time or astronomical time. And suppose that instead they used a new kind of "Railroad Time"—which could be the "Standard Time."

Suppose you managed to persuade the different cities along the railroad line to set their clocks to the same time. Take, for example, the train which ran west from Boston to Worcester. Although Worcester's astronomical time was 4 minutes earlier than Boston's, the people of Worcester might be persuaded to set their clocks to the same time as those in Boston.

For the United States as a whole, you could mark off on the map a few conspicuous time belts—up and down the whole country. You would need only four—Eastern Time, Central Time, Mountain Time, and Pacific Time—each several hundred miles wide. Standard Time would be exactly the same for all the places within each belt. At the edge of each belt, the time would change by a whole hour. These time belts would be marked on all maps, and then everybody could know exactly what time it was everywhere.

This was a sensible plan. But it took many years to persuade Americans. The leader of the campaign was William Frederick Allen, an energetic man who was not afraid to make enemies. He had seen the confusion when he had been an engineer on the Camden and Amboy Railroad before he joined the staff of the *Official Guide of the Railways*. And he made time reform the main purpose of his life. Allen aimed to provide a railroad timetable that everybody could

understand and could rely on. This would help make railroad travel safer and speedier. His plan for Standard Time finally was adopted by the railroads to go into effect at noon, November 18, 1883.

Everywhere people prepared for the dramatic moment. At 11:45 in the morning according to the old Chicago time, conductors and engineers gathered in the lobby of the railroad station in Chicago. With their old-fashioned stem-winding pocket watches in their hands they looked at the clock on the wall. When the official Chicago railroad clock reached noon, it was stopped. The switch instantly connected it by telegraph wire to the new official clock for the whole Central time belt. At what would have been 9 minutes and 32 seconds past noon by the old Chicago time, the clock was started again. The railroad men all set their watches. Now everybody was on Standard Time!

Some people still objected. They thought the railroads were trying to take the place of God. "It is unconstitutional," warned Mayor Dogberry of Bangor, Maine, "being an attempt to change the immutable laws of God Almighty and hard on the workingman by changing day into night." He told churches not to ring their bells according to the new Standard Time. The editor of the Indianapolis *Sentinel* was outraged:

> The sun is no longer boss of the job. People—55,000,000 of them—must eat, sleep and work as well as travel by railroad time. It is a revolt, a rebellion. The sun will be requested to rise and set by railroad time. . . . People will have to marry by railroad time, and die by railroad time. Minis-

ters will be required to preach by railroad time.

One minister in Tennessee was so disgusted at this effort to take the place of God's own sun time that he took a hammer into his pulpit and smashed his watch to pieces just to shock his congregation.

But others found reason to be pleased. "The man who goes to church in New York on November 18th," applauded the New York *Herald,* "will hug himself with delight to find that the noon service has been curtailed to the extent of nearly four minutes, while every old maid on Beacon Hill in Boston will rejoice to discover that she is younger by almost 16 minutes."

Gradually people forgot their outrage. They discovered that it was wonderfully convenient to have Standard Time. One city after another changed its clocks to agree with the clock on the railroad station. In 1918 Congress finally gave the Interstate Commerce Commission the legal power to mark off time belts. The government simply followed the time belts that William Frederick Allen had persuaded the railroads to adopt thirty-five years earlier.

Standard Time helped to draw all the nation's railroad lines together. But other steps were needed too. In 1860 there were about 350 different railroad companies and about 30,000 miles of railroad tracks in the United States. Yet there was not really a national railroad network.

The main reason was that the many railroad lines were not on the same "gauge." The gauge is the distance between the two rails, measured from the inside of one rail to the inside of the other. There were many different gauges. Some railroad builders put their tracks six feet apart but some put them closer together, and there were at least eleven different gauges in general use. A railroad car that would just fit the six-foot gauge would not run on the narrower gauges.

If you wanted to send a package any distance by railroad it had to be taken out of the car that fitted one gauge and moved into a car to fit the gauge of the next railroad. In 1861 a package sent by railroad from Charleston, South Carolina, to Philadelphia, had to change railroad cars eight times.

Moving a package from one railroad to another made work for porters and teamsters. At the same time the passengers, who had to wait in the town while they changed trains, made business for hotels, restaurants, and storekeepers. Naturally enough, then, town boosters were not anxious to have all railroads on the same gauge.

From the beginning, quite a few lines happened to have the same gauge. George Stephenson, the English railroad inventor, had designed his locomotive to measure 4 feet 8½ inches between the wheels—the usual distance between wheels on a wagon. When Stephenson locomotives were imported to the United States, they had this "Standard Gauge." And many early railroad lines naturally built their tracks to fit the imported trains.

By 1861 about half the railroad tracks in the United States were on Standard Gauge. These were mainly in New England and the Middle Atlantic States, where most of the early railroads had

OUR STANDARD (GAUGE) ADOPTED ALL OVER THE UNION.

Thomas Nast, who drew this cartoon, came to New York from Germany as a child. He supported the Radical Republicans, attacked corrupt politicians, and invented the Republican Elephant and the Democratic Donkey.

been built. But the other half of American railroad tracks were on every sort of gauge—from about three feet to about six feet.

The Civil War brought an urgent need to ship arms and men quickly across the country. In the Confederacy, lines which ran into Richmond on Standard Gauge were hastily connected to one another. Now passengers and freight could go straight through. In the North, too, the war hurried progress. For the first time through service connected New York City with Washington, D.C.

At the end of the war Americans, North and South, saw the overwhelming advantages of a uniform gauge. And when the transcontinental railroad was completed with Standard Gauge in 1869, that settled the question. Now if a railroad builder wanted to join the traffic across the continent, he had to set his rails 4 feet 8½ inches apart.

By 1880 about four-fifths of the tracks in the United States had been converted to Standard Gauge. Most of the other gauges were in the Old Confederate South. Finally, in 1886, representatives of Southern railroads decided to change the gauge of all their 13,000 miles of track to the national standard.

A month in advance, crews went along loosening the old track. They measured the distance for the new Standard Gauge and put spikes along the wooden ties. On May 31 and June 1, 1886, the men worked frantically. One record-breaking crew on the Louisville and Nashville Railroad changed eleven miles of track in 4½ hours. June 1, 1886, was a holiday along the Southern tracks. By 4:00 P.M. the Southern railroads had joined the Union.

CHAPTER 16
Company Towns and Garden Cities

The American West was known for its "instant cities." Even before the Civil War, these grew quickly if they happened to be located at way stations where the westward travelers passed—at the joinings of riverways, on lake ports, at railroad terminals, or near new mines. As these cities grew, their boosters competed with one another to attract new settlers who, of course, would also be new customers. Each city hoped to become "bigger and better" than all the others. Some of them—Cincinnati, Chicago, Denver, Omaha, Kansas City, and others—became the great cities of the new Middle West.

But after the Civil War, as the whole country became more citified, there grew up new kinds of instant cities. These had not been way stations on the road west. They were found all over the country. At first their aim was not to grow big, but to stay small—and so escape the troubles of the crowded metropolis. They were actually planned—by businessmen, real-estate developers, and others—and they had common patterns.

Businessmen were looking for new places to put their factories. Workers were anxious to escape the dumbbell tenements and the darkened, crowded cities. Prosperous merchants and lawyers and doctors were eager to raise their families out in the open air.

With the new railroad network there was less reason than ever for factories to stay in big cities. Almost everywhere along a railroad line would do. For raw materials could be brought in from anywhere and finished products could be transported to anyplace.

Then why not build a "Company Town"? If an industrialist built his factory away from a big city, the workers would not have to live in slums. Where land was so much less expensive, each worker could have an attractive little house with his own garden. The employer could provide parks and playgrounds, and workers might be more content. After the Civil War many energetic businessmen had this idea.

In 1881 Andrew Carnegie, a Go-Getting steel industrialist, built a steel plant and a whole new town called Homestead seven miles up the Monongahela River from Pittsburgh. Besides small houses for the workers and their families, Carnegie provided a library and even bowling alleys. Homestead was not beautiful, but at least it lacked the crowds and the filth of the city slums.

George M. Pullman, inventor of the Pullman sleeping car for railroads, also decided to build a new town ten miles outside Chicago. In 1884 he bought a tract of land on the shores of Lake Calumet. He named it after himself and hoped it would be a model for other Company Towns. Pullman's architect designed the whole town, including a central square with town hall, churches, a library, and parks. All the buildings, including the small houses for the workers, were of dark-red brick.

Then in 1893 Granite City was founded outside St. Louis, to manufacture "graniteware" pottery. The Diamond Match Company and the Pittsburgh Plate Glass Company built Company Towns near Akron, Ohio. The United States Steel Company in 1905 built Gary in Indiana (not far from Chicago), named after Elbert Henry Gary, the head of the company.

Company Towns sprang up all over the country. There workers escaped the worst horrors of the big city. But they found some new horrors. Living in a Company Town was something like being a feudal serf in the Middle Ages. The company not only controlled your job, but it also decided where you would live, where (and at what price) you could buy your food. The company controlled your schools, and even hired your police.

Some of the most violent strikes were in these Company Towns. When the Carnegie Steel Company cut wages at its Homestead plant in 1892, the angry workers went on strike. In the resulting violence a dozen men were killed. When the Pullman Company cut wages but kept up its rents during the business depression of 1893, their whole town went on strike against the company and for months the nation's railroads were paralyzed. For Americans who wanted to run their own lives the Company

Homestead, Pennsylvania, the company town built by Andrew Carnegie, where workers escaped the city slum but lived in a pall of smoke from the blast furnaces.

Town was a spiritual failure.

But the Company Town was not the only new-style instant city which appeared at the end of the nineteenth century. On the "suburban frontier" there appeared the Garden City. An English reformer, Ebenezer Howard, who had come to America as a young man and had spent five years around crowded Chicago, tried to design a suburban utopia. Howard's *Garden Cities of Tomorrow* (1898) was his blueprint for a better life. He wished to combine the best features of the city and the country. He urged people to group together to build Garden Cities—new small towns out in the country. These towns, he said, should be planned with a garden belt all around. Then, if the Garden City was

connected to the big city by a railroad, it gave its residents the best of both worlds.

Some rich men who owned summer houses in the country near cities began living out in the suburbs year-round. For example, some businessmen who worked in New York City preferred living in Old Greenwich, Connecticut, three-quarters of an hour away on the railroad. Since there was not enough traffic to persuade the railroad to stop there, they would hop on or off the train outside Old Greenwich as it slowed down for a bridge. By the 1880's when enough New York businessmen were living there, they built their own railroad station, and the train stopped for them. These rich suburban pioneers built their own country clubs, and tried to keep their communities "exclusive"— for Oldcomers.

Soon other Americans, following Ebenezer Howard's advice, were building Garden Cities. These were no longer only for the very rich, but they were not yet for people of modest means. Lake Forest outside Chicago and Shaker Heights outside Cleveland showed a special effort to make the Garden City more romantic than the big city. Instead of the monotonous parallel streets of checkerboard city blocks, the Garden City streets wound up and down the hills and by the trees of the countryside. Wide lawns separated the houses from the roads and from one another. Before long, Garden Cities like Radburn, New Jersey, were being specially planned for people of modest income. In 1910 a New York architect made a new design for space-saving "garden apartments" with "kitchenettes" (a new American word for a compact kitchen and pantry). Now you no longer needed to be rich to live out in a garden suburb.

Ebenezer Howard's diagram (1898) of the ideal arrangement of lands in a Garden City. Houses were to be built in a circle around a park. Outside the Circle Railway there were to be farms and forests.

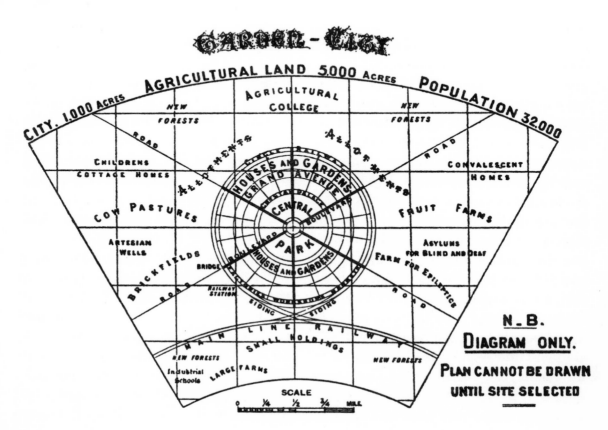

CHAPTER 17

Bridge-Building Heroes ᕙᕗᕙᕗᕙᕗᕙᕗ

Many fast-growing American cities had started on the banks of wide rivers. To expand, they had to find ways of carrying the railroad—and thousands of daily passengers—out beyond the old city limits. The growth of these American cities, and their ability to hold their citizens together, depended on their ability to span the neighboring waterway. Go-Getting American engineers transformed the ancient art of bridge building to help the cities to reach out to their new frontiers.

Something about bridge building specially attracted the American inventive genius. James Buchanan Eads, the man who built the bridge for St. Louis, had first shown his inventive talents during the Civil War as an adviser to the Union navy. In 1861 he proposed a fleet of ironclad gunboats to control the Mississippi River. When the government took up his suggestion he manufactured the needed ships in sixty-five days. After the war the people of St. Louis, which was on the west bank of the Mississippi, saw that they had to bring the railroad across the wide river and into their city if St. Louis was to grow.

Many different schemes were offered. But all were rejected until Eads appeared. As a boy he had worked on a river steamboat. When only twenty-two years old, he had invented a diving bell to salvage ships that had sunk in the river. And then he had done a lot of walking underwater on the very bottom of the Mississippi. He knew that river bottom almost as well as other men knew the city streets.

What Eads had learned was important. Building a bridge across the Mississippi depended first on finding solid support under the sandy river bottom. As Eads had moved along 65 feet below the surface of the water, he saw the swift currents churning up the sands. He knew that the supports for his bridge would have to go far below those river sands—all the way down to bedrock.

In 1867, when Eads began construction, his first problem was to lay the foundations of the two stone towers which would hold up the arches of the bridge in midstream. The towers would rise 50 feet above water level. The foundation of one would have to go down 86 feet below water level, and the other, where bedrock was deeper, had to go down 123 feet. But was this possible?

Eads's plan was to use his own diving bell together with some new caissons—watertight working chambers—that had recently been perfected in England. The 75-foot-wide caissons would keep out the water while the men dug, and the men would keep digging beneath the river sands until they reached solid rock.

Stages in the building of Eads's bridge to span the Mississippi River at St. Louis. From the two stone towers in midstream, steel arches thrust out to meet arches thrusting from other towers on the shore.

When his men finally reached bedrock, they were working ten stories below the surface of the water! Because of the great pressures at that depth, the men could stay down only 45 minutes at a time. They had to come up slowly. Between shifts they rested long periods. Despite all precautions thirteen men died of "caisson disease" (sometimes called "the bends") from too rapid change in air pressure.

The Mississippi River boatmen and ferrymen feared competition from the new railroad that would cross the bridge. They tried to persuade the Secretary of War to dismantle the towers when they were half built. President U. S. Grant knew St. Louis and he had faith in Eads. He knew the bridge would be important to the future of the city and to the growth of the Middle West. And he saw that it would help bind the nation together. He ordered the engineers in the War Department to keep the project going.

For the three vast arches of the bridge Eads decided to use steel, though it had never been used in such a large structure. When the usual carbon steel did not meet his tests, he ordered large quantities of the new chromium steel, and then supervised its production. While chromium steel was more costly, it was rustproof and needed no covering.

It took Eads seven years to bridge the Mississippi. Finally in 1874 in a grand ceremony the former Union general, William T. Sherman, pounded the last spike of the double-track railroad crossing the bridge. Then fourteen locomotives, two by two, chugged triumphantly across the river. President Grant came to St. Louis to proclaim Eads an American hero.

And there were other heroic bridge builders who helped open ways to the suburban frontiers. Few other cities were quite so hemmed in by water as New York. Manhattan Island, heart of the city, was surrounded by the East River, the Hudson River, and the Atlantic Ocean. For a half-century there had been proposals for a bridge across the East River, connecting lower Manhattan Island to Brooklyn. When the fierce winter of 1866–67 stopped all ferry

service and isolated Brooklyn from Manhattan for days, it was plain that something had to be done.

John Roebling was ready with a plan. When he came to the United States from Germany as a young man he opened the first factory for making wire rope out of many strands of wire twisted together. This new material was wonderfully suited for reaching over wide rivers where it was difficult or impossible to build masonry towers in midstream. From high towers on both ends you could suspend the strong wire rope to hold up the bridge.

If the Niagara River, for example, was to be spanned near the Falls, it would have to be by such a "suspension" bridge. In 1855 Roebling completed a wire-supported bridge over the Niagara —strong enough to carry fully loaded trains. This feat made John Roebling famous. In 1860 he completed another suspension bridge, just outside Pittsburgh, reaching a thousand feet across the Allegheny River. And by 1867 he had completed still another outside Cincinnati, across the Ohio River.

A suspension bridge, Roebling style, could solve New York's problem. For the bridge from Manhattan to Brooklyn had to stay high above water level in order to allow the sails and smokestacks of large ocean-going vessels to pass underneath. Roebling's ambitious plan in 1867 proposed towers 271 feet above water level, holding up a main suspension span of 1,595 feet.

During the very beginning of construction in 1869, a ferry crushed John Roebling's foot against the dock and he died from tetanus infection in two weeks. John Roebling's son, Washington Roebling, was ready to carry on. He too was a man of courage. He had enlisted in the Union army as a private on the day after President Lincoln's first appeal for volunteers. By the time of the Battle of Gettysburg, young Washington Roebling's services had earned him the rank of colonel. On the second day of the battle, with his own hands he helped drag a cannon up to a strategic hilltop, and so helped to prevent the defeat of the Union Army.

On his father's death, Washington Roebling at once took over the building of the bridge. In 1872, when fire in the Brooklyn caisson threatened the whole project, Roebling stayed below in the

THE EAST RIVER BRIDGE.

On this page we give several views of the Brooklyn caisson of the East River Bridge, which a few days since narrowly escaped destruction by fire. The interior of the caisson is divided into chambers by temporary partitions of planking calked with oakum. It was in one of these partitions that the fire occurred. It originated from the blaze of a candle held too near the partition by a workman. Once kindled, the fire was driven by the immense force of the compressed air within the caisson with such rapidity as to defy all ordinary methods of extinguishment; and it was not until the interior was flooded with water that the engineers of the work felt satisfied that they had effectually subdued the mischievous element. It is thought that the injury to the caisson can be paired at a very slight expense.

The caisson, as our readers will see from the sectional view, is an immense wooden box, without bottom, covering a space of 102 by 168 feet, or about three-eighths of an acre of ground—nearly seven city lots. Its present height is 24 feet 6 inches. The roof is of solid timber 15 feet thick (except that the upper ten courses have narrow spaces filled with concrete, to increase the weight). The sides of the air chamber are V shaped, and are of solid timbers bolted very firmly together. The lower edge is heavily shod with iron. This V is 9 feet 6 inches high, 8 inches thick at the bottom, and 9 feet thick at the top. The timber joints, from the edge to the top of the fifth roof course, are thoroughly calked and pitched. Between the fourth and fifth roof courses is a sheet of tin, which is continued down the sides underneath

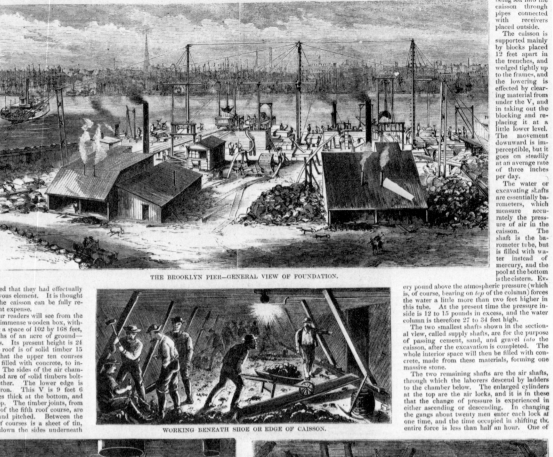

THE BROOKLYN PIER—GENERAL VIEW OF FOUNDATION.

WORKING BENEATH SHOE OR EDGE OF CAISSON.

AIR CHAMBERS FOR THE INGRESS AND EGRESS OF WORKMEN.

SENDING UP DÉBRIS THROUGH THE WATER SHAFT.

the outside sheathing; this is intended to prevent all escape of air from the inside.

The air or working chamber is divided by massive timber trusses or frames into six rooms, in each of which fifteen to twenty men are employed. Some are drilling the immense boulders preparatory to blasting, others pulling stone from the trenches by means of tackle; gangs of men are wheeling material that has been excavated and dumping it into the pools under the water-shafts, and here others are constantly shoving the material under the shafts, from whence it is taken by the dredging buckets. The interior is lighted by fourteen calcium lights; the gas

being led into the caisson through pipes connected with receivers placed outside.

The caisson is supported mainly by blocks placed 12 feet apart in the trenches, and wedged tightly up to the frames, and the lowering is effected by clearing material from under the V, and in taking out the blocking and replacing it at a little lower level. The movement downward is imperceptible, but it goes on steadily at an average rate of three inches per day.

The water or excavating shafts are essentially barometers, which measure accurately the pressure of air in the caisson. The shaft is the barometer tube, but is filled with water instead of mercury, and the pool at the bottom is the cistern. Every pound above the atmospheric pressure (which is, of course, bearing on top of the column) forces the water a little more than two feet higher in this tube. At the present time the pressure inside is 12 to 15 pounds in excess, and the water column is therefore 27 to 34 feet high.

The two smallest shafts shown in the sectional view, called supply shafts, are for the purpose of passing cement, sand, and gravel into the caisson, after the excavation is completed. The whole interior space will then be filled with concrete, made from these materials, forming one massive stone.

The two remaining shafts are the air shafts, through which the laborers descend by ladders to the chamber below. The enlarged cylinders at the top are the air locks, and it is in these that the change of pressure is experienced in either ascending or descending. In changing the gangs about twenty men enter each lock at one time, and the time occupied in shifting the entire force is less than half an hour. One of

the air pipes from the compressors enters one of these shafts, and the other one of the supply shafts.

The spaces left around the shafts are inclosed by coffer-dams, to prevent water entering from without through the masonry. There are now 18 feet of masonry completed. It is of massive blocks of limestone and granite, weighing from one and a half to six tons each. The arrangement of derricks and railway track is so complete that it is not an uncommon thing to unload and set twenty of these blocks in an hour.

There were used in the construction of the caisson over 3,000,000 feet, board measure, of yellow pine timber, and about 35 miles of bolts.

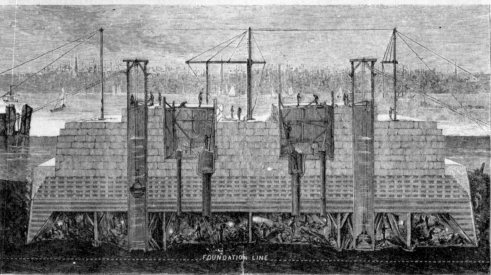

SECTIONAL VIEW OF FOUNDATION, SHOWING CAISSON AND MASON-WORK.

Building Brooklyn Bridge was one of the wonders of the age. The problems of working far underwater were just as challenging as the later problems (brought by the skyscraper) of working far into the air.

compressed-air chamber for seven hours. As a result he acquired "caisson disease."

Washington Roebling never fully recovered. Too weak to supervise the bridge on the spot, he would sit in a wheelchair in his apartment and watch the work through field glasses. Then he would give instructions to his wife, who carried them down to the bridge. All his communications with the world were through her. Efforts were made to remove him from the job, but his mind remained active and he would not give up the command.

At 1:30 on the afternoon of May 24, 1883, fourteen years after John Roebling had begun the job, President Chester A. Arthur and his Cabinet joined with Governor Grover Cleveland of New York for the formal opening of the Brooklyn Bridge. Six warships anchored below the bridge fired a resounding salute, and from the center of the bridge came a dazzling display of fireworks. The orator of the occasion declared that this, the world's greatest bridge, was a triumph of "the faith of the saint and the courage of the hero."

The "saint," Mrs. Roebling, herself attended the celebrations. But Washington Roebling, the heroic bridge-building son of a heroic father, was too ill to leave the room from which he had overseen the work. The President of the United States went to Roebling's simple apartment at No. 110 Columbia Heights to give his congratulations.

CHAPTER 18

Going Up! ঙ৩৶৩৶৩৶৩৶৩৶৩৶৩

Oddly enough, although the growing United States had lots of land to spare, the most distinctive American way for a city to grow was not to stretch *out*. After the Civil War, Americans began using their own know-how—together with materials and know-how from all over the world—to stretch their cities *up*. Although some Americans were moving to the suburbs, more people than ever before wanted to live and work right in the center. Businessmen wanted to be where the action was. And many people who could afford to live in the suburbs, still preferred to live downtown.

With old kinds of construction the tallest buildings had seldom been over five or six stories high. There were two problems which had to be solved before buildings could go higher.

The first problem—how to get the people up and down—was beginning to be solved even before the Civil War. In a few luxury hotels, elevators already carried guests up to the fifth and sixth floors. And in some early department stores the elevator was an attractive curiosity.

But elevators were thought to be dangerous. People feared that if the rope holding up the elevator cage should

On opening day at Lord & Taylor's, a new department store in New York City, the elevator was one of the chief attractions.

break, the passengers would drop to their death. Elisha Graves Otis found a way to dispel the public fears. He invented a simple automatic safety brake. If the rope broke, instead of the cage plummeting to the bottom, the brake would automatically clamp the cage safely to the sides. Otis staged a demonstration in New York in 1854. He rode the elevator to the top. Then an attendant cut the rope while breathless

spectators watched. As the cage was clamped in place, Otis bowed nonchalantly to the crowd.

Otis' early steam-driven elevators moved only 50 feet a minute, which amounted to about half a mile an hour. To Americans, who now could speed along on railroads at forty miles an hour, this steam-driven "vertical railway" seemed to climb like a snail. But before 1880 the improved "hydraulic" elevators (pushed up by water pressure in a long vertical cylinder) were climbing at 600 feet a minute. By 1892 an electric motor was carrying passengers up so fast that it "stopped" their ears.

The second problem—how to hold up the building—began to be solved when James Bogardus and others had used cast iron for their Buyers' Palaces. No longer was it necessary to build a tall building like a pyramid, with thick supporting walls on the lower floors. Cast-iron construction helped the department stores keep the lower floors wide open, with broad vistas and narrow pillars, allowing attractive show windows in between. But iron construction also made it possible to build higher and higher. Soon an eight-story building like Stewart's Cast Iron Palace would seem small.

The time was ripe for the "skyscraper." Of course Bogardus was only dreaming when he forecast buildings "ten miles high." But he was not far wrong when he told American builders that only the sky would be the limit.

Bogardus himself constructed one of the first buildings of true skyscraper design. Its frame was a tall iron cage. If the cage was strong and rigid, and solidly anchored at the bottom, then the building could go up high without needing thick walls at the bottom. This was "skeleton" construction. The building was held up, not by wide foundations at the bottom, but by its own rigid skeleton.

The first time Bogardus actually tried this, his structure did not have any rooms at all. It was a skeleton-framed tower for an ammunition factory. In those days lead shot was made by pouring molten lead through a sieve inside a

high tower. The little liquid balls of lead dripped through, a few at a time. As these plummeted down through the air they became naturally rounded. And as they fell into the tank of water at the bottom they hardened into their rounded shape—ready for use in a rifle or a cannon.

In 1855, when the McCullough Shot and Lead Company needed a new shot tower in New York City, Bogardus gave them his radical new design. He built them an octagonal iron tower eight stories high. A tall iron cage, it needed no filled-in, weight-bearing walls to hold it up. Yet it was strong. When the openings in the iron frame were covered with brick, it served just as well as any heavy column of stone.

It was one thing to build a shot tower but quite another to trust the lives of hundreds to such a newfangled way of building. The first real try was in Chicago where the pioneer was William LeBaron Jenney. An adventurous man of wide experience, he had helped build a railroad across Panama before there was any canal. In the Civil War he served on General Sherman's staff as an engineer.

In 1884 when the Home Insurance Company decided to construct a new office building in Chicago, they gave him the job. Jenney, who had probably heard of Bogardus' shot towers built twenty years before, decided himself to use an iron skeleton. In the next year his building was completed.

Even before Jenney's first skyscraper was completed, a better new material had been perfected. This new material was steel. The first six floors of the Home Insurance Building had been

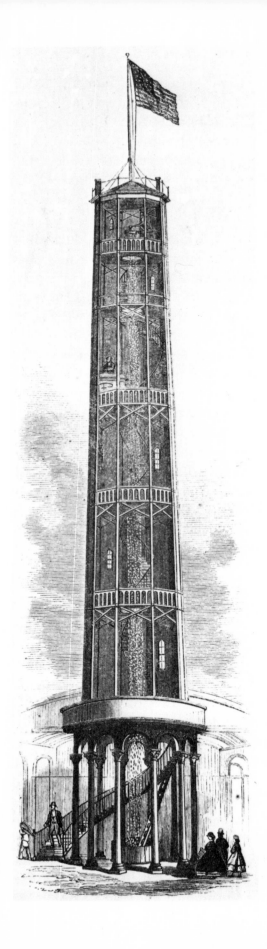

LEFT: *In the Bogardus tower, pieces of lead became rounded as they fell through the hollow center down into a well of water below.* ABOVE: *A New York City fire tower, also designed by Bogardus. The drawing is by Winslow Homer, who first became famous from his Civil War drawings for* Harper's Weekly. *Later he settled on the coast of Maine and had a second career as a painter of fishermen and the sea.*

framed with wrought iron. The top three stories were framed in steel. Steel, like wrought iron, was made almost entirely from iron ore, but steel was far superior. While wrought iron was easily shaped into beams and connecting plates, it bent readily. It was not ideal for a skyscraper frame. Steel was the answer. And it was the material that made higher and higher American skyscrapers possible.

Though men had known how to make steel for centuries, the process had been difficult and time-consuming. Therefore steel was so expensive that it was used only for small objects. The swords used by knights in the Middle Ages were made by endlessly hammering and re-heating and then again hammering the blades. Until the mid-nineteenth century this was the usual way to harden iron to make it into steel.

Then an Englishman, Henry Bessemer, invented his new mass-production steel furnace. By blowing air through the molten iron mass, the carbon in it was burnt out much more quickly. Now it was possible to produce a hundred tons of steel from a single furnace in twelve hours. Before the end of the nineteenth century, the United States—borrowing English methods, improved by American know-how—was producing about twice as much steel as Great

Steel skeleton for a pioneer skyscraper, Chicago's Reliance Building, 1894.

Britain, and now led the world. Better, cheaper steel meant more tall buildings.

Jenney's example in Chicago was followed in New York. The skeleton system was especially useful for building high structures on the tiny lots of crowded Manhattan Island. In 1888 an architect, Bradford Gilbert, was asked to design an 11-story building on Broadway, on a lot that was only 25 feet wide and 103 feet deep. With the old-fashioned heavy masonry the walls would have had to be so thick on the ground floor that there would have been no space for any rooms there. Gilbert designed a true iron-skeleton building—the first in New York City.

At first the building inspectors refused a building permit for Gilbert's Tower Building because they believed that no iron-skeleton building could stay up. Even after the building was completed, Gilbert had to show his confidence by taking the offices at the very top for himself. The age of the skyscraper had arrived.

Twenty-five years later, on the night of April 24, 1913, President Woodrow Wilson pressed a button in Washington to light the tallest habitable building in the world—the Woolworth Building in downtown Manhattan. The Woolworth Building, with its 55 stories rising 760 feet to the base of a towering flagpole, was a monument to the American Go-Getter.

The Woolworth Building was the biggest advertisement in the world. It advertised the success of Frank W. Woolworth, who had begun thirty years before as a poor farm boy in upstate New York. His empire of Five-and-Ten-Cent Stores with their brilliant red-and-gold storefronts now covered the nation. The biggest building in the world had been built from the selling of millions of little things. In that very year the 611 Woolworth stores sold 27,576,000 pairs of hosiery, 12,000 gross (1 gross = 12 dozen) of mousetraps, 300,000 gross of clothespins, 10,000 gross of tin toys, 3,000 gross of baby pacifiers, 368,000 gross of pearl buttons, and 186 tons of hairpins!

The Woolworth Building was a city in itself. With its thirty high-speed elevators it held 15,000 office workers and service employees. Its own power plant generated enough electricity to light fifty thousand homes.

Frank Woolworth wanted an office grand enough to go with the building. On a European tour in 1913 he selected the design of the Empire Room of Napoleon's palace in Paris for "the handsomest office in the country and possibly the world." For the Napoleon of American merchants, why not an office that was truly imperial? And beside his desk he placed a bust of Napoleon.

Skyscrapers still went up and up. Above the Woolworth Building rose the Chrysler Building in 1930. Then in 1931 came the Empire State Building. With its 105 stories reaching up 1,250 feet (almost twice as high as the Woolworth Building), it long remained the highest structure in the world.

PART FOUR

CHAMPIONS FOR THE PEOPLE

CHAMPIONS FOR THE PEOPLE

The Old World had long been ruled by aristocracies. In France and England and Germany, men who had inherited their titles and their lands held power over the life of the whole nation. For centuries government was by a privileged few looking after the silent many. Even after the European revolutions of the late eighteenth and early nineteenth centuries the old aristocrats still controlled the government in most countries.

In the United States, while some people were richer than others, there was no old-style aristocracy. If the people did not look after themselves, who would look after them?

In these years after the Civil War, there came a great new test for self-government. Could a nation so vast and varied find national leaders to speak for all its citizens?

The nation was growing strong and rich. It was becoming more and more citified, with bigger and bigger businesses. Could it find loud clear voices to speak for the farmer, for the small businessman, for the individual factory worker—and for all those others who had little wealth or power and who were in danger of being left out?

Grangers' meeting in Illinois. One sign says: "President $50,000 a year. Farmers 75 cents a week."

CHAPTER 19

The Farmers Find a Voice

During the Civil War many farmers—in both North and South—prospered. There was a great demand for food to supply the armies, there were fewer people working on farms, and the prices for farm products went up.

But within a few years after Appomattox the farmers' troubles began. A bushel of wheat, which in 1873 still sold for $1.21, twelve years later had gone down to 49 cents. A pound of cotton, in 1873 priced at 21 cents, in twenty years sank to 5 cents. At the same time the farmer's expenses went up.

Millions of farmers—like many homeowners today—were painfully buying their farms on mortgage loans. In good times and bad, the farmer had to make regular payments. The heartless sheriff with a long moustache who threatened to "foreclose" the mortgage was no joke to the poor farmer between about 1870 and 1900.

"In God we trusted," the farmers' saying went, "and in Kansas we busted." In the Depression of 1893 when factories closed, many unemployed workers went back to the farm and added to the farmers' burdens. Banks foreclosed their mortgages. Farm families walked the country roads in desperation.

But they did not take their troubles lying down. As early as 1867 they had begun to organize. Within ten years the Patrons of Husbandry had members all over the country in the 20,000 local lodges they called "Granges." On the Fourth of July, 1873, groups of farmers had met to hear a "Farmers' Declaration of Independence."

Farmers who believed they needed their own political party formed a "Farmers Alliance" and then organized the Populist Party in Omaha, Nebraska, in July 1892. Crusaders like the rabble-rousing Tom Watson of Georgia spoke for them in Congress, and spoke loud and clear. "Before I will give up this fight," Watson warned, "I will stay here till the ants tote me out of the keyhole."

One of the farmers' loudest demands was for "cheap money." That meant a high price for wheat and corn and cotton. For the farmers, who were always in debt, were most worried about how to keep up the yearly payments on their mortgages, so they could hold onto their farms.

Suppose for example, that a farmer owed $500 on his mortgage every year. Then if the price of wheat was $1 a bushel, he would have to raise 500 bushels of wheat to pay the $500. But if there was "cheap money"—say, if the price of wheat went up to $2 a bushel—

then the farmer could pay off his yearly debt by selling only 250 bushels of wheat. Of course the banker, to whom the farmer owed the $500 each year, would rather have seen all prices kept down, so the money he received would buy more things.

"Cheap money" meant finding ways for the government to mint as much money as possible. The more money there was around, the more likely people would pay higher prices for farm produce. On the other hand the bankers were against "cheap money" and wanted "hard money." They wanted the "Gold Standard." This meant keeping gold as the *only* basis for money. Since the amount of gold was extremely limited, and was not likely to increase much, the Gold Standard was one way of keeping prices down.

In the 1860's large new deposits of silver had been found in Nevada, Colorado, and elsewhere in the West. The farmers saw that if the government would be required to mint all this silver into money, then the quantity of money would be much increased. The price of wheat and corn and cotton would go up, and the farmers' problems might be solved. This program for minting silver was called "Free Silver" because it meant the "free," that is the unlimited, coining of silver into dollars.

Free silver, then, had a sure-fire appeal. It appealed to debt-burdened city laborers as well as debt-burdened farmers all over the country. And it appealed also to miners and prospectors in the Western States who wanted a guaranteed market for their silver. When the farmers put together their Populist Party to run their own candidates in the Presidential election of 1892, they demanded Free Silver.

The farmers' colorful leaders were not afraid to shock the comfortable people. The handsome, unladylike Mary Elizabeth Lease of Kansas was the mother of four. "What you farmers need to do," she urged, "is to raise less corn and more *Hell!*" She also said:

Wall Street owns the country. It is no longer a government of the people, by the people and for the people, but a government of Wall Street, by Wall Street and for Wall Street. The great common people of this country are slaves, and monopoly is the master.

Then, also from Kansas, there was "Sockless Jerry" Simpson. Once when he ran for Congress he accused his well-dressed opponent of wearing silk stockings. A reporter then sneered that Simpson was so crude that he wore no socks at all. Simpson made this into a boast. Always after he was known as "Sockless Jerry."

The famous farmer-orator, Ignatius Donnelly, came to be known as "the Sage of Nininger," after the town he had tried to build. Before the Civil War he had bought some Minnesota land, and hoped to get rich by making it into a boom town. When the town died, he plowed up what were supposed to be city lots and downtown streets, planted them with wheat, and so became a farmer.

Donnelly wrote many books and he loved outlandish ideas. His *Great Cryptogram* (1888) offered a secret code that was supposed to prove that the plays of Shakespeare had really been written by Sir Francis Bacon. Donnelly could attract a crowd anywhere. Some people were afraid to go hear him because they feared he would make them believe things against their will.

When the regular Democratic and Republican politicians saw the appeal of these farm crusaders, they naturally wanted to steal the Populist thunder. The Populist Platform of 1892 demanded many different reforms. But what would appeal most to the farmers was some one cure-all—a single reform that would solve all their problems at once.

It was not hard to believe that the cure-all might be Free Silver. There was something magical and mysterious about money. The amounts of money somehow seemed to change the value of everything else. Money seemed a medicine for everybody's ills.

Many Democrats and Republicans were especially afraid to see the country get into control of a third party. They called Populists the "lunatic fringe."

Inside the regular parties the most successful of the farm crusaders was William Jennings Bryan. Some called him "The Great Commoner" (because he championed the common people). Others called him "The Prairie Avenger," or "The Boy Orator of the Platte" —after the Nebraska river near his home. Born in Salem, Illinois, he studied law in Chicago and then practiced law in small towns. He distrusted rich people and people of "good family."

Bryan had a holier-than-thou way of speaking. He liked to preach against sin. Proud that he did not drink or smoke or gamble, he was always telling others how to behave. He also had a great appetite. One of his Sunday School class-

Mary Elizabeth Lease, a founder of the Populist Party, and one of the most colorful political leaders of the day.

mates recalled that Bryan was too good a boy to help steal the watermelons— "but he would enjoy eating them when the other boys had secured the booty." As a boy he would carry around bread in his pockets "for an emergency." His enormous appetite became famous. On his political campaigns it was not uncommon for him to eat six full meals a day.

A tall man of great energy, Bryan loved a political battle. And he had a talent for making every issue seem very simple. After he had explained it, every political battle seemed to be between Bryan and God on one side, and his opponents and Satan on the other. His enemies said Bryan did not really understand how complicated the problems

During the Presidential campaign of 1896, Democratic candidate Bryan traveled strenuously about the country carrying his rousing message to anyone who would listen.

were. Even his friends had to admit that what made him famous was not a sharp mind but his loud musical voice.

The "silver-tongued" William Jennings Bryan had decided that "Free Silver" would cure the ills of all mankind. When Bryan arrived at the Democratic Convention in Chicago on July 7, 1896, he was thirty-six years old—one year over the minimum age for a President. He had served only four years in Congress and was barely known outside of Nebraska. Unlike the other leading candidates, he did not have rich supporters.

As the Convention met, it was still not decided whether the Democratic Party would stay with the Gold Standard or whether they would join the farmers for Free Silver. President Grover Cleveland, the Democrat in the White House, was strong for the Gold Standard. But he had lost the support of many laborers and farmers by using federal troops against the railroad workers in the big strike at Pullman. He had a reputation as spokesman for big business.

Until Bryan came to the platform, the speakers at the Chicago convention had been dull and long-winded. Since there was no public-address system most of the speakers could hardly be heard. Bryan was the final speaker for Free Silver.

This was young Bryan's great chance. The first sound of his ringing voice awakened the perspiring audience. They responded to his words with laughter and applause, "like a trained choir" (as he said), down to his last syllable. He spoke without hesitating, for he had given substantially the same speech many times before—to farm audiences all over Nebraska. "We will answer their demand for a Gold Standard," he ended, "by saying to them: You shall not press down upon the brow of labor this crown of thorns. You shall not crucify mankind upon a cross of gold."

The crowd went wild. Their yelling and cheering lasted for an hour. The delegates from Alabama led a "grand march of glory" around the hall. Others reached for Bryan, proud even to touch his coat. They lifted him and marched him in triumph. After they put him back in his seat, admirers sat in his lap, "hugged him until his collar wilted, shook his hand, shouted into his ears, danced all over his feet, and hemmed him in until he could scarcely get his breath." This one speech had transformed a Nebraska small-town lawyer into a front runner for President!

On the next day, the Democratic Convention voted him to lead their ticket.

Bryan was a rousing candidate. From millions of admirers he received all kinds of gifts—ostrich eggs, a stuffed alligator, four live eagles, a cane supposed to have belonged to Andrew Jackson, and lots of rabbits' feet for good luck. "If all the people who have given me rabbits' feet in this campaign will vote for me," Bryan declared, "there is no possible doubt of my election."

The campaign offered one of the most spectacular contrasts in American history. "The Boy Orator of the Platte" went careering about the country by

Meanwhile Republican candidate McKinley sat calmly on his own front porch.

train, making speeches far into the night at every little town, and often in between. On some days he made thirty-six speeches. Meanwhile, his conservative Republican opponent, William B. McKinley, remained calmly seated on his front porch in Canton, Ohio. McKinley made almost no speeches. When he did, he was careful to say nothing in particular—except that he was in favor of "sound money" (the Gold Standard) and "restoring confidence."

Mark Hanna, a clever Cleveland businessman and political boss who had secured the Republican nomination for McKinley, managed McKinley's campaign. Hanna counted on letting Bryan talk himself to defeat. And he used every trick to convince voters that Bryan was a dangerous radical. For example, he persuaded some factory owners, as a stunt, to pay their workers in Mexican dollars (worth only 50 United States cents). This was supposed to show the workers what their wages would really be worth if Bryan won.

Hanna's tactics succeeded. The election went to McKinley by a narrow margin. But Bryan had attracted so many votes that the Democratic leaders could not ignore him. Twice again—in 1900 and 1908—he was named the Democratic candidate for President. Bryan never won.

The Age of Reform had arrived. Free Silver, the simple-minded cure-all, was never adopted. But other Populist reforms—the regulation of railroad rates, control of monopolies, limits on the hours of labor, and a federal income tax —all these finally became law. The Populists had done more than anybody else to advertise the farmers' troubles. And the big, old parties—the Democrats, and then the Republicans—got the message. They adopted the main Populist reforms as their own. The Populists, who had lost many noisy battles, finally won a silent victory.

CHAPTER 20

From Umpire to Guardian

Everything seemed to be growing. While at the outbreak of the Civil War, the country had numbered thirty million people, by 1900 there were over seventy-five million. From thirty-four States, the number had grown to forty-five. Before the war the nation's population was mostly between the Mississippi River and the Atlantic Ocean, plus a few sparsely settled States on the Pacific Coast. By 1900 four transcontinental railroads poured people into the great heart of the continent, filling lands between the Mississippi River and the Sierra Nevada Mountains.

There were more cities, more big cities, and the big cities were bigger than ever. In 1860 there were only nine places that contained 100,000 people or more. But by 1900 there were nearly forty. And there were three giant metropolises each with over a million people.

Businesses were growing bigger. Now you bought your clothes and furniture not from a friendly storekeeper, but from a huge mail-order house or a vast department store. In the old days, you dealt with men you knew personally. Now more and more of everybody's needs were supplied by big companies.

Your goods were manufactured in large factories thousands of miles away. Whom would you complain to? Whom could you count on? Many families who had braved the wilderness and had known loneliness, who had faced the horrors of Civil War, were now frightened by the new menace of Bigness.

What had happened to the old neighborly spirit?

The dangers of Bigness were not only imaginary. As the companies that made the things you needed became larger and larger, the number of different companies supplying your needs became

THE ROAD TO DIVIDENDS.

Newspapermen and cartoonists joined in the popular campaign against Big Business. "Muckrakers" awakened the nation's conscience by accusations, real and imaginary, against all men of wealth.

fewer and fewer. For example, by 1880 the Standard Oil Company controlled over 90 percent of the lamp-oil refining in the United States. In those days before electric light, if you wanted oil to light your house at night you had to pay whatever price that company asked.

Bigness meant monopoly. And monopoly meant that a few men had the power to dictate to everybody.

Everywhere, it seemed, some company was squeezing out its competitors. In the 1890's, if you wanted sugar for your table, you had to buy it from the company that controlled 98 percent of the sugar refining in the whole country. For tobacco, you were in the clutches of the American Tobacco Company. Almost every machine—along with the many new ships and bridges and skyscrapers—now had to use steel. In 1901

the United States Steel Company became the country's first billion-dollar corporation.

The Go-Getters (with the help of their lawyers) invented new ways to combine small businesses into big. And they found ways to keep their control secret. One new kind of company, whose only business was to own other companies, was called a "trust." The men who owned a trust really (but sometimes secretly) controlled smaller companies that still carried on under their own name.

In these ways ambitious Go-Getters built their businesses into empires. Soon there were Banking Empires and Mining Empires, Steel Empires and Railroad Empires. The men who built them were full of imagination and energy, but some of them were as arrogant and as ruthless as the despots of the Middle Ages. Some believed that the only law they had to obey was the law they made for themselves. Once when J. P. Morgan, the giant of American banking, heard that his company was being prosecuted for violating the laws, he went to see the President. "If we have done anything wrong," he explained, "send your man [the Attorney General of the United States] to my man [Morgan's lawyer] and they can fix it up."

Congress passed a law in 1890 making it a crime for businessmen to combine in order to prevent competition. This Sherman Antitrust Act was supposed to punish "restraint of trade or commerce." But like other laws, the law against trusts would work only if the government enforced it.

Presidents did not want to offend the powerful businessmen who had helped them get elected and who might help again at the next election. They pretended that the law did not exist. In the rare case when a President dared to use the law, the Supreme Court saved the trusts by thinking up technicalities. For example, in 1895 the Attorney General prosecuted the one company that controlled 98 percent of the sugar refining in the whole country. But the Supreme Court said that the company really was *not* guilty of preventing competition under the Sherman Antitrust Act—because it was in "manufacturing" and not in "commerce."

The President who actually started using the power of the national government to protect ordinary Americans was Theodore Roosevelt. He had been elected Vice-President on the Republican ticket with William B. McKinley in 1900. When President McKinley joined the festivities at the Pan-American Exposition in Buffalo on September 6, 1901, a man he had never seen before walked up and fired two shots at him. Within a week McKinley was dead.

The man who shot President McKinley called himself an anarchist, which meant that he was against all government. But by making Theodore Roosevelt President, he actually helped to give the national government strong powers.

No one who had visited Theodore Roosevelt as a child would have guessed that he would become a champion of the ordinary American. His father was a well-to-do New York banker who owned country houses and used to take his family to Europe for vacations. Among Teddy Roosevelt's early memories were seeing the Pope during a walk in Rome, and visiting the tomb of Napoleon in Paris.

Young Teddy had no worries about money. But he had other worries. He suffered from asthma, which made it hard for him to exercise, and his eyesight was poor. He became seriously interested in nature and began collecting specimens of plants and animals. When he was twelve, his mother told a maid to throw away some dead mice that the boy had stored in a dresser drawer. "The Loss to Science," Teddy lamented. "The Loss to Science!"

His father built a gymnasium at home. There Teddy worked with a punching bag and did pull-ups on the horizontal bars. He also took boxing lessons. By the time he was seventeen he was expert in track events including running, pole vaulting, and high jumping. On his grandfather's country estate at Oyster

Bay on Long Island he became an enthusiastic horseman and a crack shot. All his life Teddy Roosevelt felt that he had to make up for the childhood weakness of his body.

Roosevelt never lost his boyish excitement. He continued his boxing. After he was hit in the eye while boxing with a young army officer, his left eye became completely blind. He managed to keep this secret, and he devised ways to prevent people knowing that he could see in only one eye. He even became world-famous as an explorer and big-game hunter in Africa and South America.

From the White House he preached "The Strenuous Life." Some genteel European diplomats dreaded being assigned to Washington when "TR" was in the White House. They could not do their diplomatic duty by sipping tea and making polite conversation. TR expected them—along with panting Cabinet members and generals—to join his exhausting tramps through the countryside. "You must always remember," a British ambassador once explained, "that the President is about six years old."

TR liked a good fight—not only in the boxing arena, but also in politics. He had been shocked that earlier Presidents had not enforced the laws against monopolies, and he was disgusted by the Supreme Court's technicalities. The growing power of corporations worried him. "Of all forms of tyranny," he complained, "the least attractive and the most vulgar is the tyranny of mere wealth, the tyranny of a plutocracy."

No sooner had TR moved into the White House than he had his chance. The owners of the anthracite coal mines had become reckless about the safety

Teddy Roosevelt as a boxer at Harvard.

of their men. Workers were dying needlessly each year. In 1901 alone, 441 men were killed in mining accidents in the anthracite coal fields of Illinois, Ohio, Pennsylvania, and West Virginia.

The men had received no raise in wages in twenty years. They were paid by the weight of the coal they dug, but the companies were not weighing honestly. Sometimes they made a man dig four thousand pounds before giving him credit for a ton. Miners were forced to spend their wages in "company stores" which charged high prices.

By 1902 the miners could endure no more. The union leaders decided to take action. John Mitchell, then the energetic young president of the United Mine Workers of America, was the son of a miner who had lost his life in the mines. Mitchell himself had begun mining at the age of twelve. His union—

Membership certificate of the United Mine Workers. Labor unions in their beginnings were often organized like social clubs or lodges, and followed elaborate rituals.

150,000 strong—included thousands of Newcomers who spoke over a dozen different languages.

The coal miners went on strike in May 1902. By October, with winter coming, people feared that the railroads would have to stop running and that the nation would freeze.

President Roosevelt came to the miners' rescue. Regardless of who owned the mines, Roosevelt insisted, nobody owned the miners. He shamed the mine owners into granting most of the workers' demands. When the strike ended TR had shown how, in the new age of big business, it was possible for the federal government to help. He had proven himself a champion of the ordinary American.

This was only a beginning. President Roosevelt enforced the law against trusts—even when it offended the richest men in the country. He added to the Cabinet a Secretary of Commerce and Labor, one of whose jobs was to keep an eye out for monopolies. He sponsored a law making it a crime for the railroads to show favoritism (for example, by giving secret refunds or "rebates") to anybody.

It was just as important, Roosevelt saw, to protect future Americans against the greed of living Americans as it was to protect mine workers against greedy mine owners. This was what he meant by "Conservation." As a young man out West he had enjoyed the open spaces. From his Dakota ranch he himself had ridden the range and explored the wilderness. He loved everything about the West—the cowboys, the life of the trail, fishing and hunting. And he was shocked to see lumber companies wast-

ing forests which had taken centuries to grow. He knew that the wilderness could never be put back.

He saw some parts of the country troubled by floods while others lacked water. Saving rivers and streams was just as important as protecting the land or the forests. To the White House he called scientists, Governors, Supreme Court Justices, and others, to plan an inventory of the natural wealth. Soon "Conservation" was a popular word.

During most of American history, the money to run the federal government had been raised by selling lands from the Public Domain in the West, by customs duties on imports, and by "excise" taxes on certain kinds of goods (for example, liquor and tobacco). These taxes were not democratic enough for Roosevelt. Shocked by the "swollen and monstrous fortunes," he wanted the rich to pay a bigger share.

But the Constitution said that the only "direct" taxes Congress could pass were those apportioned according to the *population* of the States. Income was a very different thing from population. During the Civil War the government somehow had got around these technicalities and had actually passed a tax on income. But after the war the income tax was dropped.

Later, when Populists and others demanded an income tax, the Supreme Court stood in the way. The Supreme Court said that an income tax was exactly the kind of tax that the Constitution had prohibited. President Roosevelt then demanded an amendment to the Constitution. Within a few years, the required number of States had passed this income-tax amendment.

Now Congress had the power to tax the rich Americans more heavily than the poor.

Now taxes themselves would protect most Americans by making it harder for any Americans to become monstrously rich. The income tax was a "progressive" tax. The higher you progressed up the ladder of wealth the larger the *proportion* of your income you had to pay. This was a sign that Americans were beginning to think in a new way.

After Theodore Roosevelt, fewer Americans believed it was good enough for the government to be only an umpire. Even in a prosperous democracy, the powers of different citizens and corporations were not equal. In the twentieth century more and more Americans expected their government to be a guardian. They expected it actually to help protect the weak from the strong.

CHAPTER 21

Who Killed Prosperity?

During the twenty years after President Theodore Roosevelt left the White House in 1909, the United States seemed a land of miracles. Never before in history were factories making so many new things. Never before had the daily life of a nation been so quickly transformed.

At the opening of the twentieth century the automobile was still such an oddity that in Vermont the law required the driver to send someone an eighth of a mile ahead with a red flag. But before Herbert Hoover took his oath as President in 1929 the American automobiles made each year came to five million.

Back in 1900 the closest thing to a movie was the crude "nickelodeon." In return for your nickel you looked into a box to see pictures move for a few minutes. But in 1929 one hundred million tickets were being sold to the movies every week, and the movies could actually talk!

Until World War I most Americans had not even heard of the radio. But by 1929 the annual turnout of radio sets numbered over four million. Television was still in the future—but it seemed amazing enough that voices could be sent without wires.

Americans were making the highest wages in history—and working shorter hours.

The American diet was more varied. Most homes had refrigerators, and even city people could have their fill of milk and of fresh fruit and vegetables at all seasons. With advancing medical knowledge, now at last the diseases which most threatened children—typhoid, diphtheria, and measles—were coming under control. Americans were healthier and were living longer than ever before.

Education in the United States was better and reached a larger proportion of the people than in any other country. By 1928 the money that Americans

Unemployed New Yorkers in 1932 (at the Hudson River and 75th Street), using old boxes and discarded mattresses for shelter. They entertained themselves with a wind-up phonograph.

spent each year for education was more than that spent by all the rest of the world put together. In most European countries only a grade-school education was free. But in the United States a free high-school education was normal, and millions could hope to go to college.

Progress seemed endless. Then suddenly, in late October 1929, came terrifying signs that the success story might have an unhappy ending.

The first hint was the Great Stock Market Crash. The New York Stock Market was where people bought and sold stocks—"shares" in the largest American corporations. The owner of a share in a company really owned part of the company. If the company grew and made a large profit, then the owner of the share would be paid a dividend as his part of the profit. Then, too, the value of that share went up. Naturally, everybody wanted to own shares in the most profitable companies.

But by 1929 many people who bought shares hoped to make their profits, not from the earnings of the company, but from the higher price that other Stock Market gamblers would pay them for their shares. More and more people began risking their money in the Stock Market. They expected to get rich when the price of their shares would suddenly go up. And with the money they made they would buy other shares, which they hoped would also go up.

Stock Market gambling became a national mania, a contagious disease. Americans who never would have thought of borrowing money to bet on the horse races now were actually borrowing to bet on stocks. The more the stock mania grew, the less connection there was between the real value of a company and the price people were paying for that company's shares on the Stock Market. People came to expect every stock to go *up*.

The "impossible" began to happen on October 24, 1929. All prices seemed to be falling. On that day thirteen million shares were sold. Then, it seemed, *everybody* wanted to sell his stocks—and as fast as possible, before they went further down.

In the months that followed the prices of stocks sank faster than ever. A share in United States Steel which had sold for $262 soon brought only $22, while a share of Montgomery Ward sank from $138 to $4, and a share of General Motors went from $73 to $8.

In the panic, people forgot an important fact. Even though the market price of a share of General Motors went down to nearly zero (simply because Stock Market gamblers no longer bet on it) the automobile factories and the men with know-how were all still there, just as good as ever. The wealth of the land and the energy of the people were still there.

But were they? People who never really understood why American progress had seemed so endless, now, of course, had no better understanding of why prosperity had vanished. In unreasoning fear, Americans who heard of this "impossible" drop in the price of stocks began to wonder. Perhaps this was only the first signal of the collapse of all America. If stocks could so quickly lose their value (they sank by forty billion dollars before the end of 1929), maybe nothing else was worth as much as people thought.

They lost faith in their banks. Of course, one way banks make money is to lend out at interest much of the money that people deposit with them. Usually only a few people at any one time want to draw out their money, and banks keep enough on hand to take care of them.

But during the Crash nearly everybody seemed to want to draw his money out at the same time. By the hundreds, then, banks, which could not suddenly produce all that cash, failed. Many people lost their life savings. Over six hundred and fifty banks failed in 1929, thirteen hundred failed in 1930, twenty-three hundred failed in 1931. Eventually the federal government itself would provide a new kind of insurance guaranteeing the depositors their money in an emergency. But there was nothing like that at the time of the Great Crash.

After the Great Stock Market Crash came the Great Depression. Manufacturers, finding fewer customers for anything they could make, began slowing down their factories, making fewer automobiles, fewer refrigerators, and fewer radios. They laid off their workers. And workers out of a job could not afford to buy things. Then still more factories closed down. Storekeepers went bankrupt. Soon, it seemed, collapse of the prices of stocks on the Stock Market had signaled the collapse of American business and American industry.

By the end of 1932 about thirteen million able-bodied Americans—about one in every four—were out of work. They could not afford to pay their own rent and had to squeeze in with friends or relatives. Young people with no money, no job, and no prospects did not dare marry. Within three years, the number of marriages was down by one-quarter. College enrollments sank.

Millions did not have enough to eat. Children cried for the food their parents could not give them. Hungry, sad Americans were actually wandering down alleys, routing through garbage pails for scraps to keep their families alive.

Unemployed war veterans, who had joined the "Bonus March," waiting outside the Capitol as the Senate in a special night session in July 1932 debated the bonus. The Senate voted it down.

Desperate unemployed went on hunger marches. In Henryetta, Oklahoma, three hundred men broke into food stores. In Iowa and Nebraska, farmers, who could no longer pay the money due on their mortgages, used pitchforks to drive off the sheriffs who came to seize their land. In the spring of 1932 thousands of unemployed veterans formed a "Bonus Army." Demanding that the government pay them a bonus for their service fourteen years earlier in World War I, they marched on Washington. President Herbert Hoover called out the army to drive them from government buildings and parklands that they had occupied.

Where would it end?

But before Americans could cure what ailed the country, they had to know what really was the disease. Who —or what—had killed prosperity? In the panic many Americans lost their heads. Everybody wanted to have somebody to blame it on. Crackpot leaders quickly appeared with fantastic explanations and imaginary cure-alls. Abolish banks! Print more money!

The unlucky man in the White House, the Republican Herbert Hoover, had been elected President in November 1928 by the second largest popular majority until then in all American history. But he had the misfortune to be inaug-

The young Herbert Hoover as a mining engineer.

urated in March 1929, just in time to get the blame for the Great Stock Market Crash.

Never was there a more honest or a more hard-working President. Hoover, a poor boy raised in a small Iowa town, went to Stanford University where he studied engineering. Then he made a fortune working as a mining engineer—in Australia, Africa, China, Latin America, and Russia. He became world-famous during World War I, when he headed the Relief Commission that fed starving Europeans. He was also in charge of conserving food in the United States so Americans could share it with their European allies. He had proven himself a great humanitarian and a remarkable organizer.

But Hoover was no politician. He did not like to try to persuade people. He did not enjoy the arts of compromise. As an engineer, he felt he saw problems clearly. After he had carefully prepared his solution he expected people to follow his instructions without arguing. Wearing a high stiff collar, he was a stiff man who inspired respect but not love. He had none of William Jennings Bryan's eloquence, nor any of Theodore Roosevelt's pep. In ordinary times he might have been a good President to keep America on the familiar road to success.

These were not ordinary times.

President Hoover was the handiest person to blame, even though the Depression had actually begun to happen almost before he had moved into the White House. The shacks made of cardboard and flattened tin cans, where some unemployed lived, were soon called "Hoovervilles." One folk song of the unemployed declared, "Hoover made a souphound out of me." A man's empty pocket, turned inside out, was called a "Hoover flag."

But when the collapse came so unexpectedly, President Hoover did not sit still. He used all the familiar ways to relieve suffering. He called upon cities, States, and all private charities to help feed the hungry. He brought business leaders and labor leaders to the White House, where they promised to try to keep up wages and keep the factories going. At the same time he started an ambitious new plan to use government money to hold up the price of tobacco, cotton, corn, and wheat in order to help the suffering farmers. He actually cut his own Presidential salary by one-fifth.

What Hoover did helped some, but it was not enough. The disaster was more unfamiliar than President Hoover realized. And it required remedies even more unfamiliar than he could imagine.

CHAPTER 22

Nothing to Fear but Fear Itself

When the election of 1932 came around and Herbert Hoover ran for President again, almost anybody could have beaten him. Who wanted to vote *for* the Depression? But the Democrats happened to pick one of the most winning men in American history. He was a distant cousin of Theodore Roosevelt, and his name was Franklin Delano Roosevelt.

Although only a few people in the country realized it at the time, Franklin Delano Roosevelt was a man of heroic character. From his youth he had enjoyed athletics. He had always loved politics and had been the Democratic candidate for Vice-President in 1920. One August day in 1921 he was stricken with polio and left paralyzed. This single, sudden thunderclap of bad luck reduced him from a bouncy, athletic, runabout politician to a bedridden invalid. A man of weaker character might have given up.

Instead, after his misfortune, he became more determined than ever to be an active politician. An old friend who came on a sympathy visit to the hospital was surprised when FDR unexpectedly gave him a strong, good-natured wallop. "You thought you were coming to see an invalid," FDR laughed from his bed. "But I can knock you out in any bout."

People who went to cheer him up found that FDR gave them a lift instead.

Franklin Delano Roosevelt and his wife Eleanor (right), eight years before his paralysis. Eleanor, who was a niece of the Republican President Theodore Roosevelt, later became world-famous for her humanitarian activities.

Sometimes he joked about his affliction. FDR wrote a friend that he had "renewed his youth" by "what was fortunately a rather mild case of *infantile paralysis.*"

But his case really was far from mild. He was never able to walk again. Only after long and painful exercises and by wearing heavy braces did he learn to use his hips so he could get around on crutches. He told his friends that he had an advantage, because while they were running around he could sit still and think. He used his long period of recovery in bed to write hundreds of letters to politicians all over the country—not about his personal problems, but about politics and how to build a stronger Democratic party. All over the country Democratic politicians valued his advice.

FDR made a fantastic comeback. When the Democratic Convention in Chicago in 1932 nominated Franklin Delano Roosevelt to be their candidate for President, it was really not because of his heroic personal qualities. For he had already proven himself a spectacularly successful politician in New York. In 1928, only a few years after he had been stricken with infantile paralysis, he managed to be elected Governor of his State. After a successful term as Governor he ran again in 1930, and he won by the biggest majority ever.

With his broad, contagious smile, he was a wonderful persuader. He loved people, and could make them love him. People cheered up when they saw his jaunty long cigarette holder and felt his warm firm handshake. He had all the human qualities that Herbert Hoover lacked. And these were what the nation wanted in that dangerous year of 1932.

FDR was no radical. In fact, during his campaign he was careful not to offend anybody. When he made speeches, he sounded more like William McKinley than like William Jennings Bryan. Some people, who thought the nation needed strong medicine, criticized FDR.

They said he was too eager to please everybody. They were afraid that he was simply "a pleasant man who would very much like to be President."

Those critics were wrong. For FDR had courage in politics just as much as in his private life. And as soon as he took office on March 4, 1933, he showed it.

"A New Deal for the American people!" This was what FDR had announced in Chicago when he accepted the nomination. He promised to *experiment*. The nation and all its wealth were still there, he reminded people in his inaugural address. "We are stricken by no plague of locusts. Compared with the perils which our forefathers conquered because they believed and were not afraid, we have still much to be thankful for. Nature still offers her bounty and human efforts have multiplied it. Plenty is at our doorstep." He had faith that there really were lots of new ways that could be tried.

"The only thing we have to fear," he said, "is fear itself." His courage and his optimism, like his smile, were contagious. Americans were encouraged most of all because they believed that their new President really would experiment. He would try one thing, and then another—until ways would be found to put the country back on the track, and to put people back to work.

FDR began trying things from his first day in the White House. In order to preserve people's life savings, he ordered all banks closed for four days while ways were found to restore confidence in them. He called Congress into special session to pass laws for the emergency.

Congress, on his urging, arranged special loans to help people pay their mortgages so they could keep their farms and homes till the crisis was over. A fund of over two billion dollars helped citizens start new construction—of homes, offices, shops, and factories—and thus create new jobs. Over three billion dollars was appropriated for new government buildings, and a half-billion dollars for outright relief. New laws guaranteed workers their right to organize into unions. New laws prohibited child labor, set minimum wages and maximum hours. A new program was passed for the farmer, to keep up the price of his crops.

Some experiments were not so successful. For example, one of FDR's pet projects was a law—the National Recovery Act or NRA—enforcing new "codes" to be made by representatives of business and labor in each industry. These codes aimed to keep up prices and wages. They said what should be manufactured, how many of everything, and at what price. They made many of the kinds of arrangements which big businesses had been punished for making when they fixed prices by monopoly. But the new law said that the antitrust rules did not apply. Small businessmen objected. They said the big businessmen were simply using the law to protect their own monopoly profits.

The Supreme Court declared the NRA codes unconstitutional. Congress, the Court said, was trying to give away the power to make laws. But the Constitution had assigned the lawmaking power only to Congress.

Still, on the whole, FDR seemed to be making headway. By the end of his first term in office, there were fewer people without jobs. The country was looking up. When FDR ran again in 1936, he was reelected by an even bigger majority.

All over the rest of the world, desperate people were handing over their liberty to dictators who promised them food and jobs in return. In Italy, only ten years before FDR was inaugurated, Benito Mussolini and his gang of fascists marched on Rome. They seized the government, abolished democracy, destroyed the liberties of the Italian people —all on the promise that they would provide more and better jobs.

In Germany, too, in the very month when FDR took his oath of office, Adolf

President Franklin D. Roosevelt (seen here by cartoonist Gluyas Williams) reached the American people through the new and democratic devices of the press conference and the radio fireside chat.

Copr. © 1942, The *New Yorker* Magazine, Inc.

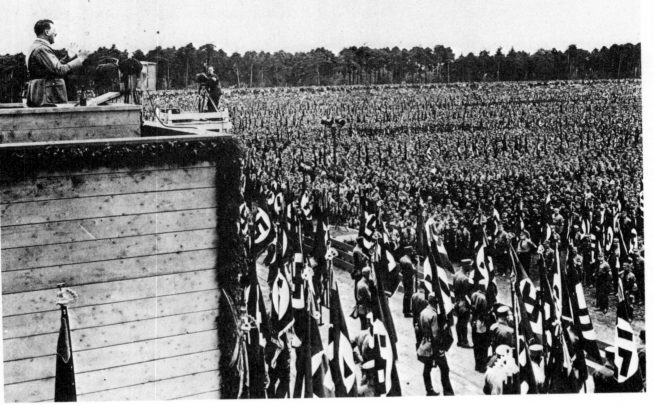

Adolf Hitler addressing the 160,000 Storm Troopers who, by spreading terror, helped "persuade" the German people to become Nazis.

Hitler, with his gang of Nazis, was made dictator. Screaming slogans of race hate and fear, the Nazis destroyed the universities. They used secret police and concentration camps. They murdered, robbed, and tortured. They abolished liberty and decency. And the civilized German people somehow tolerated it all because many of them needed jobs, their children were hungry, and they believed Hitler's promise of prosperity.

FDR had faith that it did not need to happen here. He tried all sorts of experiments—democratic experiments—to restore hope and prosperity, while strengthening American liberties. He consulted with business leaders, labor organizers, university professors, social workers, judges, scientists, lawyers, and doctors. Anybody who had an idea

knew that somebody in the New Deal would listen. Of course some people accused FDR of wanting to be a dictator. But he never lost his faith in democracy and in the ability of Americans to handle the unexpected.

"Happy Days Are Here Again!" had been FDR's campaign song. Many Americans wanted to believe that FDR was a kind of magician who could suddenly bring back prosperity. Of course, FDR did not believe government had a magic formula.

He did believe, though, that there were many helpful things the government could always do, and had to do. And he believed that the government did not need to wait till the next emergency. It ought to promise people help in advance. Then, if Americans felt sure they would get the emergency help they needed, they would be more cheerful and less worried about their future. This itself might help bring back prosperity and keep prosperity alive.

FDR therefore proposed a scheme of insurance. While a person had a job, he paid a small amount every month out of his wages, and his employer paid the same amount. This went into the federal treasury. Then when the worker was out of a job or when he became too old to work, he received back a payment every month. He could be sure that he would never starve.

The people who received their insurance payments did not feel they were charity cases. Since they had been putting in their own money when they were prosperous, they felt they were only getting what they were entitled to when times were bad. This system was called Social Security. It aimed to make everybody in the whole society feel more secure.

Following the lead of the Republican Roosevelt, FDR set up a grand new plan for conservation, to prevent the soil from being used up or washed away, and so to help farmers make a better living. And he found other ways to preserve resources for the future.

FDR enlarged Teddy Roosevelt's idea to include "People Conservation." The government spent millions of dollars encouraging artists by employing them to decorate post offices and other government buildings. Government programs also provided useful work for young people who could not afford to go to college.

One of the most ingenious plans was to "conserve" the people of a whole re-

gion. In the mountains of western Kentucky, Tennessee, and Alabama, around the valley of the Tennessee River, there lived about 3,500,000 people. Most of them lived poorly. Their land was exhausted. Electricity was too expensive, yet without electricity they could not modernize their farms or bring in the factories to provide jobs.

FDR's idea was to build a great dam on the Tennessee River. This would protect against floods. At the same time the water flowing through the dam would turn generators to make cheap electricity. And two old munitions plants left over from World War I could be made into factories for fertilizer to improve the farms. These were FDR's plans for the Tennessee Valley Authority (TVA).

The lives of thousands of people in the Tennessee Valley were brightened. Public Health doctors used this chance to rid the countryside of malaria. Librarians sent "bookmobiles" into the farms. Better houses and better schools were built. Again, some people objected that FDR was trying to be a dictator. They accused the government of competing unfairly with private electric and fertilizer companies.

Yet the experiment was a success. Of course, it did not solve all the problems of the poor farmers in the Tennessee Valley. But it showed how much *could* be done if a democratic government was willing to help.

Hope came back to America. FDR had found ways to cure the symptoms of the Great Depression. But had he cured the disease? Many Americans were not sure. Prosperity did not fully return until World War II put the fac-

These energetic young men were among the three million members of the Civilian Conserva-
tion Corps, one of many New Deal programs to put people to work. The CCC planted more
than seventeen million acres of forests, stocked over a billion fish in hatcheries, built trails in
the National Parks, fought forest fires, and worked on countless other useful outdoor projects.

tories back to working full steam. Some people said the real end of the Depression did not come till then. But Americans had learned a lot about how to deal with the dangers of unemployment and how to keep the factories working in peacetime.

Americans too had lost many of their old fears of economic Ups and Downs. That itself was a gain. The Great Depression proved that, the more people were frightened, the worse things became.

Americans had discovered a new strength. Through the crisis the federal Constitution proved adaptable, and came out stronger than ever. Americans had proved that they could survive their worst peacetime disaster—without spreading hate, without taking away liberties, without installing a dictator.

This was a great and reassuring discovery. It was as important as anything Americans had ever learned about their land or about themselves.

CHAPTER 23

Who Was Left Out?

When prosperity returned, Americans boasted that this was a land where *every*body had a fair chance. But that still was not quite correct. When you surveyed the whole country and all the people in it you had to wonder. Many Americans were not getting their full fair chance. Some were almost entirely left out.

The United States was, of course, a nation of minorities. Had there ever before been a nation built of so many different groups?

There were many kinds of minorities. Of the religious minorities, for example, in some parts of the country Catholics were commonly discriminated against. It was taken for granted that no Catholic could ever be elected President—until the 1960 election of John F. Kennedy. Although the Jews had a long tradition of learning, even before they arrived in this country, strict quotas in colleges and medical schools kept out all but a few, even if they were the best qualified. The Mormons, who were a distinctive American religion, actually had laws passed against them.

We have seen how the Oldcomers—in New England, for example—had looked down their noses at Newcomers. And it was especially easy to be snobbish when the Newcomers looked different. Mexican immigrants, who came across the border for seasonal farm work, were not allowed to buy land, or to get an education, or to find a better job. The Chinese and Japanese, who had been imported to help build the Western railroads, afterwards in some places were not permitted to live equally among other Americans, or to own land, or to become voting citizens.

The American Indians, of course, were the oldest of the Oldcomers. But they were deprived of their best land and forced onto barren "reservations" of desert wastes and rocky mountain slopes. They were not allowed to become full-fledged Americans. And there were many others.

The largest single group of left-out Americans were the Negroes. This was especially disappointing because the whole nation had fought its most terrible war and had even split families apart so that all Americans would be treated like men. While the Civil War was, of course, a war for Union, it was also emphatically a war to help the Negro. For that cause a quarter-million Union soldiers had given their lives.

Never before in history had so many people fought for the freedom of others. In relation to the Negro, the United States had shown its best and its worst. Some Americans had kept him a slave. But other Americans fought and died to make him free.

After the Civil War, as we have seen,

Some American Indians have carried on their traditional crafts. But these Americans, the oldest of the Oldcomers, were sometimes treated as if they were not Americans at all. An Act of Congress in 1924 finally admitted all Indians born in the United States to full citizenship.

the United States had as hard a job as faced any nation. The millions of Americans who had been treated as *things* were suddenly to be given their rights as *people*. They had owned no property and had not even been allowed to go to school. Now they were suddenly to become citizens with the duty to govern themselves and to help govern others. All this had to be done in the shadow of the hateful "peculiar institution," slavery, which had bred fears and hates on all sides. And all this had to be done in the aftermath of a bloody war which had bred still more fears and hates.

The mark of slavery could not be erased by magic. The South—and

Southerners—might take generations to recover. The full tragedy of slavery was only now appearing.

Yet by the early twentieth century there had been progress. When the Freedmen's Bureau ended in 1872, money to educate former slaves and their children then came from churches and missionary associations.

Wealthy men and women, mostly from the North, gave millions of dollars to help educate the Negro. By 1900 there were already about thirty thousand Negro teachers. John D. Rockefeller, for example, had contributed over $50 million of the money he had made from oil, most of it to train more teachers for

Negro schools. Every year more Negroes owned their own farms. And in the long run, better education, better wages, and more property would help the Negro to equality.

But a small number of Americans still actually *wanted* a Two-Nation America. These people were afraid that if Negroes had their share of education and owned their share of property, they really would become equal. And they were especially afraid to let the Negroes vote. Most of these fearful Americans were in the South. Less money was spent there than in other parts of the country for all kinds of education. In the South Negroes had to attend separate, and inferior, schools. There, especially, Negroes found it hard to borrow money in order to buy houses or farms.

The whole South suffered. By 1938 President Franklin Delano Roosevelt called the South "the nation's No. 1 economic problem." Almost any way you measured—by the health of the people, the quality of schools or houses, the number of automobiles, the amount of farm machinery, or the income of the families—the South was the worst-off section of the whole United States. And in the South, the Negroes were generally even worse off than others.

In 1930, 80 percent of American Negroes were still living within the boundaries of the old Confederacy. Yet new forces were working on all America. One of the most important of these was the Negro himself. Emancipation gave him a new power to be heard.

Even before the Civil War, a few eloquent Negroes like Frederick Douglass had managed to speak up loud and clear against slavery. Douglass, the slave son of an unknown white father, had been working on the Baltimore wharves. One day in 1838, at the age of twenty-one, he stowed away on a ship sailing for New York. After that he became one of the best propagandists against slavery. His books described the sufferings of slaves, and urged everybody to help them escape. Beginning in 1847, Douglass' newspaper, *The North Star,* worked for many reforms, including women's right to vote.

As more Negroes were educated and acquired property, more were able to help themselves. But how could they do it best? Negro leaders could not agree.

One way was proposed by Booker T. Washington. Born a slave, Washington was a self-made man. He worked as a janitor and at all sorts of jobs to support

---

Frederick Douglass helped recruit Negroes for the Union army. After the Civil War he became U.S. Minister to Haiti.

himself in school. Before his death he was famous throughout the world. For his own story of his life, *Up From Slavery* (1901), was read by millions.

"No man," he said, ". . . black or white, from North or South, shall drag me down so low as to make me hate him."

He preached a gospel of love and common sense. He told the Negro to make the most of himself and of his opportunities. He told white Southerners to show new respect for the Negro, to realize that only by bettering the Negro's life could they make a better South for everybody. Self-respect, self-education, and self-help, he said, would bring Negroes the opportunities they deserved. Some people thought he sounded old-fashioned. This might have been Benjamin Franklin speaking!

But Booker T. Washington did not merely talk. In 1881 he founded Tuskegee Institute in Alabama, which became one of the most powerful forces in American education. There he trained thousands of Negroes to be better farmers and mechanics, to make a good living, and to help build their communities.

He believed in a step-by-step way "up from slavery." First, he said, Negroes should get education and get property. But he believed in a special kind of education. Most important for Negroes right away was not a "liberal" education of the kind American college students were getting all over the country. He did not want Negroes to spend their efforts learning history and literature and foreign languages and science and mathematics. Instead, he said, they should train quickly for jobs—and mostly for jobs they could do with their hands. The vote, he said, could wait.

The Negro first should become a free man with a job before he became a free man with a vote.

Many who admired Booker T. Washington still did not agree with his program for the Negro. One-step-at-a-time was not good enough. Americans were quick with their know-how, quick in covering the continent and building cities. Why should they be slow to give *all* Americans *all* their rights?

Twenty-five years after Booker T. Washington started his Tuskegee Institute in Alabama, a group met at Niagara Falls. They demanded for Negroes all the rights of Americans. *Now!*

Their Negro leader was W. E. B. Du Bois. His life had been very different from that of Booker T. Washington. Born in Massachusetts after the Civil War, he studied at the University of Berlin in Germany and then received a Ph.D. degree from Harvard in 1895. While Booker T. Washington's roots were in the South, Du Bois's roots were in abolitionist Massachusetts, and in the whole world. Du Bois was a poet, and a man of brilliant mind and vast learning. Why should anyone try to tell Du Bois and others like him to be satisfied to work with their hands?

In 1905 the Declaration by Du Bois's Niagara Movement expressed outrage. It demanded for Negroes *all* their human rights, all their rights as Americans, and *at once*. It opposed all laws and all customs that treated Negroes as if they were different from other people. And, of course, it demanded the right to vote.

After the Civil War, white Southerners who believed in a Two-Nation South (run by the whites) had used all sorts of tricks to deprive Negroes of their rights

Booker T. Washington's Tuskegee Institute aimed to train its students for skilled and useful jobs. ABOVE: *Young men learn upholstering.* BELOW: *Young women learn nursing.*

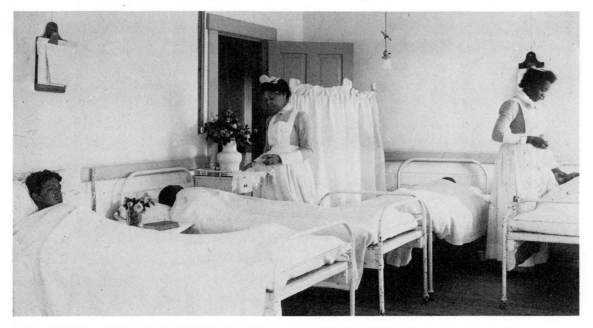

as citizens. The Fifteenth Amendment, adopted during Reconstruction, plainly declared that the right of citizens to vote should not be denied "by the United States or by any State on account of race, color, or previous condition of servitude." This set a real puzzle for the Two-Nation Southerners.

They tried using the "grandfather clause." They simply passed a law in the State Legislature giving the right to vote to those persons who *did* have the right to vote on January 1, 1867 (before the Fifteenth Amendment had been passed) and to those persons' descendants. Anybody else who wanted to vote had to pass all sorts of impossible tests. Of course that included Negroes. *They* would not be allowed to vote simply because their *grandfathers* did not have the right to vote! Beginning in 1895, seven Southern States passed "grandfather" laws. Not until 1915 did the United States Supreme Court declare

Booker T. Washington (left) believed that permanent progress must come slowly. W. E. B. Du Bois, himself a scholar, feared that Booker T. Washington's "gradualist" program would keep Negroes in lowly jobs.

that these laws violated the Constitution.

Another trick was the so-called Literacy Test. It was as dishonest as the Literacy Test which Oldcomers had tried to use to keep out immigrants from certain countries. It pretended to limit the vote to people who could read. But prejudiced election judges gave ridiculously complicated tests (which they themselves probably could not have passed) whenever Negroes came to vote. They would ask a Negro to explain the most difficult part of the Constitution. But a white person only had to read out a simple sentence.

Some Southern States also used the Poll Tax. That was a tax that everybody was required to pay before he could vote (or go to the "poll"). Most Negroes in the South were so poor they really could not afford the few dollars for the tax. And even if a Negro paid his tax, the election judge could always find some technical mistake in his tax receipt, and

so keep him from voting.

The craftiness of Two-Nation Southerners seemed endless. They even went so far as to pretend that the great political parties in the South were not political parties at all, but only private clubs. Therefore, they said, nobody except the white "members" had a right to vote in the primary election when their "club" picked its candidates.

Since the Democratic Party was in complete control in most of the South, whoever won in the Democratic primary automatically won the office. By keeping a person from voting in the primary, then, you would actually be taking away his vote. Finally, in three separate decisions—in 1944, 1947, and 1953—the United States Supreme Court declared that these laws violated the Fourteenth Amendment to the Constitution. But it took a special Twenty-fourth Amendment to the Constitution, adopted in 1964, to outlaw the Poll Tax.

CHAPTER 24

"A Triumph for Freedom"

Intelligent citizens all over the country were beginning to be ashamed and disgusted that the nation had been so slow to give all Americans their simple rights. The Niagara Movement, sparked by Du Bois and aided by white Americans who gloried in the anti-slavery tradition, became stronger. To help prevent shameful race riots like the one in Springfield, Illinois (Lincoln's birthplace) in 1908, a new organization, the National Association for the Advancement of Colored People (NAACP), was founded in 1909 on Lincoln's birthday.

Americans of all races and religions, from all parts of the country, joined hands. People like Jane Addams, who already were working for the poor of all races in the northern city slums, gave money to pay for lawyers to help Negroes secure their rights in the South. The president of the NAACP, a famous Boston lawyer, argued the case before the Supreme Court in 1915 when the "grandfather" laws were declared unconstitutional. The NAACP also won other important cases. One of these declared that no trial of a Negro could be a fair trial (as the Constitution required) if Negroes were kept off the jury. During the next years the NAACP was the most important group trying to awaken all Americans to the rights of Negroes.

Things were getting better for the Negro. But the progress was painfully slow—even considering the long distance the Negro needed to rise from slavery.

For millions of Negro Americans—especially in the South and in the big city slums in the North—there still seemed almost no change. Negro workers were the last hired and the first fired. Negro children still had less money spent on their education. Negroes were not allowed to live wherever they could afford, but had to live in special neighborhoods. Even under the New Deal, Negroes were not always given their share. For example, they were not allowed to live in the model towns built with government money in the Tennessee Valley. Most of the Negroes whom Du Bois called the "Talented Tenth" still had to take lowly jobs.

Some, in fact, gave up. Du Bois, for example, joined the Communist Party and then renounced his United States citizenship. In 1961 at the age of 93 he moved to the new African country of Ghana, which before 1957 had been a British colony. Others kept their faith in America and struggled for new ways to keep the nation true.

During two World Wars, Negro Americans fought for their country. In World War I, Negro soldiers numbered over a third of a million. In World War II they numbered a million. In both wars they proved their bravery and their loyalty. The wars gave them other chances, too—to move outside the South, away from their farms and villages, into the larger world.

They discovered that the prejudices which some white Southerners had inherited from the days of slavery were not found everywhere. They mixed with other Americans from all over the country, and they went abroad. They had new experiences and new adventures.

Yet, even in the army and navy and air force, Negro Americans still were not given equal rights. In World War I, Negroes found it difficult to become officers. They were not allowed at all in the Marines, and in the navy they had no hope for promotion. Even in uniform, they were often insulted. It took great faith and patriotism, then, for a Negro American to risk his life for a country that was not yet giving him his full rights as a citizen.

President Woodrow Wilson was leading the country in a war "to make the world safe for democracy." Yet President Wilson himself, born in Virginia before the Civil War, had never outgrown the feelings of the Two-Nation South. Though elected on the slogan of the "New Freedom," after he came to Washington he actually segregated Negroes working in the government. And he took government jobs away from Negroes in the South.

In World War II things were better for the Negro soldier. The Marines no longer kept him out, and before the war was over there were 17,000 Negro "Leathernecks." It became easier for qualified Negroes to become officers. Even the navy, which before had taken in Negroes only for kitchen work and as waiters, began to open up. The air force trained Negro officers and pilots, and more than eighty won the Distinguished Flying Cross.

But the long shadow of the Two-Nation South remained. Negroes, once more fighting for democracy, were usually still segregated.

Finally, though, the stain of slavery was washed away in the armed services. President Harry S Truman in 1946 appointed a national committee to recommend action. By 1949 the army, navy, and air force had all abolished racial quotas. They made it their policy to give all Americans an equal chance. By the time of the Korean War in 1950–1953 *all* Americans were fighting for democracy side by side.

During these later wars, even more than during the Civil War, Americans moved all around the country. Many went to new war jobs. Returning soldiers settled in new places. Before World War I only about 10 percent of Negro Americans lived outside the South. After that war the number rose to 20 percent. And after World War II about one-third of all Negro Americans were living outside the Old Confederacy.

Negro Americans, like other Americans, were becoming more and more citified. Outside the South nearly all of them were living in cities. Even in the South they too were moving off the countryside. Many Americans—including, of course, more Negroes—were churning quickly and easily around the whole country. It was harder than ever for the South to keep its old ways.

In Africa, new republics were declaring their independence from the old colonial powers. First came Ghana in 1957, and by 1965 there were over thirty new African members of the United Nations. When they sent their ambassadors to the United States, the discrimination against Negroes here was more embarrassing than ever.

Then, too, the United States Supreme Court began to wake up. In a series of decisions it began to outlaw those Southern practices and laws which had taken from the Negro his full rights as an American. Back in 1896 the Court actually had declared that laws which required Negroes to stay separate—to use separate washrooms, separate schools, and separate railroad cars—did *not* violate the Fourteenth Amendment. It was all right, the Court said, for any services to be separate so long as they were "equal." But this was a trick argument. Anyone who knew the South could

have known that the white Southerners who ran the government would *say* they were providing "equal" schools. But who had the power to complain if the schools were not really equal? Negroes, who still were not allowed to vote, had no way of forcing government officials to listen. The Supreme Court had okayed the Two-Nation South.

In the South, Negroes continued to have the worst of everything. Their schools and hospitals, and even their washrooms and water fountains, were inferior.

Anyway, the whole idea of "separate but equal"—even if it could have been enforced—was wrong. It was not only wrong, it was nonsense. Because, in a democracy, people who are forced to be separate, forced to use washrooms and water fountains and schools not used by other Americans, are not being allowed

Segregated water fountain.

"Freedom Riders" in a Montgomery, Alabama, bus station (May 1961) integrating a lunch counter with a nonviolent "sit-in."

to be equal. The special separate schools for Negroes could not possibly be equal —simply because they were separate.

Finally in 1954, in one of the most important decisions it had ever made, the Supreme Court ordered that, under the Constitution, public schools could not be separate. Americans had a right to go to school with all other Americans of their age and grade. This was a part of their education. No American should be deprived of that right. The opposite of separation was "integration"—bringing together into one. And the Supreme Court ordered that all public schools in the United States had to be "integrated."

These changes in American life, in American thought and feeling all over the country, made the time ripe for the work of Martin Luther King, Jr. His work began in a small way and in one place. Within only a few years his message had carried to the world.

Born in Atlanta in 1929, son of a minister, he attended Morehouse College and received a doctor's degree from Boston University. He was a natural leader, American to the core. He combined the common sense of a Booker T. Washington with the impatient visions of a Du Bois.

On December 1, 1955, a tired Negro seamstress returning from work boarded a crowded bus in Montgomery, Alabama. She took a seat. But the seat she took was in the part of the bus reserved for white passengers. When she was asked to give up her seat to a white person, she refused. The police arrested her for violating the law.

Martin Luther King, who was then a Baptist minister in Montgomery, decided it was time for action. It was time to stop any Americans from being degraded.

Although King was indignant and saddened, he was not angry. He was a thoughtful man, and a Christian, and he decided to try a new way. He called it the only true Christian way. It was the way of nonviolence.

He did not tell people to burn the buses or to fight the police. No, he said. All people need to be educated in the ways of peace and decency. If you fight your enemies with violence, you are using their weapons and brutalizing yourself. But if you are peaceful and simply do not go along with them, you will eventually prevail. And if you win this way, your victory will not merely be the truce in a running battle. It will actually be peace. Your enemies then

will understand, and they will begin to be decent, too.

So he preached to the Negroes in Montgomery. He told them to stop using the buses until the buses gave them their place as Americans. Of course many Negroes were angry. But Martin Luther King begged and pleaded with them to keep their heads, and to keep love in their hearts, even while they joined the bus boycott.

For 381 days the Negroes of Montgomery refused to ride the buses. It was inconvenient. Some formed car pools. Many were given rides by friendly white neighbors. Many walked miles to work. Others simply did not get to their jobs and had to lose their wages.

And the bus company was about to go bankrupt.

In the end the Negroes and all the decent people of Montgomery won. When the buses ran again, every passenger was treated like all the others. Martin Luther King called this a "Stride Toward Freedom." And he was right.

It was not only a stride toward freedom. It was a step along a new path. Many Americans were encouraged to walk along that path in the years that followed. By 1960 many Negroes in the South were using this new way to fight segregation. They sat down at lunch counters where they had not been allowed to sit. They swam in public swimming pools that had been denied to Negroes. And they worshiped in churches that had kept out Negroes. They did not fight the police or strike out at anyone. Quietly and peacefully, they simply acted like decent Americans who knew their rights.

The movement spread. In 1963—a

full century after the Emancipation Proclamation—there came a climax. In February, the season of Lincoln's birthday, President John F. Kennedy sent a Civil Rights Bill to Congress. The bill would guarantee the vote to all Americans, outlaw segregation in all public places, and protect the right of all Americans to use motels and hotels and barber shops and restaurants. But Congress did not act. The Two-Nation Southerners and a few of their Northern supporters blocked the law. They acted as if the Civil War had never been fought—or as if it had been won by the South.

Americans of all races became impatient. Members of all religious groups—Catholics, Protestants, and Jews—leaders of labor unions and many others decided to show Congress how strongly Americans felt. They planned a "March on Washington." The purpose of their march was peaceful, entirely in line with Martin Luther King's ideas. They did not want to fight the police or take over the government. They simply wanted to use their democratic right to show their representatives in Congress how many Americans were demanding equality for everybody.

On August 28, 1963, nearly a quarter-million Americans gathered at the Lincoln Memorial in Washington, D.C., within sight of the White House and the Capitol where Congress met. The meeting was orderly and eloquent. It was the largest number of Americans until

The March on Washington, August 1963. Americans of all faiths and races and several labor unions joined hands in demanding equal rights for all. In the center of the front row was Dr. Martin Luther King.

President Lyndon B. Johnson speaking with Dr. Martin Luther King during the televised ceremony at the signing of the Civil Rights Act of 1964.

that time ever gathered in one place for any purpose in peacetime.

Some were afraid there might be trouble. But trouble did not come. Americans could ever after be proud that so many of their countrymen cared enough for the rights of all Americans to

make that meeting possible, and to keep it peaceful.

Congress still delayed. They did not want to act when it might seem they were acting under threat. Then, on November 22, 1963, the nation was shaken by tragedy. While riding in an open car in Dallas, Texas, President Kennedy was shot. He was dead within a few minutes. But the spirit of all who believed in America, and in the promise of equality, lived on.

The new President was Lyndon B. Johnson. His first act was to address Congress demanding immediate passage of the Civil Rights Bill. He also offered a new Voting Rights Act, with effective new ways of protecting the right of everybody to vote—even in the South.

These acts meant business. The day of legal trickery had passed. "Today is a triumph for freedom," President Johnson declared when these acts became law, "as huge as any victory that's ever been won on any battlefield. . . . Today the Negro story and the American story fuse and blend." He could have called it a bigger victory than the victories in war. This peaceful victory had taken a century to win.

Still, the forces of hate and fear—of a Two-Nation America—were not yet dead. Martin Luther King himself was shot while he stood on the balcony of a Memphis motel on April 4, 1968. No American who knew history could be surprised that the spirit of hate still walked the land—and it found new preachers of hate in all races.

Just as after the Civil War many white Southerners would not accept their defeat, so after the Civil Rights revolution of the 1960's some Americans would not accept their victory. Their festering hate had gathered strength. A new "black" racism, a new version of the Ku Klux Klan, began to threaten the land. It was organized by Negroes and supported by others who had lost their faith in America. They still would not believe in the victory which had come to them and to all Americans. Like the white Southerners after the Civil War, now some Negro Americans boasted that their race was better. But both white and black racism were a disease which the nation would have to cure.

The twentieth-century battle for rights left new wounds, stirred new fears and hates. The future of the nation would depend on the ability of all Americans to remember the long struggle which *all* Americans shared. And also on their ability to forget—to forget harsh words and old insults. The nation needed a renewal of the generous, forgiving spirit of Lincoln.

PART FIVE

TO THIS WHOLE WORLD —AND BEYOND

TO THIS WHOLE WORLD—AND BEYOND

Until the Civil War the United States had seemed a world of its own. It had been easy for Americans to imagine that they really did not need the rest of the world. The continent was so large. It offered so many different climates. Almost every needed crop or animal, almost every mineral, was found somewhere within the nation and its territories. When the first settlers had called this a New World they were speaking the sober truth.

Then after the Civil War, more and more Americans discovered that America needed the world. The nation still wanted to import people by the millions. And it needed the outside world for many new reasons.

The prosperity of American farmers and factory workers and businessmen now depended on faraway customers and on the ability of Americans to deliver their goods overseas. American consumers were coming to rely on silk from Italy and China, on rubber from the Congo and Sumatra, on coffee from Brazil, on tin from Malaya, on gold from Rhodesia—and on a thousand other items from across the oceans.

The United States became the world's know-how center—for trying new ways of making and doing.

And people everywhere expected to learn from America. Americans began to feel it their duty to help make the whole earth into a New World.

But could the United States preach democracy and help other nations become democratic without trying to choose other peoples' governments for them?

Could Americans take their place in the world competition for customers and for raw materials without making remote peoples into a new kind of colonies?

Could the most powerful nation on earth resist the temptation to run the affairs of mankind?

Could the nation do its duty in the battles of the Old World and yet stay free of the Old World curse of endless wars?

Could the nation become the most modern, most intricately organized people on earth, and yet preserve self-government and the spirit of adventure?

CHAPTER 25
Ocean Paths to World Power

After the Civil War, Americans realized that the United States had become a two-ocean nation. The Atlantic seaboard looked eastward toward Europe and Africa. The Far Western States looked across the Pacific toward Australia and Asia.

Some Americans were beginning to think differently about their place in the world. An Annapolis graduate, Admiral Alfred T. Mahan, wrote a powerful book called *The Influence of Sea Power Upon History* (1890). What *Uncle Tom's Cabin* was to the Civil War, Mahan's *Sea Power* would be to the Spanish-American War.

Sea Power, Mahan said, was the key to all history. A nation became great and kept its greatness only if it ruled the waves. Americans, he said, had long shown "the instinct for commerce, bold enterprise in the pursuit of gain, and a keen sense for the trails that lead to it." Yet these were not enough. The nation also needed to be rich in all kinds of ships. Then, of course, she would need colonies in faraway places where her ships could refuel and find protection.

A few years after Mahan began preaching Sea Power he found one of his strongest allies in Theodore Roosevelt, whom President McKinley appointed Assistant Secretary of the Navy in 1897. Even before he had finished at Harvard,

Teddy had begun writing *The Naval War of 1812*, which was published in 1882, only two years after he graduated. He remained fascinated by ships. And he was especially intrigued by the puzzle of power. What really made a nation strong? He was delighted by Mahan's writings.

At that time trouble was brewing only a few miles off the coast of Florida. The island of Cuba had been a colony of Spain ever since it was first sighted by Columbus. In the nineteenth century Spain was tyrannizing over the inhabitants. And the Cuban rebels declared their independence in February 1895.

The Spanish government sent out troops and put the island under a ruthless general, Valeriano "Butcher" Weyler. On February 10, 1896, General Weyler ordered that "all the inhabitants of the country" who were still outside the towns should "concentrate themselves in the towns." Anybody found outside a town would be shot. This made Cuban towns into "concentration camps." The whole island became a prison. Men, women, and children were herded together. Some were tortured, others died of disease and starvation— including some United States citizens.

American newspapers splashed the stories of "Butcher" Weyler's atrocities on the front pages of papers which went out in six editions a day to the cities and at least once a day (by RFD) even to remote farms. Joseph Pulitzer, an energetic Hungarian immigrant who had bought the New York *World,* was anxious to make his paper popular. The more copies he sold, the more he could charge for advertising—and advertising supported the paper.

Pulitzer was brilliant at finding new ways to attract readers. For example, he hired a clever cartoonist, Richard F. Outcault, to make the first color comic strip. It showed the adventures of a bad boy called the "Yellow Kid" who ap-

in whether they were true. Because they featured the Yellow Kid these newspapers—and others like them—were soon called the "Yellow Press."

The United States had a long-standing interest in Cuba. Back in the early nineteenth century Thomas Jefferson himself had said he hoped to see Cuba become part of the United States. Now American businessmen had invested over fifty million dollars in Cuban sugar. In 1895 the rebels destroyed sugar plantations and mills, hoping to prod the United States to intervene. Then, in 1896, William McKinley was

Sensational headlines in Hearst newspaper.

peared regularly in the Sunday edition. Outcault's cartoons were so successful that Pulitzer's leading competitor, the Go-Getting William Randolph Hearst, hired the same cartoonist to do another Yellow Kid series for the Sunday edition of *his* paper, the New York *Journal.*

While on Sundays both papers used the Yellow Kid to attract readers, every day they competed by printing shocking stories. They were more interested in whether the stories were shocking than

elected President with a promise to help Cuba become independent.

When Spain began to negotiate with the United States about freedom for the Cubans, it seemed there would be no need to fight. But on February 9, 1898, the New York *Journal* printed a stolen letter in which the Spanish ambassador called President McKinley a coward and other nasty names.

To protect American lives and property, the United States battleship *Maine* had been sent to Havana harbor. At 9:40 P.M. on the night of February 15, 1898, the *Maine* was shattered by an explosion, and 260 officers and men were killed. The navy's court of inquiry reported that the cause was an underwater mine, but they could not say for sure whether the Spanish were to blame. Anyway the Yellow Press called for war against Spain, and headlined the slogan, "REMEMBER THE MAINE!"

When the excitable Assistant Secretary of the Navy, Theodore Roosevelt, heard that McKinley was hesitating, he said the President "had no more backbone than a chocolate éclair." On February 25 the Secretary of the Navy made the mistake of taking the afternoon off. That left impatient Teddy as Acting Secretary—in charge of the whole United States navy. Without consulting anyone, he instantly cabled his friend Admiral George Dewey, who commanded the United States fleet in Asiatic waters. Make sure, he ordered, that Spanish ships do not leave the coast of Asia. Begin "defensive operations" against the Spanish colony out there—the Philippines!

When the Secretary of the Navy returned to his office next day, he was astonished. "Roosevelt," he wrote in his diary, "has come very near causing more of an explosion than happened to the *Maine*." But it was too late to change the order. And even *before* war had begun in nearby Cuba, Teddy had arrayed the United States fleet for war on the other side of the world.

If President McKinley had been a stronger man he would not have been afraid to keep the peace. The government of Spain now actually told him

Joseph Pulitzer, a painting by John Singer Sargent, who was famous for his portraits of notable Americans.

they would give Cuba her independence. But the Yellow Press was still demanding Spanish blood. The "jingoes" —the people who loved to see a fight— wanted war. On April 11, the day *after* President McKinley learned that Spain would agree to do everything Americans said they wanted, he asked Congress to declare war.

The war lasted only a few months— but that was long enough to create the greatest confusion. At the training camp in Tampa, Florida, commanding officers could not find uniforms, while for weeks fifteen railroad cars full of uniforms remained on a siding twenty-five miles away. The commander of United States troops in Cuba, Major General W. R. Shafter, weighed three hundred pounds and was therefore "too unwieldy to get to the front." Unprepared for combat,

"Charge of the Rough Riders at San Juan Hill," a painting by Frederic Remington, who went to Cuba as an artist-correspondent. The "Rough Riders" had to run up the hill on foot. Teddy Roosevelt, leading them on horseback, made himself the most conspicuous target.

the army committed every foolishness known to man.

The navy was in better shape. On May 1, when Admiral Dewey, following Roosevelt's impulsive orders, attacked the Spanish warships in the Philippines, he finished off the Spaniards in seven hours. The remnant of the Spanish fleet, which was in North American waters, then sneaked into Santiago harbor on the southeastern tip of Cuba.

Meanwhile Teddy Roosevelt had himself appointed lieutenant colonel of a new regiment of cavalry. At a training camp in San Antonio, Texas, he gathered cowboys, sheriffs, and desperadoes from the West, and a sprinkling of playboy polo players and steeplechase riders from the East. They came to be known as Roosevelt's Rough Riders.

Roosevelt himself was preparing for serious combat. What worried him most was his bad eyesight. If he broke or lost his glasses he could not see where he was going, much less find the Spaniards

to shoot. He ordered a dozen extra pairs of steel-rimmed eyeglasses. He then stowed them separately all over his uniform and even put several extra pairs inside the lining of his campaign hat.

On June 22, Roosevelt's Rough Riders arrived in Cuba. They were given the job of storming San Juan Hill, which overlooked Santiago bay. To capture the steep hill his "Rough Riding" cavalry (who had been selected for their horsemanship) actually had to dismount. "I waved my hat and went up the hill with a rush," Roosevelt recalled. After a bloody fight, they reached the top.

Theodore Roosevelt never suffered from modesty. When Roosevelt published his book *The Rough Riders,* the humorist "Mr. Dooley" said Teddy should have called it "Alone in Cuba."

The decisive naval battle occurred even before the Americans could place their big guns on San Juan Hill to bombard the enemy navy below. When the Spanish fleet tried to run for the open sea the United States navy exterminated every last warship of Spain. All over the United States, enthusiastic Americans celebrated their victory.

By the standards of American history, this had not been a full-size war. There were 385 battle deaths—less than one-tenth the deaths in the American Revolution, and only one-twentieth the deaths at the Battle of Gettysburg alone. While the American Revolution had lasted nearly eight years and the Civil War had lasted four years, the Spanish-American War lasted only four *months*. Even this "little" war cost a quarter-billion dollars and several thousand deaths from disease.

And the little war marked a big change in the relationship of the United States to the world. The tides of history were turned. Cuba, given her independence, became an American protectorate.

The defeated Spain forfeited to the United States an empire of islands. This nation, born in a colonial revolution, would now have her own colonies. All were outside the continent, some were thousands of miles away. The United States acquired Puerto Rico at the gateway of the Caribbean, along with Guam, important as a refuelling station in mid-Pacific. The Philippine Islands (there were seven thousand of them, of which over one thousand were inhabitable) off the coast of China were sold to the United States for the bargain price of twenty million dollars.

These new American colonies added up to one hundred thousand square miles, holding nearly ten million people. That was not much, compared to the vast empires of England, France, or Germany. But for the United States it was something quite new.

The meaning of this Spanish-American War in American history, then, was actually less in what it accomplished than in what it proclaimed. The American Revolution had been our War of Independence. Now the Spanish-American War at the threshold of the twentieth century, was our first War of Intervention. We had joined the old-fashioned race for empire—on all the oceans of the world.

Many Americans were worried. Some were saddened, and even angry. They called themselves "Anti-Imperialists," for they hated to see the United States become an empire. To be an empire, they said, meant lording it over people in faraway places. Anti-Imperialists included Democrats and Republicans, of all sections and classes—labor leader Samuel Gompers, industrialist Andrew Carnegie, President Charles W. Eliot of Harvard and President David Starr Jordan of Stanford, the philosopher William James, the social worker Jane Addams, and the popular writer Mark Twain.

Theodore Roosevelt, however, believed that the United States could accomplish her mission only if she was a great world power. We must be willing to have colonies, he said, while we help the people learn to be democratic.

He built a great navy. In the Spanish-American War we had only five battleships and two armored cruisers. But before Roosevelt left the White House in 1909, we had twenty-five battleships and ten heavy cruisers. We had become, next to the British, the strongest naval power in the world.

President Roosevelt foresaw some grand accomplishments which would never have been done by stay-at-homes. For years Americans going westward had tried to find ways to shorten the voyage to California. Now, as a world power, the United States had to be able to move its navy speedily from one ocean to another. This was an urgent new reason to cut a waterway through Central America.

When TR came to the White House, a French company had already been working on a canal for twenty years. But they were stymied by tropical disease. Their progress was slow and international complications seemed to make the whole enterprise hopeless.

TR would let nothing stop him. First he tried to make a treaty with the little Republic of Colombia, which then included the part of the Isthmus of Panama where the canal had to be built. When the government of Colombia blocked Roosevelt's treaty in 1903, a revolution suddenly occurred in Panama. A lucky coincidence for the United States! But there was evidence that American money had helped the "coincidence" to happen. Immediately, the new "independent" Republic of Panama made a treaty granting the Canal Zone to the United States.

Within only ten years after construction began, ships were actually passing through the canal. The canal cost over a half-billion dollars.

Building the canal had produced some world-wide benefits that even TR had never dreamed of. In order to build the canal through the fever-infested swamps, the Americans had to conquer tropical diseases. When Americans occupied Havana after the Spanish-American War, Dr. Walter Reed had discovered the mosquito that carried the deadly yellow fever. Then Dr. William Gorgas, who had worked with Reed in Cuba, applied this discovery in Panama. His work finally made the canal possible —and incidentally helped conquer that tropical disease all around the world.

CHAPTER 26

How Submarines Killed the Freedom of the Seas

With world power and an island empire came a greater need to use the ocean highways. Ever since the eighteenth century, the civilized nations had agreed on certain rules. Since wars were always going on somewhere in the world, the purpose of these rules was to allow the neutral countries to carry on their commerce in peace.

The countries that were not fighting had certain Neutral Rights. The most important was their right to send their ships anywhere, and to have their citizens be safe wherever they traveled.

Warring nations were allowed to seize certain war materials ("contraband"— explosives, guns, and ammunition) even from a neutral ship. But they were not supposed to seize the other goods carried by neutrals. Before sinking any

ABOVE: *The luxury liner Lusitania at the dock in New York. When launched in 1907 it was the largest steamship in the world.* BELOW: *A German submarine in World War I. Posing a new threat to warships and passenger vessels, it was too small and crowded to rescue its victims.*

passenger ship, the attacker was required to give warning, to take the passengers on board, and do everything else reasonable to save civilian lives. Since warships were large vessels, they could normally be seen at a great distance, which automatically gave some warning. And anyway it was not too inconvenient for large warships to carry some extra passengers.

Such rules as these were what people meant by International Law. There was no court or police force to make nations obey. But the rules were still called "Law" because so many people believed they ought to be obeyed. The special rights of neutrals were also called Freedom of the Seas.

In 1914, when World War I broke out in Europe, these rules were still substantially the same as they had been for about two centuries. But the navies had changed. Most important was a new kind of ship—the submarine. The submarine's great strength was its new power to surprise. At the same time, however, the submarine was a crowded, tight-packed little vessel. With barely enough room for its own crew and food and ammunition, it had nowhere to put passengers from the ships it sank.

To say that all warring nations still had to follow the old rules would automatically outlaw the submarine. This would not have bothered Great Britain, for she had the greatest navy in the world. She commanded the seas anyway. But for Germany, with her relatively small navy, submarines would make all the difference. To forbid the submarine, then, was only another way of saying that Britain must forever rule the waves.

Great Britain made it plain that she had no intention of giving up her control of the oceans. She declared a blockade of Germany and enlarged the list of contraband to include all sorts of goods that neutrals had always been allowed to carry. Britain declared that she would even stop ships from carrying goods to neutral countries if any of those goods would eventually get to Germany. None of this was according to International Law.

Germany could hardly be expected to sit still and let herself be strangled. Her submarines could do their deadly work only if they, too, disobeyed International Law. Germany therefore decided to use the submarine for all it was worth, and to let others worry about the old rules. The Germans advertised in American newspapers urging Americans not to travel on British ships.

Then, on the night of May 7, 1915, the British luxury liner *Lusitania* was sunk without warning off the coast of Ireland by the German submarine U-20. Of nearly two thousand persons on board, 1,198 died, including 128 Americans. The ship sank within eighteen minutes of the time she was torpedoed. She was carrying 4,200 cases of small-arms ammunition and 1,250 shrapnel cases (which under International Law made the whole ship contraband and liable to be sunk).

President Woodrow Wilson sent a strong protest to Germany. He insisted on Neutral Rights. And he said this meant the right of Americans to travel wherever they pleased—even on the ships of the fighting nations, and right into the war zone. Wilson said this was a matter of national honor.

Woodrow Wilson's family background had not aroused his interest in naval or military affairs. His father, a Presbyterian minister who taught in a seminary, wanted young Woodrow to train for the ministry. Although Woodrow Wilson decided against becoming a minister, in some ways he always thought and talked like an old-fashioned minister.

Like Theodore Roosevelt, Wilson was a literary President, the author of many books. But in almost every other way he was TR's opposite. While TR's first book was on sea power, young Wilson wrote about moral questions for the North Carolina *Presbyterian*. While TR adored "The Strenuous Life," Wilson lived in the world of ideas, "longing to do immortal work." At the age when TR was learning to ride broncos and was bunking with cowboys, Wilson was sitting in post-graduate seminars on political science at Johns Hopkins University.

Wilson was an indoor sort of man. After a bright career as a professor he was elected president of Princeton University, where his educational reforms made him nationally famous. Then in 1910 he was elected Governor of New Jersey, and in 1912 he received the Democratic nomination for President. He could inspire people in large groups or from the printed page. But face to face he was stiff and stand-offish.

While Wilson had some of William Jennings Bryan's religious appeal, his tone was very different. Bryan sounded like the preacher at a country tent meeting, but Wilson could have been the minister of the best church in town. Both could persuade voters that they were joining the Army of the Lord. Wilson, like Bryan, championed the

Woodrow Wilson as president of Princeton University.

struggling farmers and underprivileged workers. As a more moderate kind of Bryan, Wilson had a wider appeal.

In 1916, two years after the outbreak of war in Europe, Wilson was reelected on the slogan, "He Kept Us Out of War!" But one thing after another was taking Americans further down the road. The German foreign minister, Arthur Zimmermann, sent a foolish message to the German ambassador in Mexico. Zimmermann asked Mexico to join the German side, and in return Germany promised to help the Mexicans recapture from the United States all of Texas, Arizona, and New Mexico. The message was intercepted and decoded by the British, who then eagerly relayed it to the United States.

Meanwhile, powerful unseen forces were drawing Americans naturally like a magnet toward the British. After all, we spoke the English language, our laws were built on English foundations, and we had fought our American Revolution to preserve our rights as Englishmen. Early in the war, the British succeeded in cutting the transatlantic cable that brought news to America direct from Germany. After that, all news from Europe was channeled through England. This gave the British a great advantage that very few people noticed.

Even before we declared war the United States was already supporting the British side. Because of the British blockade against Germany and her allies, the value of American goods sent to Germany and Austria plummeted from nearly $170,000,000 in 1914 to about $1,000,000 in 1916. During the same two years, American trade with Britain and her allies rocketed from $800,000,-000 to over $3,214,000,000. While the United States was still technically neutral, American bankers had actually loaned the British allies $2,300,000,000 to buy war supplies.

On April 2, 1917, within a month after the Zimmermann Note was published, President Wilson went to Congress to demand a declaration of war against Germany. He no longer spoke only about Neutral Rights. He would not ask Americans to die for a technicality. "The world," Wilson said, "must be made safe for democracy." Americans must fight "for the rights and liberties of small nations," to "bring peace and safety to all nations and make the world itself at last free."

There was, in fact, a good reason why the United States did not want to see the British lose. While European nations had spent their treasure on armies and navies, Americans had put their own wealth into schools and factories and railroads, into a better life for all citizens. Why had Americans been allowed to go about their business in peace? One reason was that the United States had the good luck to be protected by British Sea Power.

While the friendly British ruled the waves, they let us carry our cargoes and our people all over the world. The British, like the Americans, did not want to see other European nations build new empires in North or South America. The Monroe Doctrine—that European countries should not make new colonies in America and should not interfere in American affairs—had actually been enforced by the British navy. It had been very economical and extremely convenient, then, for Americans to have the British control the seas. But no one could predict what might come from a victorious Germany, with its new imperial ambitions.

In January 1918, President Wilson went before Congress again—to explain the American program for the future of the world. He listed Fourteen Points. They were a noble list. And if they could have been lived up to, there would never have been any more wars. All secret diplomacy was to be abolished— to make statesmen ashamed to barter away other people's lives and liberties. Freedom of the Seas would be restored. National boundaries would be adjusted so that all peoples could govern themselves. And, finally, there would be a League of Nations to preserve peace and insure justice.

The Fourteen Points impressed the world. They meant more to people outside the United States than any American statement since the Declaration of Independence or the Emancipation Proclamation.

President Wilson had proved himself one of the greatest preachers in modern history. He had lifted the spirits of the battle-worn, and he expressed the hopes of millions everywhere. But to make even half his dreams come true required a master politician. Could Wilson do the job?

CHAPTER 27

Winning a War, Losing a Peace ✑✑✑

When the United States entered the war in April 1917, our Allies had almost lost.

In Europe the land war was in a new style. The trench warfare was like nothing ever seen before. When the war broke out in 1914, both German generals and French generals had their own plans for a knockout blow to end the war in a hurry. But the new automatic weapons were deadly and accurate against attack. The advantages of the defensive had so increased that *both* armies immediately went on the defensive.

This was Stationary Warfare. Both armies dug their trenches, lived underground, and fired at each other from fixed positions. For three and a half years, the trenches stretched from the Swiss border to the North Sea. The battle lines had hardly moved.

On both sides the trenches became elaborate systems. There was usually a line of front trenches, held as outposts. Behind were networks of supply and command trenches, sometimes stretching back as far as five miles. These were connected by complicated tunnels, and sometimes even by specially designed railways. Soldiers became human moles,

hiding by day and digging by night. As soon as darkness fell, they went to work, digging new trenches, stringing barbed wire, and connecting telephone lines.

Instead of the higher officers leading their men into battle, these officers often stayed far back in command posts located in comfortable chateaus. Men in the front trenches had a terrible feeling of isolation. They were threatened not only by enemy gunfire, but by darkness, cold, and mud. Out of the filth and fatigue arose new ailments, which came to be called "trench fever," "trench foot," and "trench mouth."

In this kind of warfare, a "battle" was when large numbers of men from one set of trenches rushed out and tried to break through the enemy's trenches. The hope was always to force a big gap so your troops could pour through and then attack the whole enemy line from the rear. But advancing soldiers were tangled in barbed wire and mowed down by deadly machine-gun fire.

In the opening battles in 1914, even before the trenches were dug, each side lost a half-million men, which was more men than had been in the entire German army fifty years before. Then, during the whole year of 1915, the British and French did not advance more than three miles at any point. Still the French lost nearly a million and a half men in 1915, and a million in 1916. At the Battle of the Somme alone, the Germans lost more men than had been killed during the whole four years of the American Civil War.

Never before had so many men been slaughtered so rapidly or so senselessly. Before the war was over, the soldiers killed on both sides would number ten million, and another ten million civilians would die from disease, starvation, and the revolutions that grew out of the war.

When the United States finally plunged in, both sides were weary and sick of the bloodshed. In May 1918, the Germans had pushed their trenches to within fifty miles of Paris. They aimed at all costs to reach Paris and so force the surrender of the Allies before American troops could make a difference.

But the Americans came just in time. In July, 85,000 Americans arrived to help save Paris and to join a new counter-offensive. By August an American army of a half-million under General John J. Pershing advanced against the Germans on the southern front. Before the end of September a million and a quarter Americans were fighting in France.

After a bloody battle in October, the Americans advanced to Sedan, fifty miles behind the trenches which the Germans had held for three years. The Americans then cut the railroad line that

"Battle of the Marne," an eyewitness drawing by an artist-reporter. In the days of Stationary Warfare armies advanced on foot with fixed bayonets, hoping to break through the enemy's entrenchments.

had supplied the German army, and the whole German defense disintegrated. With this American encouragement, the French and the British were advancing too.

The German generals and the German Emperor had badly miscalculated. They had thought they would win the war before the United States came in. They could not imagine that American help at the last moment could possibly turn the tide. Though the Americans arrived late in the battle, they actually made the difference that decided the war. The United States lost 50,280 men in action.

That bloodiest war yet in history ended with the Armistice on November 11, 1918. In New York and San Francisco and Dallas and Chicago and Atlanta, Americans danced in the streets.

The Germans, in agreeing to an Armistice in November, believed that the peace would be based on Wilson's generous Fourteen Points.

When President Wilson himself decided to go to a Peace Conference in Paris, he gave ammunition to his critics. They said he was more anxious to be the Preacher to the World than to be the Protector of the United States. No President while in office had ever before gone to Europe.

In Paris, the three Allied leaders whom Wilson had to bargain with—the Prime Ministers of Great Britain, France, and Italy—were clever and tough. Each of them remembered the enormous cost of the war to his country during the four bloody years. Each wanted to get as much as possible in lands and wealth

"Blitzkrieg," Hitler's new technique of warfare in World War II, sent motorcycles and tanks speeding over highways to get behind the enemy's lines before he knew what was happening. Support by airplanes (not shown here) was crucial. This scene: Poland, 1939.

and power for his own country, and hoped to punish the enemies so they would never rise again.

The victorious European statesmen were irritated by the self-righteous American President who always said he was worrying about "all mankind." They compared the Points that Wilson had announced from Washington with the Commandments given to Moses on Mount Sinai. "Mr. Wilson bores me with his *Fourteen* Points," the French Prime Minister, Georges Clemenceau, sneered. "Why, God Almighty has only *ten!*"

The treaty that came out of the Paris conference rooms was not as selfish or as vengeful as the European leaders would have wished. Nor was it nearly as just and noble as President Wilson might have hoped. Each victorious power got territories it had been promised in secret treaties. The German colonies were parceled out among the Allies. At the same time, some new smaller republics—like Czechoslovakia and Poland—were created so that at last these people could govern themselves.

The provisions most poisonous for the future of Europe had to do with "reparations." These were payments the Allies demanded from Germany to "repair" all the war damage. When the Germans signed the Armistice they did understand they might have to pay for the damage to civilians.

But the British and the French raised the damages to include the *total* cost of the whole war to all the Allies. This meant not only the homes and farms and factories destroyed, but also the cost of guns and ammunition, the uniforms and pay for soldiers, and even the pensions to wounded Allied soldiers and to their

relatives. This sum was so vast and so hard to estimate that the Allies refused to name a figure—or even to name a time in the future when the Germans would be allowed to stop paying.

President Wilson did manage to put his own scheme for permanent peace— the League of Nations—in the very same package with all those things the other Allied powers really wanted. He believed that, even if the whole treaty was not perfect, his new League of Nations could correct the mistakes later.

When President Wilson returned to the United States, he was greeted like a returning hero. An escort of festive warships accompanied him into New York harbor. Ten thousand people welcomed him at the Union Station in Washington.

His triumph was short. Now his political mistakes came home to roost. When Wilson had appointed the American Peace Commissioners to go to Paris, he snubbed both the Republican Party and the Senate. Yet the Republicans held the majority in the Senate. And before any treaty became law, the Senate would have to approve it by a two-thirds majority.

President Wilson simply could not believe that there were reasons why sensible Americans might not want to approve his treaty. What frightened Americans most was the plan for a League of Nations—but especially Article 10. Wilson, with typical obstinacy, said that Article 10 was the heart of the whole League, and that the League was the heart of the treaty.

In Article 10 each League member promised to respect and preserve all the other members of the League against "external aggression." At first sight that looked harmless enough. But the real purpose of the Article was to make each member of the League regard an attack on any other member as an attack on itself. And in that case, each League member would be expected to prepare for war.

To agree to this would overturn one of the oldest American traditions. Should the United States let herself be *required* to plunge into some future European war?

Two able, contrasting Republican statesmen led a relentless battle against allowing the United States to join Wilson's League. One was William E. Borah, Senator from the Far Western State of Idaho. Borah, like President Wilson himself, was the son of a Presbyterian minister, who wanted him also to go into the ministry. A graduate of the University of Kansas, he was as eloquent as Wilson, but had more experience in politics. Although technically a Republican, he supported many Democratic measures when he happened to agree with them. He had worked for the income tax and had fought against trusts and monopolies.

Just as Senator Borah's own personal rule in politics had been to stay independent, and then support whatever measures were best, so he believed the United States should always stay independent in her relation to other countries. He bitterly opposed our joining the League of Nations, for fear it would take away our independence.

The other leader of the anti-League forces was the learned Senator Henry Cabot Lodge of Massachusetts. He, too, had had a long career as a politician.

But he came from a wealthy and aristocratic New England Oldcomer family. After attending Harvard, he wrote many books on American history. At the time of the World War he was chairman of the Senate Committee on Foreign Relations, which had the power to recommend to the Senate whether or not they should adopt the treaty. Unlike Senator Borah, he was a man of strong personal hates. He distrusted Woodrow Wilson and so he feared Wilson's League.

Then President Wilson made his fatal decision to appeal direct to the American people. In early September 1919, though already in ill health, he traveled eight thousand miles, visited twenty-nine cities, and gave forty speeches in twenty-two days. At Pueblo, Colorado, he collapsed and had to be taken back to the White House. For nearly eight months President Wilson could not even meet his Cabinet. His wife carried messages back and forth from everybody else to the President—and it was never quite clear which messages actually reached him.

Before the election of 1920 Wilson made another grave political blunder. If he had been willing to work with Senator Lodge, he might still have found some compromise and so might have passed the Treaty and the League through the Senate. Instead Wilson once again became the preacher. "Shall we," he asked "or shall we not, redeem the great moral obligation of the United States?" He declared that the Presidential election of 1920 would be a "solemn national referendum" on the League of Nations.

The Democratic candidate for President, Governor James M. Cox of Ohio, stood up for the League. The weak but likeable Republican candidate, Senator Warren G. Harding of Ohio, opposed the League and said vaguely that he favored some sort of "association of nations." Americans chose the Republican Harding by a resounding majority of seven million votes.

The United States never joined Wilson's League of Nations. Wilson was saddened that the American people chose a "barren independence." But he did not give up hope that what a union of States had accomplished in North America, a union of nations might someday accomplish for the whole world.

CHAPTER 28

The Battlefield Is Everywhere

When Franklin Delano Roosevelt moved into the White House in March 1933, the world prospects once again were grim. Italy, Russia, and Japan—three former American allies in the war "to make the world safe for democracy"— had become threats both to democracy and to peace. Germany, the leading enemy in that war, had risen from defeat, was building an enormous new army, was manufacturing weapons at frightening speed, and soon proclaimed her intention to rule the world. Any one of the new military powers had a bigger army and was beginning to have stronger armaments than the old democracies. Each proclaimed its intention to fight.

In the United States the national slogan had become, "Never Again!" Many Americans were becoming pacifists, saying they would never go to war for *any* reason. Others were becoming Isolationists, looking for ways to fence off the New World. And others refused to give up the old-fashioned hope that the country could always stay neutral. But by

1935 the idea that neutrals had rights which everybody would respect was more unrealistic than ever.

Each of the new warlike powers wanted not just a bigger empire for itself. It wanted its own kind of world —Communist, Fascist, or Nazi. All were battling for the minds of men. The winner aimed to take all.

This meant that, whether Americans liked it or not, the battlefront was everywhere. Now the airplane had made nearly all traditional thinking about war out-of-date. What the submarine had done to Freedom of the Seas, the airplane was doing to almost all the other rules of warfare.

Just as Admiral Mahan had once argued for the decisive influence of Sea Power on history, so during World War I the brilliant and energetic Billy Mitchell began to advertise Air Power.

Air Power was still so new that few took it seriously. In the Spanish-American War one light observation balloon had actually been used in Cuba. But "military ballooning" (as it was

Billy Mitchell, commander of United States aviators in France during World War I, was a bold and enthusiastic pioneer of Air Power.

called) was considered mostly a sport or a hobby. In 1913 when Mitchell was a young officer in the Signal Corps he began to be intrigued by the airplane's military possibilities. Then, during World War I, as General Pershing's Chief of Air Service he was impressed by the effectiveness of British and French warplanes.

At the end of the war, American generals and admirals still considered the airplane at most merely another new weapon. Like a new machine gun, it was to be used by either the army or the navy in their own regular operations.

Billy Mitchell had other ideas. His experience as a flyer and his other wartime observations persuaded him that airplanes really ought to be organized into an entirely new military unit, under a command all their own. So long as Americans thought of airplanes as only helpers in traditional army and navy maneuvers, he argued, Americans were sure to be left behind. They would lose the next war to nations who recognized that Air Power was something new and world-shaking.

Air Power, Mitchell said, had actually shifted the main targets. No longer were they the enemy *armies*. Now the most important targets were the "vital centers"—the centers of industry, the centers of supply, and the centers of the enemy's will to resist. "Armies themselves can be disregarded by air power," he explained, "if a rapid strike is made against the opposing centers."

Americans could not bear the thought of a new warfare that was so horrible. They hated to believe that whole cities might have to be destroyed.

Mitchell was an expert at getting publicity. He wrote magazine articles and books, and made speeches to alert all citizens to the importance of Air Power. Many of his fellow officers disliked him for it. Some called him "General of the 'Hot Air' Force."

But Mitchell was not discouraged. To prove that airplanes were an effective and economical force against battleships, he planned a spectacular demonstration. He arranged to have the German battleship *Ostfriesland*, which had been surrendered at the end of World War I, hauled to a position sixty miles off the Virginia coast. The battleship had a reputation for being "unsinkable." Now it was a ghost ship, with not a soul on board.

Just before noon on July 21, 1921, a flight of Mitchell's army bombers left Langley Field eighty-five miles away. As they arrived over the battleship, they dropped six 2,000-pound bombs. Within twenty minutes the "unsinkable" battleship was at the bottom of the ocean. It was the first time a battleship had ever been sunk by planes.

When admirals and generals still refused to grasp the full meaning of Air Power, Mitchell tried other tactics. He publicly denounced "the incompetency, criminal negligence, and almost treasonable administration of the National Defense by the Navy and War Departments." This was the sure road to court-martial—and that seemed to be his purpose. On December 17, 1925, a panel of generals found Brigadier General Billy Mitchell guilty of "conduct which brought discredit upon the military service." They sentenced him to a five-year suspension from active duty.

But his publicity campaign had already forced President Calvin Coolidge to take some action. The committee he appointed did not support all of Mitchell's demands, but they did urge the buildup of an American air force.

Then, on May 21, 1927, a young airmail pilot named Charles A. Lindbergh surprised and delighted the world by flying his light monoplane, *The Spirit of St. Louis*, nonstop from New York to Paris. Americans were proud of his courage and his modesty. He called his book *We* (meaning his plane and himself).

Charles Lindbergh at Curtiss Field, New York, before beginning his solo flight across the Atlantic. When he arrived at Le Bourget Airport outside Paris, to his astonishment he was greeted by 100,000 people.

As the military meaning of Lindbergh's feat sank in, Americans began to realize that Billy Mitchell's "wild" ideas no longer were so wild. Now it seemed quite possible that some day the United States might be attacked by airplanes which came nonstop across the ocean. The nation began to take Mitchell, and Air Power, seriously.

In 1935 the new American long-range B-17 bomber (soon called the "Flying Fortress" and equipped with the super-accurate Norden bombsight) first went into the air. Now it was hard for Americans to doubt that Air Power would change the meaning of war. Air war against "vital centers" would be as different as possible from the old stationary trench warfare.

Adolf Hitler's shocking new strategy depended on Air Power. The German name for it was *Blitzkrieg*, which means "lightning war." The idea was to strike with lightning speed. Using the fastest new vehicles (airplanes, tanks, trucks, and even motorcycles) the Nazis would rush quick and deep into enemy territory. The sluggish, unprepared enemies would be overwhelmed.

Blitzkrieg also meant war that struck like lightning—from the sky. Air Power made it possible. Leaping over "standing" armies, over water barriers and coastal fortifications, the Nazi air force would strike abruptly at the heart of the defenseless nations.

On September 1, 1939, Hitler invaded Poland, which fell before the end of the month. Then, on April 9, 1940, he horrified the world by invading Denmark and Norway. One month later he rushed into the Netherlands, Belgium, and Luxembourg, and then lunged deep into France around the "impregnable" Maginot Line. On June 14 his Nazis marched into Paris. Thousands of weeping Frenchmen lined the streets, helpless against this lightning barbarian invasion.

Luckily, President Franklin Delano Roosevelt recognized the Nazi menace. Even before the Nazis had overrun France he had sent a special message to Congress warning the nation to rearm. He announced his plan to turn out fifty thousand planes in the next year and every year until the Nazis were beaten. In one of his most effective "fireside chats" over the radio, he alerted the nation:

> The Nazi masters of Germany have made it clear that they intend not only to dominate all life and thought in their own country, but also to enslave the whole of Europe, and then to use the resources of Europe to dominate the rest of the world. . . . We cannot escape danger, or the fear of danger, by crawling into a bed and pulling the covers over our heads. . . . No nation can appease the Nazis. No man can tame a tiger into a kitten by stroking it. . . . Let not the defeatists tell us that it is too late. It will never be earlier.

But still there were those who believed they could ward off the Nazi menace by the old-fashioned magic word, "Neutrality!"

The Isolationists had passed a Neutrality Law requiring that all military supplies sent abroad had to be "cash-and-carry." This law required all the warring countries to pay for the goods they bought here before the goods left our shores and then also required them to carry the goods in their own ships. The Isolationists hoped this would keep the United States out of the war.

The British had run out of cash and were running out of ships. If this law was not quickly changed the United States might not be able to get help to the British before they were defeated by the Nazis.

President Franklin Delano Roosevelt showed his usual genius for compromise and for persuasion. He offered a clever plan called "Lend-Lease." We would "lend" or "lease" to the British—or any other country whose defense the President considered vital to the defense of the United States—whatever war supplies we could make. In that way the British would not need cash, and the hesitating Congressmen might be persuaded that we were getting value in return.

At the same time, in January 1941, in his annual message to Congress, President Roosevelt proclaimed the Four Freedoms. After the war he hoped for "a world founded upon four essential human freedoms"—freedom of speech, freedom of religion, freedom from want, and freedom from fear. Later that year, after a secret meeting with British Prime Minister Winston Churchill on a warship off the coast of Newfoundland, the two men issued the Atlantic Charter. This was an up-to-date version of Woodrow Wilson's Fourteen Points.

Meanwhile Hitler made his fatal blunder. In his maniac belief that all battlefields were alike and that *Blitzkrieg* could conquer all, on June 22, 1941, only

The bombing of Pearl Harbor by Japanese war planes helped convince all Americans that the age of Air Power had arrived.

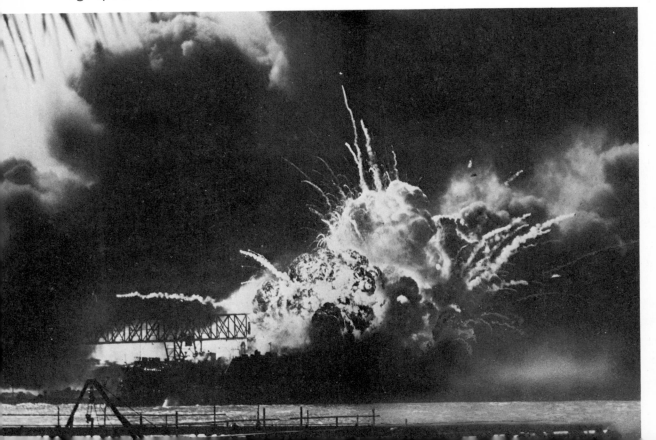

a year after mastering France, he suddenly invaded Russia. But Russia was bigger—and colder—than Hitler had imagined. When the Russian winter arrived, the fingers of Nazi soldiers became numb. Frozen oil paralyzed the motors of his tanks. The Russians counterattacked and Hitler's *Blitzkrieg* was buried in the snow.

At the same time, halfway around the world, the Japanese suddenly forced even the most Isolationist of Americans to realize that Air Power had already put them on the battlefield. On the morning of December 7, 1941, while Japanese diplomats were pretending to discuss peace at the White House, a fleet of 189 Japanese warplanes attacked American airfields at Pearl Harbor in Hawaii. Then they attacked the ships of the United States navy anchored in the harbor. An hour later came a second fleet of 171 Japanese warplanes.

The surprise had been perfect. 150 American warplanes—the bulk of our air force in the Pacific—were destroyed on the ground. It was a better demonstration than Billy Mitchell could have imagined, and the fulfillment of his direst prophecies. There were eighty-six American ships in Pearl Harbor at the time. The most powerful of these, the eight battleships, were put out of action, together with three cruisers and three destroyers, and one battleship was actually sunk. 2,323 men were killed. This was the worst naval catastrophe in American history.

The very next day Congress announced that we were at war.

CHAPTER 29

The Exploding World of the Atom

As soon as Americans had been plunged into battle by this lightning stroke of Air Power, it was plain that the new kind of war was even newer than anyone had imagined. Now the battlefield was everywhere—but especially in the hearts of civilians. Warplanes sometimes flew so high they could not be seen and could barely be heard, to strike at homes and factories.

At first the bombing of Germany followed an American plan of "pinpoint" daylight attacks. Since daylight bombers could actually see their targets they could focus their bombs on the crucial factories. But at the same time the Germans could see the approaching planes, and they downed a disastrous number. The damage to the whole German war machine was slight.

By contrast with the American scheme of "precision" bombing, the British bombers went over at night and bombed whole areas. Incendiary bombs set fire to entire cities. Since these attacking bombers could not be seen, the British losses were much lower. And the damage to the "vital centers"—to the enemy's production, communication, and transportation and the enemy's will to

Massed United States bombers attacking a target in Germany in World War II.

resist—was far greater.

Now the war came home to the people on both sides. Never before in the history of warfare was there so much suffering by civilians. The Germans sent their bombers over London and other British cities, killing thousands. The Americans and British sent their bombers back over Germany. Finally it was the destruction of factories and cities behind the lines that broke the Nazi will to war. Allied planes had killed nearly a third of a million Germans and had destroyed over five million homes.

When the defeat of the Nazis appeared to be in sight, in February 1945, President Roosevelt met with the Allied leaders, British Prime Minister Churchill and Russian Dictator Josef Stalin. They met at Yalta, a Russian summer resort on the Black Sea. There they agreed on their plans for the Nazi surrender. Germany was to be taken apart. The Germans once again would have to

pay enormous "reparations," with Russia receiving half.

At first Stalin demanded that Poland, on the Russian border, be put under a Communist puppet government. Then when Roosevelt and Churchill objected, Stalin promised to let the Polish people choose their own government by free elections.

The Russians agreed to declare war against Japan soon after the defeat of Germany, and they agreed that they would join the United Nations. In return the Russians gained certain Japanese islands and would be allowed to conquer Outer Mongolia—a vast area twice the size of Texas—on the Russian border in central Asia. At the same time, Stalin solemnly promised not to interfere in the countries along the Russian border in eastern Europe. He promised to let those countries choose their own governments.

Of course Churchill and Roosevelt

knew that for years the communist leaders had called democracy a fraud. But since the Russian armies still had unrivaled power in eastern Europe, the British and American leaders did not have much choice. From their Russian ally all they could expect was promises. They considered themselves lucky to get those. Soon enough they would discover what Stalin's promises were really worth.

Within one short month the Nazi armies crumbled—caught between the Russian communist armies speeding westward and the Anglo-Americans speeding eastward.

General Dwight D. Eisenhower was Supreme Commander of Allied forces. Now his decision could change the history of Europe. If he wanted, he could quickly move his forces into Berlin, the capital of Germany, and also into Prague, the capital of Czechoslovakia.

In Anglo-American hands, Berlin and Prague would be strongholds to help the democracies enforce the Russian agreement to let eastern Europe decide its own fate.

On the other hand General Eisenhower could wait to mop up the German troops behind his own lines—meanwhile letting the Russians overrun more of eastern Europe and consolidate their positions in the capitals. In communist hands, those capitals would help the Russians to foist their dictatorship on all the surrounding peoples. The Russians could make Poland, Czechoslovakia, Hungary, Rumania, and Bulgaria into "satellites" revolving around Moscow.

The far-sighted Winston Churchill saw the threat. "I deem it highly important," he warned General Eisenhower, "that we should shake hands with the Russians as far to the east as

General Eisenhower talking to American paratroopers in June 1944 just before "Operation Overlord"—the successful landing on D-Day of Allied troops on the German-held coast of France. The paratroopers were assigned to drop behind enemy lines before the Allied landing.

possible." But General Eisenhower was anxious to avoid the loss of more American soldiers. Instead of rushing his democratic forces eastward, he decided to halt fifty miles west of Berlin at the River Elbe. Stalin applauded this decision, for now both Berlin and Prague were left to the Russians.

Until the last minute, Churchill was still trying to warn President Roosevelt. The new "mortal danger to the free world," he said, was our "ally," Russia. It would be tragic, after the long struggle against the Nazi tyranny, to hand over half of Europe to a communist tyranny.

Before Churchill's wisdom could prevail in Washington, President Roosevelt was dead. Worn down by wartime burdens, he had gone for a rest to Warm Springs, Georgia, where he often went for treatment of his paralyzed limbs. On April 12, 1945, he complained of a bad headache, and within a few hours a blood vessel had burst in his brain. The cheerful leader, who had helped raise his fellow Americans from the depth of their Great Depression and who had organized their battle against Nazi barbarism, finally did not have the satisfaction of receiving the Nazi surrender.

The nation grieved as it had grieved for few Americans since Lincoln. Men and women wept in their offices, at home, and in the streets. They felt they had lost not only a national leader, but a personal friend.

To the White House in his place came the courageous, peppery Vice-President, Harry S Truman. He was destined to make some of the most fateful decisions in the history of modern warfare. But when he solemnly took his oath of office

and asked the nation to pray for him, he could not have imagined what was in store. He still had not even heard of the super-secret project that was already nearing completion—to build an atomic bomb.

Those who made the American bomb possible (in addition to many American scientists) were a "Who's Who" of world science. From Germany came the greatest physicist of the age, Albert Einstein. Because he was a Jew, the Nazis had taken away his German citizenship and seized his property. From Italy, as a refugee from Mussolini, came the brilliant Enrico Fermi, who was one of the first to propose an atomic bomb as a practical possibility. Scientists, engineers, and mathematicians came also from Hungary, Austria, Denmark, and Czechoslovakia—refugees from all the enslaved parts of Europe.

To build the atomic bomb certain theoretical questions first had to be answered. Was it really possible to achieve "the controlled release of atomic energy"?

The answer came at 3:25 on the afternoon of December 2, 1942, in a squash court on the campus of the University of Chicago. Professor Enrico Fermi supervised the experiment. When everything was prepared, he gave the signal to pull out the control rod. Suddenly the Geiger counters resounded with telltale clicks from the radiation made by the successful breaking up of uranium atoms. The dignified scientists let out a cheer. They had produced a chain reaction that transformed matter into energy! The Atomic Age had begun.

One of the physicists hurried to the long-distance telephone and gave the code message to be relayed to the President of the United States.

"You'll be interested to know," he reported with mock casualness, "that the Italian navigator has just landed in the New World. The Earth was not as large as he had estimated, and he arrived in the New World sooner than he had expected."

"Is that so?" he was asked. "Were the natives friendly?"

"Everyone landed safe and happy." This meant that Professor Fermi (the "Italian navigator") had succeeded even ahead of schedule. The "New World" was, of course, the uncharted world of Atomic Power.

In May 1942, seven months before the Fermi experiment succeeded, President Roosevelt had set up the super-secret "Manhattan Project" to be prepared to build a bomb. Within less than three years and at a cost of two billion dollars, "Manhattan Project" did its job.

At 5:30 on the morning of July 16, 1945, in the remote desert near Alamogordo, New Mexico, the moment came to prove that the bold thinking of the scientists could be matched by the practical know-how of engineers. The answer required no delicate Geiger counter to detect it. The world's first atomic bomb exploded—with a blinding flash and a mushroom cloud such as had never been seen before.

By the time the bomb was perfected, the Germans and Italians had already surrendered. Of the enemies now only Japan remained. On July 26, the Allied leaders gave the Japanese a solemn warning that "the alternative to surrender is prompt and utter destruction."

Still they did not surrender.

Should the United States use the atomic bomb? President Truman alone had to decide. No one knew how long Japan would hold out. Despite the terrifying fire raids of March 1945, when much of Tokyo was destroyed, the Japanese militarists showed no signs of giving up. If the war dragged on and Americans had to invade Japan, it might cost a million lives. The atomic bomb, President Truman knew, might kill hundreds of thousands of innocent Japanese. But life for life, the odds were that it would cost less.

Devastation at Nagasaki, Japan, after the dropping of the second United States atomic bomb on August 9, 1945.

On August 6, 1945, three weeks after that first blinding blast on the New Mexico desert, a single American plane dropped an atomic bomb on Hiroshima. About eighty thousand people were killed. The Japanese still held on. A few days later another plane dropped an atomic bomb on Nagasaki. The Japanese caved in. They announced their surrender on August 14, 1945.

CHAPTER 30

"Little" Wars and Big Risks

World War II was over. The menace of Nazi barbarism and of Japanese militarism was destroyed. But the world was haunted by new fears. Could democracy survive in a world where the Russian communists were more powerful than ever before—and more determined than ever to conquer the world?

By now the United States had joined a modernized version of Wilson's League of Nations. The United Nations had been organized in San Francisco in 1945 even before the German surrender. President Truman hoped the United Nations would help keep the world at peace. But he had fought in France in World War I and he remembered the letdown after that war. Therefore he scaled down his hopes and made plans to fit. He did not promise perpetual peace or freedom for all men on earth.

Instead President Truman offered a simple two-pronged plan. People weakened by the war would receive American machinery and food and money. This would make them stronger to resist tyranny. He would also use American force, wherever it was needed, to help any particular country fight off a takeover by the communists from the outside. This was called "Containment" because it aimed to "contain" the communists and prevent them from taking over the world.

The Truman Doctrine was not as inspiring as Wilson's dream of an entirely democratic world. It was a country-by-country approach. It aimed to help free people stay strong and to help weak people stay free.

And, on the whole, it worked. The exhausted countries of western Europe —Great Britain, France, West Germany, and Italy—which might have been easy pickings for the Russian communists, became stronger in these postwar years. On the shaky borderlands of Greece and Turkey, the communist threat was held back.

The first armed test of the Truman Doctrine came in far-off Korea. The communists set up a puppet government in North Korea—like the puppets they had already set up in eastern Europe— and they claimed the right to rule the whole country. The United Nations (supported by the United States) proposed free elections so all the Koreans could choose their own government. But the Russians objected. And on June

American troops like these, fighting in Korea under the United Nations command, struggled over a hilly country, often barren and frigid.

25, 1950, an army of 100,000 men, who had been armed and trained by the Russian communists, swooped down to take possession of South Korea.

President Truman instantly sent in American troops. The United Nations condemned North Korea as an aggressor. And a United Nations army was organized with troops drawn from fifty-three member nations, commanded by the American General Douglas MacArthur. At first the United Nations forces drove back the invading North Korean communists.

Then suddenly the whole picture changed. Communist China, aided by the Russians, poured in masses of its own troops against the United Nations. They came down from north of the Yalu River. Now the Chinese communists threatened a third World War—if the United Nations forces stepped over the Yalu River into Chinese territory.

On March 24, 1951, General MacArthur, supreme commander of American forces in Korea, publicly warned that he would attack communist China if her forces did not withdraw from South Korea. Unlike President Truman, General MacArthur was willing to risk World War III.

But President Truman had not forgotten the powers of the President. The Constitution said that the President was Commander in Chief of all the United States armed forces. And the general had disobeyed the President's orders by refusing to keep the war inside Korea. President Truman called a surprise press conference at one o'clock in the morning on April 11, 1951, to announce that General MacArthur had been removed.

When the picturesque General MacArthur returned to the United States, admiring crowds greeted him in San Francisco, Chicago, and New York. In

Washington on April 19, he gave an oration to Congress. "In war," he urged in his deep baritone voice, "there can be no substitute for victory."

But even as the sound of the general's voice died away, more and more Americans saw that President Truman was talking common sense. You could no longer talk about "victory" in the general's simple phrase. Communist Russia now had its own atomic bomb. If there was another World War both "winners" and "losers" would go up in atomic blasts. The only hope for mankind, said President Truman, was to keep the fighting limited. Now even "little" wars carried big risks.

When General Eisenhower campaigned for President in 1952, he promised that if he was elected he would go to Korea to find a way to end the war. And the Korean War ended in a compromise, arranged by President Eisenhower, on July 27, 1953. The American dead numbered thirty-five thousand. The Korean peace was no "victory" for the United States. But since it removed the most immediate threat of an atomic war, it was a kind of victory for mankind.

The expanding forces of communism had been warned that any attempt to conquer their neighbors would be extremely costly. They had not been defeated, but they had been held back. It was not all that Americans really wished

An American military adviser in Viet Nam (third from right) with South Vietnamese Marines at the edge of a rice paddy. At far left are two enemy (Viet Cong) prisoners.

but it was probably the best that could be expected for some time to come.

Within a few years after the Korean truce, again on a peninsula which bordered on communist China, came another test of Containment. In April 1954 the United States met at Geneva with communist Russia, communist China, and countries that once had colonies in Southeast Asia. They agreed that Indochina, the old French colony, should be divided into new independent nations. The people in the area called "Viet Nam" were already split between the communists in the north (on the border of communist China) and the anticommunists in the south. It was therefore agreed to set up *two* Viet Nams.

But then, as in Korea a few years before, communist forces from the North began invading the South.

Would the United States again try to hold back the expanding forces of communism?

In October 1961, President John F. Kennedy made the decision to intervene. Then, after the assassination of President Kennedy in November 1963, Congress on President Lyndon B. Johnson's request voted to use American forces. By 1967 there were nearly a half-million American soldiers in Viet Nam.

This new War of Containment was in many ways similar to the war in Korea. But there were some important differences. Now it was not the whole United Nations but the United States forces with only a few allies who were fighting.

And now many more Americans had their doubts. On October 15 and on November 15, 1969, hundreds of thousands of Americans came to Washington, D.C., and marched peacefully to

During an enemy attack in Viet Nam, a United States Marine carries frightened children to safety.

protest the official United States policy. They demanded immediate withdrawal of American troops from Viet Nam. Some thought that the Vietnamese people should be left to settle their own affairs—even with interference or domination by the neighboring communist Chinese. Some now wondered if the United States really could police the whole world. A new spirit of Isolationism was growing.

The answer, at the start of the 1970's, was still not clear. The United States was willing to compromise. But the North Vietnamese communists, supported by communist China, would not compromise. They demanded power to impose their will on the whole nation.

CHAPTER 31

Windows to the World ༄༅༄༅༄༅༄༅༄༅༄༅

By 1960 there were many more automobiles in the United States than in all the rest of the world put together. Two-thirds of American households had at least one automobile.

Perhaps more than anything else that Americans had made by the millions, the automobile expressed their new civilization. All American wealth and ingenuity and organizing ability had been required to give Americans their cars.

The automobile was democratic. Just as ready-made clothing had made it harder in the United States than anywhere else to tell a man's occupation or social class by what he wore, so it was harder than anywhere else to guess an American's bank account by the car he drove.

The automobile was a symbol of freedom. A man who owned a car was free to live at a considerable distance from where he worked. He could take his family to the country on weekends, and to far parts of the continent on vacations.

The automobile was a symbol of speed. With it a man could go as fast as the fastest locomotive, and he could make his own timetable. Americans had always valued their ability to go where and when they wanted. In the twentieth century it was the automobile that helped make this possible.

While automobiles took Americans all around their own country, they no longer had to be rich to vacation abroad. In 1930 less than a half-million Americans traveled overseas, but in 1970 the number reached three million. Jet airplanes took them on three-week holidays to all the continents. And the enormous jumbo jet began to carry four hundred passengers from New York City to London in less time than a farmer used to spend on his weekly drive to the village post office.

Each American felt closer to others, too, when messages came to him more quickly and more easily. But it was almost the time of the Civil War before the U.S. mail had begun to be speedy and reliable. Before Lincoln came to the White House, Morse's telegraph had made it possible for Americans to share the news, which reached newspaper readers throughout the whole nation within a day after it happened. In 1866 the transatlantic cable, which had taken twelve years to complete, brought messages instantly from the Old World.

Then came the telephone. Alexander Graham Bell was twenty-three when he immigrated from Scotland with his family in 1870. Young Bell, following his father's interests in helping the deaf, studied acoustics (the science of sound) and electricity.

Bell determined to find a way to use

American automobiles, about 1913, on a group excursion to the Great Oregon Caves. Some critics feared that Americans would stop going to church and instead would spend Sundays in their automobiles.

electricity to carry the human voice. For Morse's telegraph would carry nothing but dots and dashes.

By 1876 Bell's new electromagnetic telephone was being displayed at the Centennial Exposition in Philadelphia as a great curiosity. Bell, like Edison, was a skillful organizer, and in the early twentieth century his telephone company had overtaken U. S. Steel to become the largest corporation in the United States.

On remote farms and ranches, medical-care-by-telephone saved the life of many a child—and incidentally saved the doctor a long ride. New businesses were started by new-style Go-Getters who sold their goods exclusively by telephone. The telephone (like the typewriter, which was perfected about the same time) provided new jobs for women.

Within a century after Bell made his invention, it was unusual for any American family to be out of reach of a telephone. The nation's hundred million telephones were more than half of all those in the world. By 1970 three hundred million separate phone conversations were carried on in the United States each day.

Back in the 1880's it was hard enough for people to imagine that a voice could be sent on a wire. But how much harder to imagine that messages could be sent even *without* a wire!

Before 1890 a German physicist, Heinrich Hertz, had discovered the existence of radio waves. At first people called them "Hertzian waves." These had the amazing quality of being able to pass through solid objects—even through wooden and brick walls.

In 1894 a young Italian named Guglielmo Marconi, still in his teens, happened to see a magazine article on "Hertzian waves." The idea fascinated him. He retreated to his room on the third floor of the family home near Bologna, locked the door, and experimented with "Hertzian waves" for hours

A boy learning to draw by listening to lessons broadcast over the newfangled invention, the radio (about 1924). The term "broadcast" (used on page 32) now had a new meaning.

on end. His first success was to use these waves to ring a bell across a room or downstairs. The very next year, when he was still only twenty-one, he succeeded in sending these waves outdoors (the distance of a twenty-minute walk) and even across the neighboring hill.

In 1896 Marconi and his mother went to England with a "little black box" containing his invention. Encouraged by the chief of telegraph in the British Post Office, he pursued his experiments and soon was sending messages nine miles. In 1897 Marconi received a British patent for his "wireless telegraph" and founded Marconi's Wireless Telegraph Company in London. His company was a great success.

His wireless equipment was installed in three British battleships in 1899. And in that year Marconi came to the United States.

Americans, with their new colonial empire, had special reasons to want news quickly from everywhere. During the Spanish-American War, when Admiral Dewey reported his victory at Manila Bay, he first had to send dispatch boats to Hong Kong. There the news was telegraphed westward (on British-controlled cables) by way of the Indian Ocean, the Red Sea, the Mediterranean, and then across the Atlantic, before it finally reached the President in Washington. Now wireless might make it possible (without depending on cables owned by the British or by anyone else) to get messages to Washington instantly from anywhere. The American Marconi Company prospered.

But Marconi's wireless still sent only dots and dashes. It would not send voices or music. The next step was taken by Reginald Aubrey Fessenden, a Canadian who had worked with Edison in his "invention factory" in the 1880's.

Fessenden had a simple but revolutionary idea. Marconi, using wireless waves, had sent out dots and dashes by stopping and starting electrical signals. Suppose, said Fessenden, the wireless message was sent out in a *continuing* wave of radio rays. Then, by making the waves correspond to the vibrations made by sounds, you could actually transmit speech and music. Fessenden experimented with this idea at the laboratory of the General Electric Company, which had grown out of Edison's invention factory.

The startling result occurred on Christmas Eve, 1906. That night, wireless operators on ships at sea, wearing their earphones, were listening for the usual stream of dots and dashes. To their amazement, they suddenly heard a human voice. A woman sang a Christmas carol, someone played a violin, then someone read a passage from the Bible, and finally Fessenden's own voice wished them Merry Christmas.

The very word broadcast took on a new meaning. In the 1901 dictionary it usually meant "the act or process of scattering seeds." But by 1927 *broadcast* usually meant "to scatter or disseminate, specifically, radio messages, speeches, etc."

Within the twenty years after Fessenden's first Christmas broadcast in 1906, events moved with a peculiarly American speed. Many other Go-Getters, inventors, and adventurous businessmen joined in.

One of the most remarkable of these Go-Getters was Lee De Forest, born in Council Bluff, Iowa, in 1873. His father went to Alabama, to be president of Talledega College, which had been founded by missionaries just after the Civil War to help educate the Negro freedmen.

Like Marconi, young De Forest began to read about the new "Hertzian waves." His summer job pushing a chair for sightseers at the World's Columbian Exposition in Chicago in 1893 gave him the opportunity to study the electrical exhibits. He worked his way through Yale College, sometimes rising at 4:00 A.M. to mow lawns. And he studied hard. But he was not popular with his classmates, who voted him both the "nerviest" and the "homeliest" of their year.

After graduation—and for the rest of his life—De Forest gave his enormous energies to inventing ways to improve radio. His new radio tube which he patented in 1906 was called the Audion. It was based on a tube that Edison had made in his laboratory when working on the incandescent lamp. With the Audion tube it was easier to tune in, all reception became louder and clearer, and the broadcast of voice and music was much improved. Before his death De Forest had received over three hundred patents.

The man who did more than anyone else to bring radio and then television into American homes was David Sarnoff. He showed that the Go-Getting spirit was as alive in the mid-twentieth century as it had been in the days of the trailblazer John Iliff or the merchandising giants, Montgomery Ward and Richard Sears.

David Sarnoff's life was an American saga. He was born in southern Russia in 1891, to a poor family who intended him to become a rabbi. Even before he was nine he was reading the sacred texts in Hebrew. Then his father, who had gone to America a few years before, sent back money for the family's transatlantic passage.

When the Sarnoffs settled in a crowded immigrant section of New York City, David still did not know a word of English. But he went to public school and soon spoke like an American. When his father became too sick to earn a living, David at the age of ten began supporting the whole family with the profits from his newsstand on Tenth Avenue.

David was ambitious. Deciding to become a wireless operator, he taught himself the Morse code and was hired by the American Marconi Company.

Then, by luck, Sarnoff happened to be the only operator at a New York wire-

David Sarnoff as a teen-age telegraph operator working for Marconi.

less receiver when word came dimly through on the afternoon of April 15, 1912, that the luxury liner *Titanic* had struck an iceberg and was sinking in mid-Atlantic. He gave the news to the press, and stayed at his instrument (while all other stations were ordered off the air) to alert other ships to send help. The name of David Sarnoff reached everyone who read the newspapers.

When the American Marconi Company was taken over by the Radio Corporation of America (RCA), Sarnoff joined the new firm. By 1921 Sarnoff was running the large company, making plans to sell the new "radio music boxes" by the millions.

During World War I the soldiers hidden in trenches had needed the radio to keep in touch with their units. And radio sets improved in wartime, when the different manufacturers had been required to pool their know-how. After the war, radio entered American homes. With the new sets listeners no longer had to wear earphones. Now they could receive the program over a loudspeaker.

In 1920 the Department of Commerce issued the first license for a regular commercial broadcasting station to KDKA in Pittsburgh. Within two years there were over five hundred licensed commercial broadcasting stations, and over a half-million radio sets were being produced annually. Before World War II, the annual production of radio sets numbered ten million.

Sarnoff was just as bold in forecasting the success of television. He invested large sums in the RCA television research laboratory where another Russian immigrant, Vladimir Zworykin, was making remarkable progress.

While Zworykin was collaborating

with a large staff in the costly RCA laboratory, another inventor was working quietly by himself. Philo Taylor Farnsworth, born to a large Mormon family on a farm near Beaver, Utah, in 1906, began studying electronics on his own when he was still in high school. Encouraged by his science teacher, he tried to make a television set. Then a businessman furnished a small laboratory for him in California. Philo worked alone and in secret, with the blinds drawn. Once the police (suspecting he was building a still to make illegal whiskey) raided his laboratory. At the age of only twenty-four, Farnsworth had patented his own new system for television.

World War II delayed the manufacture of television for the home. But out of wartime needs came "radar"—a word made up from *ra*(dio) *d*(etecting) *a*(nd) *r*(anging). Radar used radio waves to locate enemy planes and ships. The many returning servicemen with radar experience were well prepared to work on television.

By 1948 television was booming. Sarnoff's foresight had paid off. In that year nearly one million television sets were produced, in the very next year production reached three million, and in the year following 7,500,000. By the mid-1960's it was hard to find an American household without a television set.

When people could see a movie at home free, why should they go to the movie theater? Thousands of movie theaters closed. But many new movies —including new series, documentaries, and shorts—were made especially for television. While fewer movies were made for the theater each year, the movie spectaculars (like *Ben Hur* or *Cleopatra*) were as successful as ever. Old movies, especially Westerns, found a new life on television. And there was a new interest in experimental movies. Though shown in small theaters they aroused widespread interest. And then "underground" movies—which went on for hours—showed that the new movie audience was more patient than ever.

Television gave everybody a window to the world. Now everyone—whether he lived on a farm or in the city, whether his neighborhood was rich or poor, whether in Oregon, New Mexico, Maine, or Florida, whether young or old, sick or well—could look through the television window at the very same world. Now, as never before, Americans shared their experience.

Even in the days before television, when President Franklin Delano Roosevelt broadcasted his first inaugural address on radio he received in response a half-million pieces of mail. During the Great Depression and World War II he skillfully used his radio "fireside chats" to bring all Americans together.

Now with television all Americans could actually see their candidates in action. They could watch the expression on a candidate's face and could follow his gestures. In this new way, American voters could feel personally acquainted with their leaders.

In 1948, for the first time, the National Party Conventions were telecast. While sitting in the White House, President Truman saw the nomination of his Republican rival, Governor Thomas E. Dewey, in Philadelphia. During the campaign President Truman seemed relaxed and homey on television while

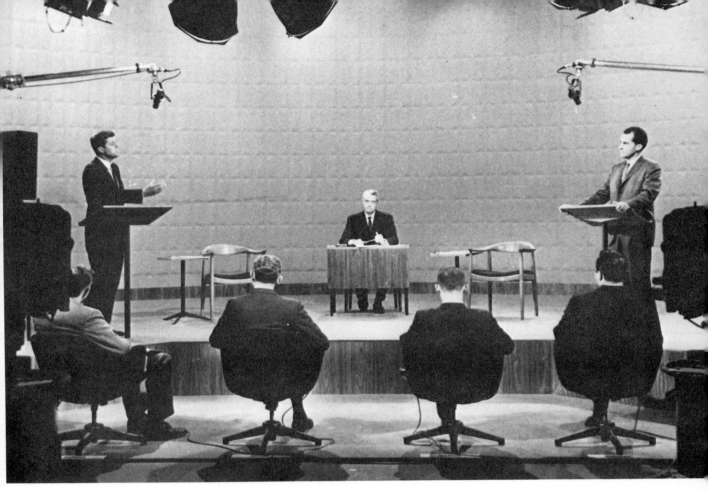

One of television's "Great Debates" in 1960. LEFT: *John F. Kennedy.* RIGHT: *Richard M. Nixon. Presiding: Howard K. Smith of ABC. William Jennings Bryan's strenuous campaigning had brought his voice to a few million Americans; each of the Great Debates reached about seventy million.*

Governor Dewey (his opponents said he looked like the bridegroom on a wedding cake) appeared stiff and formal. This new opportunity for American voters to size up the personalities of the candidates on television helped explain why President Truman won reelection.

In the Presidential campaign of 1960 the two candidates appeared together on television. In the "Great Debates"—a series of four one-hour programs—John F. Kennedy, the Democratic candidate, and Richard M. Nixon, the Republican candidate, discussed the issues. These were not really "debates" like the old-fashioned Lincoln-Douglas Debates a

century earlier. For now newspaper reporters put the questions. Each Presidential candidate had 2½ minutes in which to give his answer. Then he had 1½ minutes for reply after the other candidate had made his brief statement.

These "Great Debates" probably reached the largest audience in history up to that time. Seventy million people were watching each program. Television's new window to the world had made American life more democratic. Television showed more Americans more about everything and everybody in their country. American technology—drawing on the know-how of Americans and of the whole world—had come to the service of American democracy.

But there were dangers. The man who showed up best on television was bound to be the man who was the best "performer." He was the man who could give the cleverest response in 2½ minutes to questions he had just heard. But was that the best test of a President?

"Telstar," an American satellite, made it possible to exchange television programs between continents. With television Americans could even reach out beyond this world. And by looking through the window in his living room every American would join the nation's adventures to the New Worlds of outer space.

CHAPTER 32

Footprints on the Moon

When the first Europeans came to America, they came in their familiar ships "over the vast and furious ocean." They feared the ocean, but they knew its perils. When the first Americans pushed off into outer space, they had to invent new kinds of ships. And they had to brave the unknown perils of a new kind of ocean.

By the time of World War II, of course, a great deal was known about airplanes. But airplanes would not work in outer space. For every airplane engine then known—whether an internal-combustion engine like an automobile's that used gasoline to turn a propeller, or a jet engine that pushed ahead by burning gases—depended on the air. From the air came oxygen to explode the gasoline or to burn the gases. But in outer space there is no air. Out there you would need a very special kind of engine.

The pioneer American space scientist, Robert H. Goddard, proposed propelling spacecraft by rocket. A rocket carries its own fuel, and also carries its own "air"—usually in the form of liquid oxygen—which it uses to burn the fuel. The shooting of the rocket behind pushes the spacecraft forward.

In 1914 Goddard received a patent for his liquid-fuel rocket engine. In 1920 he wrote a technical report for the Smithsonian Institution in Washington explaining how his rocket engine worked. He said it might even be possible someday to reach the moon by rocket. The New York *Times* and other respectable newspapers wrote editorials ridiculing his idea. For the rest of his life Goddard distrusted newspapers. Unlike Billy Mitchell he kept his work secret and hated publicity. And he went ahead perfecting his rocket engine. He finally secured 214 patents on rocket improvements.

When he died in 1945, few Americans yet believed that man would ever travel through interplanetary space.

The people of London, however, already had sad reason to know that rock-

Robert Goddard with his first successful rocket. His imaginative experiments with small rockets laid the groundwork for later American achievements in space.

ets provided a fantastic new source of Air Power. Raining down from the skies in 1944 came thousands of German V-2 rockets. Aimed from distant launching pads in Germany they did not carry pilots but still reached their English targets with terrifying accuracy. They traveled at a speed of 3,500 miles an hour and each dropped a ton of explosives.

The V-2 rockets were the work of a group of German scientists who had been experimenting since 1932. When the Nazis came to power and plunged the world into war, the Nazis had provided these scientists with a secret new laboratory in Peenemuende, a little fishing village on the Baltic Sea in northeastern Germany.

By 1944, about twelve thousand Germans were engaged in making the V-2 rockets which were pouring down

on England every day. The name "V-2" came from a German term meaning "Vengeance Weapon, No. 2." It was the most terrifying weapon of the war because no defense against it had been found. If the Nazis had only perfected this weapon earlier, they might have won the war. But by mid-1944 Germany was near collapse.

When the Russians speeded westward across Europe in their final triumphal march, they hastened to Peenemuende to capture the German rocket factory—for their own future use. When they arrived they were dismayed to find that the most valuable resource, the rocket scientists themselves, had already fled westward.

"This is absolutely intolerable," Dictator Stalin complained in a rage. "We defeated the Nazi armies; we occupied Berlin and Peenemuende; but the Americans got the rocket engineers!" Stalin was especially irritated because the Russian communists were not strong in big bombing planes. Their only weapon, then, for a possible long-distance attack on the United States was transatlantic rockets.

Some far-sighted American generals organized a new project under the code name "Operation Paperclip." They collected 118 of the best German rocket scientists (including Wernher von Braun), and signed them up to work on rockets and space travel for the United States. Wernher von Braun became head of the U.S. Army rocket research.

The United States and communist Russia began a competition in rockets. By 1956 the chief of the Russian Communist Party boasted that soon Russian military rockets would be able to hit any target on the earth. The Russians had improved the old V-2 into a new weapon called the T-1.

Then, on October 4, 1957, the Russians sent up the first man-made earth satellite. It was a package of instruments weighing 184 pounds. They called it "Sputnik" which in Russian meant "fellow traveler" (of the earth). One month later they launched a much heavier satellite, Sputnik II. It weighed 1,120 pounds and for experimental purposes carried a dog named Laika.

The Space Race was on!

Early American efforts were not always successful. The White House announced that on December 6, 1957, the United States would launch its own satellite with a Vanguard rocket. While the whole nation watched on television this much-advertised rocket collapsed on the wet sand around the launching pad.

The next try did succeed. Two months later Explorer I, the first American satellite, went into orbit. And it made some important scientific discoveries.

But Americans still worried about the "Space Gap." Within the next few years, both Russia and the United States performed spectacular feats in space.

On April 12, 1961, the Russians sent up Yuri Gagarin, the first man in space. He went whirling around the earth in a satellite, and made nearly a full orbit —in 89 minutes. A year later the United States sent John H. Glenn, Jr., into orbit in the American spaceship called Friendship 7. Probably Russia and the United States each would have lagged if it had not been for the competition of the other.

President John F. Kennedy at first had doubts about space exploration. He doubted whether man could survive outside the earth's atmosphere. He feared another Vanguard fiasco. And he thought that the enormous sums of money might be better spent on earth. But his persuasive Vice-President Lyndon B. Johnson was a great space enthusiast. After the Russians had sent Yuri Gagarin into orbit, President Kennedy announced that the United States would aim to land a man on the moon before 1970. When President Johnson came to office, he gave space exploration his strong support.

The moon-landing project did need all the support it could find. For there were great risks and vast expenses. When a fire exploded in 1967 during tests of a spaceship, three of the most experienced astronauts were killed. The costs of preparing for the moon shot came to over $25,000,000,000. But this meant new industries, new products, and employment in new jobs for a third of a million people all over the country.

"We work in a place," boasted someone at the Manned Spacecraft Center in Houston, Texas, "where 13,000 men can feel like Columbus."

Finally, after nine years of preparation and two voyages around the moon and back, on July 16, 1969, Americans set out to land on the moon. Neil Armstrong commanded the mission, Michael Collins piloted the command ship Apollo 11, and Edwin E. Aldrin, Jr., was to work with Armstrong when they landed on the moon.

None of them was a great scientist. None came from a family that was rich or famous. They all had a passion for

American on the moon, July 20, 1969.

flying. Armstrong had made a reputation as a daring yet reliable test pilot. Aldrin's father, an army colonel, had studied with the space pioneer Goddard. Aldrin himself, after graduating from West Point in 1951, piloted a Sabrejet in the Korean War, and then earned a doctor's degree in aeronautics at Massachusetts Institute of Technology. Collins had been born in Rome while his father, a professional army officer, was stationed there. He graduated from West Point, joined the Air Force, and became a test pilot. As an astronaut, he had taken a 5½-hour space walk, the longest ever. All three men were athletes, in top physical condition. They were all modest men, who had practiced working together.

The moon trip was unlike earlier explorations of unknown lands. For this voyage was watched on television by the whole world—including the explorers' own families. Hundreds of millions of people could share the adventure and the suspense.

The three astronauts shot up in the command ship Apollo 11, which took them orbiting around the earth. Then, after 2½ orbits, they steered Apollo 11 off toward the moon, over two hundred thousand miles away. After a three-day journey through interplanetary space, they arrived in their moon orbit. Armstrong and Aldrin climbed into a small "lunar module" attached at the nose of Apollo 11. They called this little ship "Eagle."

They separated Eagle from the mother ship. After orbiting the moon to the agreed position, they landed Eagle on the moon at 4:17 P.M. Eastern Daylight Time on July 20, 1969.

There were risks till the last instant of the landing. As the computer guided them down, Armstrong noticed they were about to settle in a deep crater about the size of a football field, filled with large boulders. He seized the controls and guided Eagle to a safe, smoother site.

By the original plan, Armstrong and Aldrin were supposed to take a long nap within their Lunar Module before risking the strain of the moon walk. But they were impatient and in no mood for napping. After receiving permission from the Mission Control Center in Houston and putting on their complicated space suits, they opened their hatch, six and a half hours after landing.

The first man, an American, stepped out on a heavenly body. For that moment the whole world, except those whose dictators forbade them to know, watched proudly together.

Surrounded by the footprints of the first earthlings on the moon is the launching stand from which Armstrong and Aldrin took off from the moon, in their Lunar Module. And on it is a plaque that may remain forever. For on the moon there is no oxygen to rust and no water to erode. The message on the plaque boasts an American achievement and proclaims the hope of the world. "Here men from the planet earth first set foot upon the moon, July 1969, A.D. We came in peace for all mankind."

But already—long before American dreams to make the world safe for democracy could come true, long before world-wide peace was in sight—Americans back on earth were asking the familiar American question, "Where next?"

Postscript: The Mysterious Future

When we look back on the story of America we feel very wise. In some ways we really are even wiser than William Bradford or Benjamin Franklin or George Washington or Abraham Lincoln.

We know what they did not know. What for us is history, for them would have been prophecy.

For we know how it turned out. They had to guess.

We can see how right it was for the Pilgrims to risk the long voyage across the wild ocean. We see how lucky it was that the thirteen little colonies somehow united for Independence. We can see how much better the American Revolution would have been fought with a stronger, more unified Continental army.

We can see how futile were all the "compromises" on slavery before the Civil War. We can see, too, the Civil War toll in blood and hate. We can see that while the Civil War abolished slavery and saved the Union, it cost over a half-million lives and created new hates that would not quickly die.

From American history we can learn that the future is always full of surprising secrets. This New World has been such an exciting place because it has been so new. The great achievements of America are mostly things that never before really seemed possible.

Which signers of the Declaration of Independence in 1776 could have imagined that their feeble little confederation, in less than two centuries, would be the world's greatest democracy—a continent-nation of over two hundred million people, the refuge of the world, the strongest nation on earth?

Of those fifty-five men in Philadelphia struggling in the hot summer of 1787 to agree on how to prevent the colonies from falling apart—how many would have believed that their work would become the longest-lived written constitution in history?

Who would have imagined that a nation of immigrants, the most miscellaneous people on earth, would someday be the most powerful? Or that men and women from all over Europe, from Africa and Asia—of many races and religions and traditions—would adopt one language, and become loyal builders of one new nation?

Who would have guessed that out of the American wilderness (still only half-explored in 1850) so soon would come men to explore the moon, and then to plan voyages to the farther planets of outer space?

These were some of the happy surprises. But there were others not quite so happy, and to the founders of our nation just as secret.

Who would have guessed that, within less than two hundred years, a trackless, half-mapped continent could be criss-crossed by superhighways, defaced by billboards and tin cans? Who would have guessed that Americans would perfect horseless carriages to go a hundred miles an hour—and yet be stuck in traffic jams where they could not even move as fast as a walking horse? Or that ten times as many would be killed by these horseless carriages every year as were killed in all the battles of the American Revolution?

Who would have imagined that the fresh air of a New World would begin to become smoke-filled? Or that the sparkling waters of lakes and rivers would become so darkened and dirtied by factory sewage that even the fish found them unlivable and the birds no longer enjoyed their shores?

Who would have believed that the wonderful American silences—once broken by Indian chants or the songs of birds or the call of the coyote—would be shattered by the roar of supersonic jets strong enough to break windows as well as eardrums? Who would have believed that a continent, once frightening by its emptiness, would now terrify men by crowding them together?

Who would have believed that a Nation of Nations, created by peoples of all races from everywhere, which had suffered through a bloody war for Union and for Freedom, would see new forms of racism?

Who would have believed that a nation designed to be a refuge for all people from the violence of the Old World could ever be plagued by reckless violence within?

Americans, even more than other people in the world, love the adventure of the unexpected. The future is just as much a mystery story as it ever was.

Jetliners waiting for takeoff.

A few of the hundreds of thousands of young Americans who gathered near Woodstock, New York, in August 1969 for a festival of rock music.

Americans have been planters in this faraway land, builders of cities in the wilderness, Go-Getters. Americans—makers of something out of nothing—have delivered a new way of life to far corners of the world. Americans have been adventurers—to this New World, within this New World, and out to even newer New Worlds.

If the future is a mystery story, then, that does not frighten Americans. For Americans have always lived in the world's greatest treasure house of the unexpected.

Index

Abilene, Tex., 6–7
Abraham & Straus department store, 24
Adams, Andy, 6
Addams, Jane, 69–71, 133, 147
Air power, 163
    Hitler's strategy based on, 161
    Mitchell's views on, 158–61
Akron, Ohio, 90
Alabama, 109, 125, 130
Alamogordo, N.M., 167
Aldrin, Edwin E., Jr., 181, 183
Allegheny River, 95
Allen, William Frederick, 86–87
Amalgamated Clothing Workers, 72
American Federation of Labor, 64, 72
American Marconi Company, 174–76
American Revolution, 25, 55, 147, 152, 184–85
American Tobacco Company, 111
Anglo-Saxon superiority, ideas of, 66–67, 71
Annapolis Junction, Md., 77
Antitrust Act, Sherman, 112
Apollo 11, 183
Appomattox, Va., 41, 43–44, 51–52, 105
Arizona, 72, 151
Armstrong, Neil, 181, 183
Arthur, Chester A., 97
Assembly line, 35–37
Associated Press, 78
Atlanta University, 49
Atlantic Charter, 162
Atomic bomb, 166–68, 170
Audion tube, 175
Austro-Hungarian Empire, Americans from, 55, 58
Autobiography (Franklin), 83
Automobile, 116, 172
    assembly line for making, 35–37
Aviation, 172, 185

Baltimore, Md., 9, 77–78, 85
Baltimore and Ohio Railroad, 64
Banks, 111, 118
    closing of (1933), 122
Bell, Alexander Graham, 172–73
Bessemer, Henry, 101

Bethlehem Iron Company, 34–35
Big business, 110–11
Bissell, George H., 10
Black Codes, 48
Blitzkrieg, 155, 161–63
Bogardus, James, 22–23, 99
Bogardus towers, 99–100
Bonus March, 119
Booth, John Wilkes, 44
Borah, William E., 157
Boston, Mass., 9, 28, 58, 64, 66, 74, 78, 85–86
Bradford, William, 184
Brady, Mathew, 41
Bridge building, 93–97
Brooklyn, N.Y., 94–95
Brooklyn Bridge, 96–97
Bryan, William Jennings, 107–10, 120, 122, 151
Buffalo, N.Y., 58, 112
Bulgaria, 165
Bullock, William, 78
Business, big, 110–11

Cable, transatlantic, 152, 172
California, 148
    Gold Rush in, 2
Calumet, Lake, 90
Camden and Amboy Railroad, 86
Canada, Americans from, 58
Canton, Ohio, 109
Carnegie, Andrew, 90, 147
Carnegie Steel Company, 90
Catalogs, mail-order, 16–21, 27
Catholics, 127
Cattle, Longhorn, 5–7
Cattlemen, 3–8
Centennial Exposition (1876), 30–33, 64, 79, 173
Central Time, 86
Charleston, S.C., 41, 78, 87
Cheyenne, Wyo., 5, 7
Chicago, Ill., 6–7, 17, 19, 64, 74, 78, 81, 85–86, 89, 99, 102
    University of, 71
Child labor, prohibition of, 123
China, 14, 147
    Communist, 169, 171
    Americans from, 58, 127
Chinese Exclusion Act (1882), 68

Chrysler Building, 102
Churchill, Winston, 162, 164–66
Cigarmakers Union, 72
Cincinnati, Ohio, 89
Cities, 110
    immigrants in, 58–62, 72
    "instant," 89, 91
    as "melting pots," 60
    of Middle West, 89
Civil rights, 46, 138, 140
Civil War, 2–3, 15, 17, 25–26, 33, 40, 42–44, 52, 58, 71, 78, 81, 89, 93, 95, 99, 105, 110, 115, 127, 134, 138, 143, 147, 154, 184
Civilian Conservation Corps (CCC), 126
Clay, Henry, 77
Clemenceau, Georges, 156
Cleveland, Grover, 68, 97, 108
Cleveland, Ohio, 13, 58
Clock manufacture, 32
Clothing industry, 26–30
Colleges, land-grant, 71
Collins, Michael, 181, 183
Colorado, 4, 106
Colorado River, 2
Colt, Samuel, 15
Columbian Exposition (1893), 64, 81, 175
Columbus, Christopher, 81
Command of the Army Act, 46
Communism, 158, 170
    containment of, 168, 170–71
Communist Party
    Russian, 180
    U.S.A., 133
Company towns, 90–91
Confederacy, 41, 43, 45, 89
Conservation, 115, 125
Constitution, U.S., 42–43, 46–48, 50–51, 70, 80, 115, 123, 126, 132, 136, 169
Coolidge, Calvin, 160
Corliss, George H., 32
Corliss steam engine, 32
Corporations, 113, 117
Cowboys, 3, 5–8
Cox, James M., 157
Craig, Daniel, 75
Crazy Horse, Chief, 65
Crime rates, 64
Cuba, 143–48, 158
Czechoslovakia, 156, 165–66

Dallas, Tex., 140
David, 20
Declaration of Independence, 153, 184
De Forest, Lee, 175
Democratic Party, 52, 108, 110, 122, 132
Denver, Colo., 4, 74, 89
Department stores, 22–24, 27, 99
Depression, Great, 118–21, 125–26, 166, 177
Detroit, Mich., 58, 64
Dewey, George, 145–46, 174
Dewey, Thomas E., 177–78
Diamond Match Company, 90
Distinguished Flying Cross, 134
Diving bell, invention of, 93
Dodge City, Kans., 7
Donnelly, Ignatius, 106
Douglass, Frederick, 129
Drake, Edwin L., 10–12
Du Bois, W. E. B., 130, 132–33, 137
"Dumbbell" tenement, 62, 90

Eads, James Buchanan, 93–94
East River, 94
East St. Louis, Ill., 65
Eastern Time, 86
Edison, Thomas A., 28, 36–38, 173, 175
Education, 116–17
    See also Public schools; Universities
Einstein, Albert, 166
Eisenhower, Dwight D., 165–66, 170
Electric light, invention of, 38
Elevators, for buildings, 97–99
Eliot, Charles W., 147
Ellis Island, 72
Emancipation Proclamation, 138, 153
Empire State Building, 102
England. *See* Great Britain
Explorer I, 181

Factory organization, 33, 35
Farmers, 105–06
    and mail-order firms, 16, 19–21
    and RFD, 82
Farmers' Alliance, 105
Farnsworth, Philo Taylor, 177
Fascism, 123, 158
Fermi, Enrico, 166-67
Fessenden, Reginald Aubrey, 174–75
Fifteenth Amendment, 51, 131
Fisk University, 49
Five-and-ten-cent stores, 102
Florida, 2, 51

Ford, Henry, 28, 36–38
Ford's Theater (Washington, D.C.), 44
Forrest, Nathan Bedford, 50–51
Fort Sumter, 44
Four Freedoms (Roosevelt), 162
Fourteen Points (Wilson), 152, 155–56, 162
Fourteenth Amendment, 51, 132, 135
France, 76, 104, 147, 155–56, 168
    in World War I, 154–55
    in World War II, 161
Franklin, Benjamin, 80–81, 84, 130, 184
Free silver, 106–08, 110
Freedmen's Bureau, 40, 48–49, 128
"Freedom Riders," 136
Frelinghuysen, Theodore, 77
Frontier, 66

Gagarin, Yuri, 181
Garden cities, 91–92
Garden Cities of Tomorrow (Howard), 91
Gary, Elbert Henry, 90
Gary, Ind., 90
Gasoline, 15, 38
General Electric Company, 174
General Motors Corporation, 118
"Gentlemen's Agreement," 68
Georgia, 40
Germany, 66, 104, 147, 156, 164
    Americans from, 29, 55, 57–58, 60, 69, 72
    Nazis in, 123-24, 161, 166, 180
    in World War I, 150-52, 154–55
    in World War II, 155, 161–65
Gesner, Abraham, 10
Gettysburg, Battle of, 40, 95, 147
Ghana, 133, 135
Gilbert, Bradford, 102
Glenn, John H., 181
Goddard, Robert H., 179–80, 183
Go-Getters, 2, 4, 8, 19, 22, 111, 175, 187
Gold Rush
    in California, 2
    in Colorado, 4
Gold standard, 106, 108–09
Gompers, Samuel, 72, 147
Goodnight, Charles, 5, 8, 13
Gorgas, William, 148
"Grandfather" laws, Southern, 131, 133
Grange Clubs, 17, 82, 105

Granite City, Ill., 90
Grant, Ulysses S., 41, 44, 51, 65, 94
Great Britain, 32–33, 66, 104, 147, 152, 155–56
    in World War I, 150, 152, 154–55
    in World War II, 162–64
Great Cryptogram (Donnelly), 106
Great Lakes, 2
Greece, 168
    Americans from, 67
Guam, 147

Hall, Prescott Farnsworth, 66–67
Hamburg-Amerika Steamship Line, 53
Hampton Institute, 49
Hanna, Mark, 109
Harding, Warren G., 158
Harvard College, 66, 71
Haymarket Massacre, 64
Hearst, William Randolph, 144
Henryetta, Okla., 119
Herald, New York, 87
Hertz, Heinrich, 173
Hillman, Sidney, 72
Hine, Lewis W., 62
Hiroshima, bombing of, 168
Hitler, Adolf, 123–24, 161–63
Hoe, Richard, 78–79
Hoe rotary press, 78
Hoffman, Adon J., 29
Hoffmann, Francis, 57
Home Insurance Company, 99
Homer, Winslow, 100
Homestead, Pa., 64, 90–91
Homestead Act, 54–56
Hoover, Herbert, 116, 119–22
Hotels, 22
House of Representatives, 42, 45–47, 76
Houston, Tex., Mission Control Center in, 181, 183
Howard, Ebenezer, 91–92
Howard University, 49
Howe, Elias, 27–28
Hudson River, 94
Hull-House, 69–70
Human Proportions in Growth (Ryan), 27
Hungary, 165–66
Hunt, Walter, 27

Iliff, John Wesley, 3–5, 175
Illinois, 56, 85, 113
Illinois Central Railroad, 56–58
Illustrated Police News, 66
Immigrants, 29, 40, 52–53, 55–56, 58, 63, 66–67
    in cities, 58–62, 72
    as Reformers, 71

Immigration Restriction League, 67–68
Income tax, 115–16, 157
Indian Territory, 54
Indiana, 85
Indianapolis, Ind., 85
Indianapolis *Sentinel*, 86
Indians, American, 4, 6, 8, 40, 65, 72, 127–28
Industrial Revolution, 15
Influence of Sea Power Upon History (Mahan), 143
International law, 150
International News Service, 78
International Workers of the World, 64
Interstate Commerce Commission, 87
Iowa, 119
Ireland, Americans from, 58, 67
Isolationism, 158, 161–62, 171
Italy, 76, 155, 158, 166
  Fascism in, 123
  Americans from, 58, 60, 67, 69, 72, 74

Jackson, Andrew, 109
Jackson, Charles T., 76
James, William, 147
Japan, 158, 164
  and "Gentlemen's Agreement," 68
  Americans from, 127
  in World War II, 162–65, 167
Jefferson, Thomas, 65, 84, 144
Jenney, William LeBaron, 99, 102
Jennings, Isaiah, 9
Jetliners, 172, 185
Jews, 53, 69, 127
Johns Hopkins University, 71, 151
Johnson, Andrew, 42, 44–48
Johnson, Lyndon B., 139–40, 171, 181
Jonathan, 24
Jordan, David Starr, 147
Journal, New York, 144

Kansas, 105–06
Kansas City, Mo., 89
Kansas Pacific Railroad, 6–7
Kennedy, John F., 127, 138, 171, 178, 181
  assassination of, 140
Kentucky, 8, 125
Kier, Samuel, 8–10
Kinetoscope, 38
King, Martin Luther, Jr., 136–39
  assassination of, 140
Knights of the Black Cross, 51
Korean War, 134, 169–70, 183
Ku Klux Klan, 50–51
Ku Klux Klan Acts, 51

Labor unions, 30, 63–64, 71
La Guardia, Fiorello, 71–72
Lake Forest, Ill., 92
Land, homestead, 54–55
Law, international, 150
League of Nations, 152, 156–58
Lease, Mary Elizabeth, 106–07
Lee, Robert E., 41, 44
Leland Stanford Jr. University, 71
Lend-Lease, 162
Lincoln, Abraham, 42–48, 54, 95, 138, 140, 184
  assassination of, 44–45
Lindbergh, Charles A., 160–61
Literacy Test, 67–68
  in South, 132
Little Theater movement, 70
Lodge, Henry Cabot, 157
Longhorn cattle, 5–7
Long's Peak, 2
Los Angeles, Calif., 74
Louisiana, 2
Louisiana Knights of the White Camelia, 51
Louisiana Purchase, 55
Louisville and Nashville Railroad, 89
Lunar Module, 183
Lusitania, 149
  sinking of, 150

MacArthur, Douglas, 169–70
McCoy, Joseph G., 6–7
McCullough Shot and Lead Company, 99
Machine tools, 32–33
Machinery Hall, at Centennial Exposition (1876), 32, 79
McKinley, William B., 109–10, 112, 122, 143–45
Magnetic Telegraph Company, 78
Mahan, Alfred T., 143, 158
Mail-order firms, 16–21, 27
Mail system, 80–83, 172
Maine, U.S.S., 144–45
Malmborg, Oscar, 57
Management, scientific, 34–35
Manhattan Island, 61, 63, 94–95, 102
Manhattan Project, 167
March on Washington (1963), 138–39
Marconi, Guglielmo, 173–74
Marne, Battle of, 154
Massachusetts, 40, 130
Metal-cutting tools, 32–33
Mexican War, 25, 57, 78
Mexico, 55, 151
  Americans from, 127
Michigan, 55

Micrometer, invention of, 32
Middle Atlantic States, 87
Middle West, 89, 94
Milwaukee, Wis., 58, 78
Miners, 64, 113, 115
Minimum-wage laws, 123
Minnesota, 55, 74, 106
Mississippi, 48
Mississippi River, 93–94, 110
Mitchell, Billy, 158–61, 163, 179
Mitchell, John, 113
Molly Maguires, 64
Money, "cheap," 105–06
Monongahela River, 90
Monopoly, 111, 123, 157
Monroe Doctrine, 152
Montana, 7
Montgomery, Ala., 136–37
Montgomery Ward & Company, 118
Moon, landing on, 181–83
Morgan, J. P., 112
Mormons, 127
Morrill, Justin S., 71
Morrill Act, 71
Morse, Samuel F. B., 74–78, 172–73
Morse code, 76, 175
Mountain Time, 86
Movies, 116, 177
Mussolini, Benito, 123, 166

Nagasaki, bombing of, 167-68
Napoleon Bonaparte, 55, 102, 112
Nast, Thomas, 88
National Association for the Advancement of Colored People (NAACP), 133
National Museum of History and Technology, 76
National Recovery Act (NRA), 123
Natural resources, conservation of, 115, 125
Naval War of 1812, The (Roosevelt), 143
Nazis, 123–24, 158, 161, 166, 180
  defeat of, 164–66, 168
Nebraska, 7, 108–09, 119
Negroes
  and Black Codes, 48
  and civil rights, 46, 138, 140
  education of, 49, 128–30, 136
  and Fifteenth Amendment, 131
  and Fourteenth Amendment, 132, 135
  as freedmen, 40, 46–52
  in Korean War, 134
  and Niagara Movement, 130, 133
  and poll tax, 132

and Thirteenth Amendment, 48
and voting rights, 48, 131–32
in World Wars I and II, 133–34
Neutral Rights, 148, 150, 152
Neutrality Law, 161
Nevada, 106
New Bedford, Mass., 26
New Deal, 122, 124, 133
New England, 26, 58, 66, 74, 87, 127
New Freedom, 134
New Jersey, 151
New Mexico, 151
New Orleans, La., 51, 58
New York City, 9, 57–59, 64–65, 72, 74, 78, 85, 89, 94, 102
immigrants in, 60–61
New York *Herald,* 87
New York *Journal,* 144
New York State, 22, 122
New York *Sun,* 75
New York *Times,* 179
New York *World,* 144
Newspapers, 65, 75, 78–79, 82, 143–44, 172
Niagara Movement, 130, 133
Niagara River, 95
Nickelodeon, 116
Nineteenth Amendment, 70
Nixon, Richard M., 178
Norden bombsight, 161
North Carolina, 49
North Dakota, 74
North Redwood, Minn., 19
North Star, The, 129
Norway
Americans from, 57–58
invaded by Hitler, 161

Official Guide of the Railways, 86
Oglala Indians, 4
Ohio, 14, 113
Ohio River, 95
Oil towns, 12–13
Oil wells, 11–12
Oilmen, 12–14
Oklahoma "Land Rush," 54
Old Confederates, 48, 50–52
Old Greenwich, Conn., 91
Omaha, Nebr., 53, 89, 105
Ostfriesland (German battleship), 159
Otis, Elisha Graves, 98
Outcault, Richard F., 144
Pacific Coast, 110
Pacific Time, 86
Panama, 99, 148
Panama Canal, 148
Pan-American Exposition (1901), 112
Patrons of Husbandry, 17, 105

Paul, 26
Pearl Harbor, Japanese attack on, 162–63
Peenemuende, 180
Pennsylvania, 10-11, 13, 40, 64, 113
Pennsylvania Railroad, 85
Pennsylvania Rock Oil Company, 10
Pershing, John J., 154, 159
Petroleum (rock oil), 8–10, 15, 38
Philadelphia, Pa., 30–34, 64, 74, 78, 80, 87, 184
Philippine Islands, 145–47
Phonograph, 36–38
Pigeon Express, 75
Pilgrims, 184
Pittsburgh, Pa., 64, 90, 176
Pittsburgh Plate Glass Company, 90
Plains Indians, 6
Plumber and Sanitary Engineer, The, 62
Poland, 156, 164–65
Americans from, 29, 58, 60, 69
invaded by Hitler, 161
Poll tax, 132
Pond Freshet, 12–13
Populism, 82, 105–07, 110, 115
Portland, Me., 78
Post Office, 80–82
Press, Hoe rotary, 78
Presser, steam, invention of, 29
Princeton University, 151
Proclamation of Amnesty and Reconstruction (Lincoln), 43
Public domain, 54–55, 115
Public schools, 61
integration of, 136
Puerto Rico, 147
Pulaski, Tenn., 50
Pulitzer, Joseph, 144–45
Pullman, George M., 90

Quincy Hall Clothing Manufactory, 28

Racism, 47–48, 66, 123, 140, 185
Radar, 177
Radburn, N.J., 92
Radical Republicans, 42–48, 51
Radio, 116, 173–76
Radio Corporation of America, 176-77
Railroads, 4, 55–56, 80, 85, 90, 110
gauge of tracks for, 87, 89
land grants to, 56
and rebates, 13, 115
Railway Mail Service, 81–82

Reconstruction, 41, 43, 45, 131
Red Jackets, 51
Reed, Walter, 148
Reformers, 68, 71
Refrigerator, 116
Reinhart, Charles S., 67
Reliance Building, 101
Relief Commission (World War I), 120
Remington, Frederic, 3, 146
Republican Party, 52, 109–10, 112, 156
Richmond, Va., 89
Riis, Jacob, 62
Rock oil (petroleum), 8–10, 15, 38
Rockefeller, John D., 13-15, 38, 71, 128
Rockets, 179–81
Rocky Mountains, 2
Roebling, John, 95, 97
Roebling, Washington, 95, 97
Roebuck, Alvah Curtis, 19
Roosevelt, Eleanor, 121
Roosevelt, Franklin D., 121–25, 129, 158, 161–62, 164–67, 177
Roosevelt, Theodore, 63, 68, 112–13, 115–16, 120, 125, 143, 145–48, 151
Rough Riders, 146
Rough Riders, The (Roosevelt), 146
Rumania, 165
Rural Free Delivery (RFD), 82, 144
Russell, C. M., 4
Russia, 53, 69, 158, 170–71, 180
Americans from, 29, 58
Sputniks launched by, 181
in World War II, 163–66
Ryan, Daniel Edward, 27

Safety pin, invention of, 27
St. Louis, Mo., 74, 78, 93–94
San Antonio, Tex., 146
San Francisco, Calif., 64, 168
San Juan Hill, Rough Riders' charge at, 146
Sargent, John Singer, 145
Sarnoff, David, 175–77
Satellites, earth, 179, 181
Schools, public. *See* Public schools
Screws, manufacture of, 33
Sea power, Mahan's views on, 143, 158
Sears, Richard, 19–21, 175
Sellers, William, 33
Semaphore system, messages sent over, 75
Senate, U.S., 42, 46–47
Seneca Indians, 8
Seneca Oil, 8

Sentinel, Indianapolis, 86
Settlement houses, 69–70
Sewing machine, invention of, 27–28
Sewing Machine Combination, 28
Shafter, W. R., 145
Shaker Heights, Ohio, 92
Sharon, 25
Sherman, William T., 94, 99
Sherman Antitrust Act, 112
Shoe manufacture, 26
Silliman, Benjamin, Jr., 10, 38
Silver, free, 106–08, 110
Simpson, "Sockless Jerry," 106
Singer, Isaac Merrit, 28
Sitting Bull, Chief, 65
Skyscrapers, 99–102
Slavery, 43, 47–50, 52, 128–30, 184
Slopshop clothing, 26
Slums, 61, 63, 69, 133
Smith, "Fog," 77
Smith, "Uncle Billy," 11
Smithsonian Institution, 179
Social Security, 125
Social work, 69-71
Somme, Battle of, 154
South Carolina, 49
South Dakota, 74
Southeast Asia, 171
Space exploration, 180-84
Spain, 69, 143–45, 147
Spanish-American War, 143, 145–48, 158, 174
Spirit of St. Louis, The, 169
Springfield, Ill., 64, 133
Sputniks, 181
Stalin, Josef, 164–66, 180
Standard gauge, for railroad tracks, 87, 89
Standard Oil Company, 14, 111
Standard Time, 86-87
Stanford, Leland, 71
Stanton, Edwin M., 46
Steam engine, Corliss, 32
Steam presser, invention of, 29
Steamships, 52–53
Steel production, 101
Stephenson, George, 87
Stevens, Thaddeus, 42–45, 48, 52
Stewart, A. T., 22–24
Stewart's Cast Iron Palace, 22, 24, 99
Stock Market, 117
   and crash (1929), 117–18, 120
Strikes
   in company towns, 90
   Pullman (1894), 64, 90, 108
   railroad (1877), 64–65
Submarines, German, in World War I, 149–50

Sully (ship), 76
Sun, New York, 75
Supreme Court, U.S., 112–13, 115, 123, 131–33, 135–36
Sweatshops, 30, 72
Sweden, immigrants from, 57–58, 74
Swift Bird, Chief, 4
Syracuse, N.Y., 29
System of Screw Threads and Nuts (Sellers), 33

Taft, William Howard, 68
Tampa, Fla., 145
Taxation, 115–16
Taylor, Frederick W., 34–35
Telegraph, 77–78, 172–73
   invention of, 74, 76–77
Telephone, 172–73
   invention of, 173
Television, 116, 175–79
   "Great Debates" on (1960), 178
Telstar, 179
Tenement design, 61–63
Tennessee, 44, 51, 87, 125
Tennessee River, 135
Tennessee Valley Authority (TVA), 125
Tenure of Office Act, 46
Terry, Eli, 32
Texas, 5, 45, 151
Texas Knights of the Rising Sun, 51
Thirteenth Amendment, 48, 51
Time, Standard, 86–87
Times, New York, 179
Titanic, sinking of, 176
Titusville, Pa., 11
Trench warfare, in World War I, 153
Truman, Harry S, 134, 166–70, 177–78
Truman Doctrine, 168
Trusts, 111–12, 157
Turkey, and Truman Doctrine, 168
Turner, Frederick Jackson, 66
Tuskegee Institute, 130–31
Twain, Mark, 147
Twenty-fourth Amendment, 132
Typewriter, 173

Unemployment insurance, 125
Union Pacific Railroad, 4, 53
Unions, labor, 30, 63–64, 71
United Mine Workers of America, 113
United Nations, 135, 164, 168–69
United Press, 78
United States Steel Corporation, 90, 111, 118, 173

Universities, 71
Up From Slavery (Washington), 130

Van Buren, Martin, 77
Vanguard rocket, 181
Vermont, 71, 116
Vicksburg, Miss., 49
Viet Nam, 170–71
Virginia, 134
Von Braun, Wernher, 180
Voting Rights Act, 140
V-2 rockets, 180

Wade-Davis Bill, 43–45
Wall Street, 106
Wanamaker, John, 82
War of 1812, 25
Ward, Montgomery, 15–17, 19–20, 175
Ward, Robert De Courcy, 66–67
Warren, Charles, 66–67
Washington, Booker T., 129–30, 132, 137
Washington, D.C., 76–77, 89, 171
   March on (1963), 138–39
Washington, George, 80–81, 84, 184
Watson, Tom, 105
We (Lindbergh), 160
West Virginia, 64, 113
Weyler, Valeriano "Butcher," 143
Whig Party, 77
Whitney, Eli, 15
Williams, Gluyas, 123
Wilson, Woodrow, 68, 102, 134, 150–52, 155–58
Wireless telegraph, 174
Wisconsin, 55, 85
Women's suffrage, 70
Woodstock, N.Y., 186
Woolworth, Frank W., 102
Woolworth Building, 102
Worcester, Mass., 85–86
World, New York, 144
World War I, 119–20, 133–34, 150–55, 158–59, 168, 176
World War II, 125, 133–34, 155, 161–68, 177
Wyoming, 5, 7

Yale College, 175
Yalta Conference, 164
Yalu River, 169
Yellow fever, conquest of, 148
Yellow press, 144–45

Zimmermann, Arthur, 151
Zimmermann Note, 152
Zworykin, Vladimir, 176

Daniel J. Boorstin, as Director of the Smithsonian's National Museum of History and Technology, plays host to 6,000,000 visitors a year.

He was appointed to the President's Bicentennial Commission by Lyndon B. Johnson and reappointed by Richard M. Nixon. Formerly Distinguished Service Professor of American History at the University of Chicago, Mr. Boorstin was the first holder of the chair of American History at the Sorbonne, as well as Pitt Professor of American History and Institutions at Cambridge University. He has lectured in far corners of the world, including Nepal and the Fiji Islands.

Among his books are *The Americans: The Colonial Experience* (which received Columbia University's Bancroft Prize) and *The Americans: The National Experience* (honored by the Society of American Historians with its Parkman Prize). He is the editor of *An American Primer* (in two volumes) and of the 30-volume *Chicago History of American Civilization*.

Born in Georgia and raised in Oklahoma, with degrees from Harvard and Yale, Mr. Boorstin taught at Harvard and at Swarthmore before going to the University of Chicago. His wife, Ruth, and their three sons have shared his enthusiasm for seeing the world.